MASONIC QUIZ BOOK

"Ask Me Another, Brother"

A MASONIC PRIMER

I0126727

A Thousand and One Answers to Questions, Compiled from Scriptural References and the Best Masonic Authorities

Edited by
Wm. O. Peterson, P.M. 32°

THE BOOK TREE
San Diego, California

Originally published
1949
by Charles Powner, Chicago

Republished 2006
The Book Tree

ISBN 1-58509-255-X

The Arms of y^e most Ancient & Honorable Fraternity of Free and Accepted Masons.

Holiness to the Lord.

The Arms of the Operative or Stone Masons.

Frontispiece to "Ahiman Rezon," 1764

ADOPTED BY THE GRAND LODGE OF PENNSYLVANIA, 1783

The title "Ahiman Rezon" is derived from three Hebrew words, אחים, *ahim,* "brothers," מנה, *manah,* "to appoint," or "to select," and רצן, *ratzon,* "the will, pleasure or meaning;" and hence the combination of the three words in the title, Ahiman Rezon, signifies "the will of selected brethren" = the law of a class or society of men who are chosen or selected from the rest of the world as brethren. The written laws of Freemasonry are contained in the "Ahiman Rezon" or Book of Constitutions.

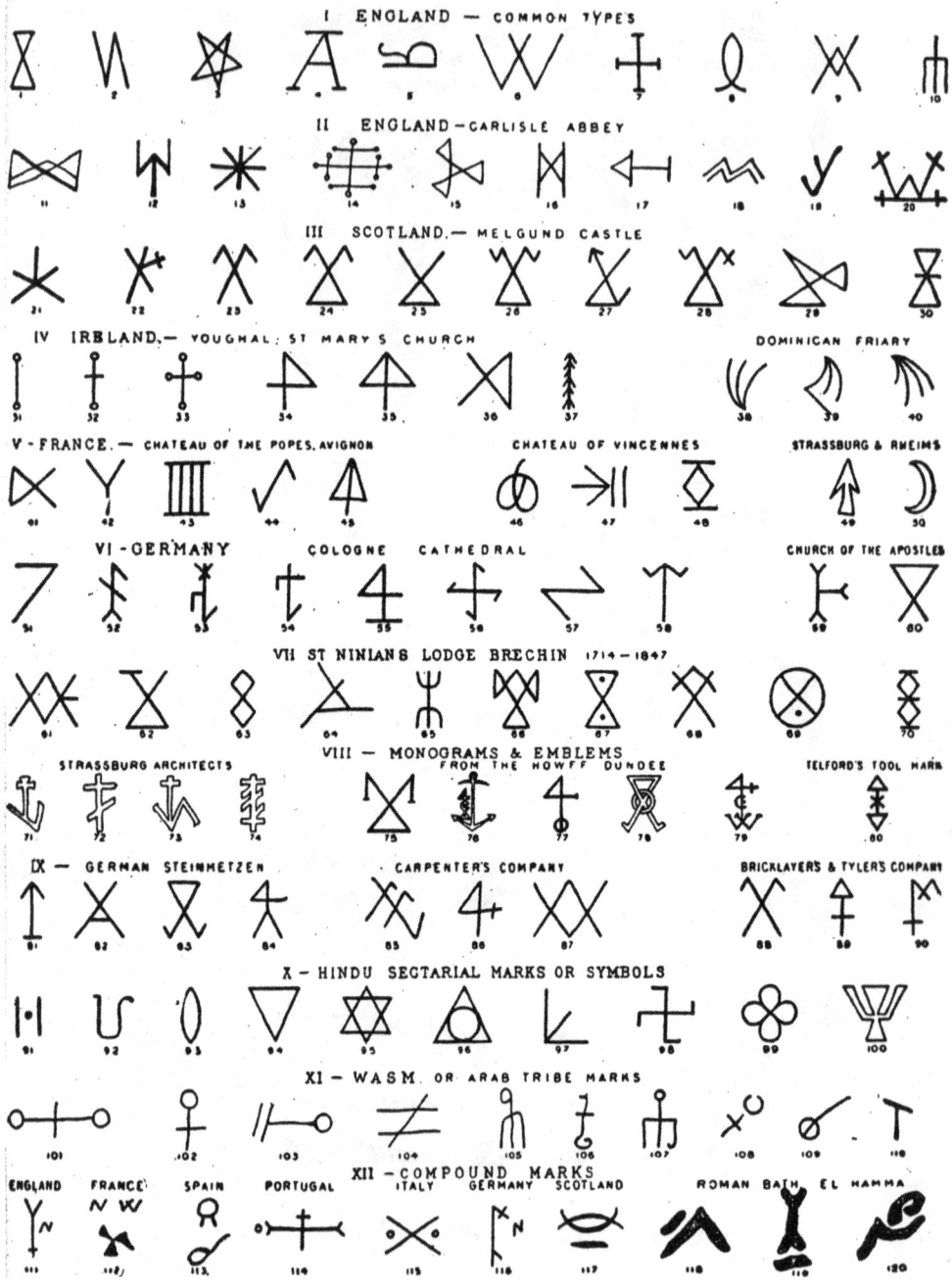

I ENGLAND — COMMON TYPES

II ENGLAND — CARLISLE ABBEY

III SCOTLAND. — MELGUND CASTLE

IV IRELAND. — YOUGHAL: ST MARY'S CHURCH   DOMINICAN FRIARY

V - FRANCE. — CHATEAU OF THE POPES, AVIGNON   CHATEAU OF VINCENNES   STRASSBURG & RHEIMS

VI - GERMANY   COLOGNE CATHEDRAL   CHURCH OF THE APOSTLES

VII ST NINIANS LODGE BRECHIN 1714 - 1847

VIII — MONOGRAMS & EMBLEMS FROM THE HOWFF DUNDEE
STRASSBURG ARCHITECTS   TELFORD'S TOOL MARK

IX — GERMAN STEINMETZEN   CARPENTER'S COMPANY   BRICKLAYERS & TYLERS COMPANY

X — HINDU SECTARIAL MARKS OR SYMBOLS

XI — WASM. OR ARAB TRIBE MARKS

XII — COMPOUND MARKS
ENGLAND FRANCE SPAIN PORTUGAL ITALY GERMANY SCOTLAND   ROMAN BATH, EL HAMMA

Masons' Marks

FROM THE ORIGINALS ON THE BUILDINGS,
AND IN THE COLLECTION OF MR. GEORGE GOODWIN, EDITOR OF "THE BUILDER,"
AND OTHER AUTHORITATIVE SOURCES

The seizing and the giving
The fire of living
Tis thus at the roaring loom of time
I ply and weave for God
The garments thou seest Him by

--Goethe, from *Faust*

Acknowledgments

From those who found the publisher and commissioned this printing,
to those who helped: Thanks to David and Pat Watson for the
original book; to worshipful Michael Allen for the artwork; and to
the brothers of Pt. Loma Lodge #620 for making this all possible.

CONTENTS

FOREWORD

To the newly inducted candidate who has just completed his final impersonation in the third degree, myriads of questions come to mind as to the significance of the ceremonials through which he has passed, and the incidental events in which he presumably has been an active participant.

In recent years "quizzes" of many kinds have become exceedingly popular. Many daily papers for years have conducted question boxes covering every conceivable topic of human interest. For some time the radio has introduced many "quiz" programs which are not only rewarding as a fund of information but have a pecuniary value as well.

To the recent initiate who has spent a number of evenings in the role of a candidate, there is such a wealth of scriptural fact, symbolism and tradition, that almost without exception, he is unable to absorb but a small portion of the knowledge which was imparted to him by the various officers in the several degrees.

For this reason there has been a long felt want for a "quiz" book or Masonic Primer, on the thousand and one facts, symbols, traditions and historical data concerning the fraternity. No secret matter is divulged in the slightest degree, but there have been so many distortions, exaggerations and fantastic tales concerning the elemental data of the institution, its genesis, its growth, its fundamental principles, and its function in the welfare of mankind, that it is hoped that the facts in this volume will assist in clearing away some of the fog of superstition, misstatement and error.

The first three degrees are based principally on the Old Testament of the Scriptures. This is primarily a narrative of a great event in the lives of the Hebrews of antiquity. This serves to explain the wealth of Biblical data given concerning that people from the dawn of recorded history. With the exception of the Knights Templar degrees and several in the Scottish Rite, the rituals are not based on New Testament occurrences, consequently there are fewer references to that portion of the Bible.

Brief mention is given to the female degrees, also to the appendant "fun" or "hilarity" degrees, but it is hoped that the data included will be of general interest. To the brother who has attempted to digest the three day induction in the Scottish Rite Degrees in one of the spring or fall reunions, the synopsis compiled for the Henry L. Palmer Class of the Wisconsin Consistory will be of inestimable value. The abridged Masonic dictionary which completes the book will be found to be an encyclopedia and gazeteer of Masonic information combined. Statistical matter of membership, etc., is from records available early in 1949.

There have been so many books published on the subject drawn from different sources that at times there may appear to be a conflict of fact. In compiling this book, many authorities have been consulted, and we find that even so meticulous a writer as Dr. Mackey, sometimes errs. In one section of his Encyclopedia he states "that the use of bells in the third degree is an anachronism, because they were not invented until the fifth century;" then later in his description of the priestly robes of Aaron, he gives the biblical reference of Exodus xxviii-34 which states the robe had "a golden bell upon the hem, that he might be heard when he went into the temple." In the spelling of Athol in the same volume by others, is sometimes spelled Atholl.

However Dr. Mackey is one of our best authorities and his history ranks with Gould's as the best Masonic history written. Findel, the German historian, whose work has been translated into English is another fine authority. To the brother who wishes to delve deeply into the mysteries and the more profound philosophy of Masonry, a study of Albert Pike's "Morals and Dogma" is suggested, but to the vast majority of the fraternity, who were prompted simply by the spirit of good fellowship to become Masons, we believe this volume will be of sustaining interest.

> *The roads we travel so briskly lead out of dim antiquity, and you study the past chiefly because of its bearing on the living present and its promise for the future.*
> — Lt. Gen. James G. Harboard, U.S.A., 1866-1947

Answers to questions in first chapter will be found, beginning on Page 109. Answers to chapters following, will be found in numerical sequence thereafter.

CHAPTER I

Relating to Masonry during the Colonial Period and the Revolutionary War.

1. Who was the first native born American to be made a Mason? . . . . •

2. Who was the first Mason recorded as coming to this country and when? . . . .
. . . .

3. Who was the first Mason, of whose *affiliation we have positive evidence,* to come to the colonies? . . . .

4. What is the oldest thing in the Western Hemisphere of Masonic interest? . . . .

5. What is the oldest Masonic document in the Western Hemisphere? . . . .

6. Did Masons hold meetings in the Colonies p r i o r to receiving dispensations from the Grand Lodge in London? . . . .

7. American Freemasonry originally came from what other country? . . . .

8. When was the "First Lodge in Boston" or "Holy Lodge of St. John" constituted? . . . . .
. . . .

9. When and where was the first Lodge meeting held in America with a record better than that of pure tradition? . . . .

10. What is the first regular and duly constituted Lodge in America? . . . .

11. Give the date of the oldest existing Masonic record in America. . . . .

12. How many Lodges were formed in Massachusetts by Grand Lodges of foreign jurisdiction? . . . .

13. What did Masons have to do with the Boston Tea Party? . . . .

14. What happened to St. Andrews Lodge on the night of the Boston Tea Party? . . . .

15. What well known Mason and patriot was killed at the battle of Bunker Hill? . . . .

16. Was Paul Revere our Revolutionary hero and Grand Master of Massachusetts, of English descent? . . . .

17. To what Lodge did Gen. Dr. Joseph Warren, John Hancock and Paul Revere belong? . . . .

18. What action did the Lodges in the Colonies take during the War of Independence? . . . .

19. What is the earliest known use of the word "Freemason" in printing or writing in America ? . . . .

20. How were Lodges operating in the Colonies prior to 1730? . . . .

21. Was Benjamin Franklin a Mason? . . . .

22. What Lodge did Benjamin Franklin join during his long residence in Paris? . . . .

23. What famous French nobleman who was an officer in the American army was a Mason?

24. In what historic public event did General Lafayette last appear in this country as a Mason? . . . .

25. Who was Joseph Brant? . . . .

26. What American minister to France found his Masonic affiliation exceedingly congenial? .

27. In which of the American Colonies was Masonry first established? . . . .

28. What did Daniel Webster once call the Green Dragon Tavern (the meeting place of the early Masonic Lodges)? . . . .

29. When and where was the first Masonic public procession in America? . . . .

30. Was Masonry practiced in the Continental Army? . . . .

31. How did the Colonial Lodges take sides in the Revolutionary Wars? . . . .

32. Did these two Grand Lodges have representation in America? . . . .

33. What was the alleged reason for the secession of the Ancients at the time of the schism in 1738? . . . .

34. When did the "Ancients" begin to operate in the state of Pennsylvania? . . . . : . . .

35. Do any of the States continue to use the work of the "Ancients"? . . . .

36. What Lodge in Virginia has the distinction of holding the oldest charter in that state? . . . .
. . . .

37. How many Lodges have been chartered in the original thirteen colonies at the close of the Revolution in 1783? . . . .

38. What is the first Lodge of which we have documentary evidence in Canada? . . . .
. . . .

39. What is the first instance of the adoption of By-Laws or Regulations in America? . . . . . .
. . . .

40. When was the corner-stone of the Capitol laid? .
. . . .

41. Give location of the first Masonic Temple in America. . . . .

42. Name some of the prominent leaders in the American Army of the Revolution who were Masons, besides Washington and LaFayette.
. . . .

43. What state in the Colonies was the first to organize and confer Degrees? . . . .

44. Give the names of some of the signers of the Declaration of Independence who were Masons.

45. How many of the deputies to the Constitutional Convention were Masons? . . . .

46. How many military Lodges were there in the Colonial Army during the Revolution? . . . .

. . . .

47. Which is the best known of the military Lodges? . . . .

48. Did the British and Colonial troops exchange Masonic courtesies during the War of Independence? . . . .

49. Were Masonic suppers or banquets common in Colonial times? . . . .

50. When did Massachusetts discontinue giving numbers to Lodges under its jurisdiction? . .

. . . .

51. Is there any historic record of a Mason saving his life through the use of a Masonic sign? . .

. . . .

52. What were the fees for Degrees in Colonial Masonic Lodges? . . . .

53. Did the Masonic Fraternity help to promote the public school system? . . . .

54. Do the Lodges in Massachusetts have numbers similar to other states? . . . .

CHAPTER II

Masonic data concerning George Washington, our first President, from his initiation to his funeral.

1. Where was George Washington made a Mason? . . . .

2. When and where did George Washington take his first degree? . . . .

3. When did George Washington take his Fellowcraft degree? . . . .

4. Who was the Charter Master of Alexandria Lodge No. 22 at Alexandria, Virginia? . . . .

5. What change in the name was later made in this Lodge? . . . .

6. Did George Washington have a Masonic burial? . . . .

7. What other President besides George Washington took his oath of office on the Bible belonging to St. John's Lodge, of New York City? . . . .

8. Of what Lodge was George Washington Worshipful Master? . . . .

9. Where did George Washington first take his oath as President? . . . .

10. Who administered the oath of office to George Washington as first President of the United States and when? . . . .

11. What is the Presidential Bible? . . . .

12. Who now owns the President's Bible? . . . . .

13. Did George Washington ever attain the position of Grand Master? . . . .

14. Who gave General Washington a beautiful embroidered Masonic Apron? . . . .

15. What was the last public occasion w h e r e George Washington acted as Master of Ceremonies? . . . .

16. Is it true that George Washington consented to Washington College being named for him?

17. Did Washington adhere to the Masonic tradition when he laid the cornerstone of the Capital building in 1793? . . . .

18. What is considered the outstanding achievement of Masons in the United States in the 20th Century? . . . .

19. How many Presidents of the United States have been Masons, up to 1949, inclusive? . . .

20. What Grand Lodge has possession of the Washington "Golden Urn"? . . . .

CHAPTER III

Historical references contemporary with the reign of King Solomon.

1. Who was Solomon? ....

2. How old was Solomon when he became King of Israel? ....

3. What variation of descent occurred in the birth of Solomon, from that of his father, King David? ....

4. How long was Solomon King of Israel? ....

5. What did Solomon ask of God after he became king? ....

6. How long after he became king, did Solomon build the Temple? ....

7. Where in the Bible do we find the narrative of the census King Solomon had made of the workmen of the Temple? ....

8. Who was Solomon's Captain of the Guards? ....

9. Who was Aholiab? ....

10. Who was Adoniram? ....

11. Who was Ornan? ....

12. Are any of the cedars of L e b a n o n still remaining? ....

13. What were the boundaries of King Solomon's Temple? . . . .

14. What does the historian, Josephus, say the style of Solomon's Temple was? . . . .
. . . .

15. What has been computed as the value of gold and silver talents at the time King Solomon was king? . . . .

16. Have any models of King Solomon's Temple been constructed? . . . .

17. What is a footstone? . . . .
. . . .

18. When was the erection of King Solomon's Temple begun? . . . .

19. When was the erection of King Solomon's Temple completed? . . . .

20. The construction of King Solomon's Temple took less than eight years. How many years was necessary for the construction of four other well known edifices? . . . .
. . . .

21. What is the area covered by St. Peter's Cathedral, at Rome? . . . .

22. What celebrated Queen of sacred history, having heard of his wisdom, paid a visit to King Solomon? . . . .

23. Why did the Queen of Sheba visit K i n g Solomon? . . . .

24. What was the Queen of Sheba reputed to have exclaimed when she beheld the magnificence of the Temple for the first time? . . . .
. . . .

25. How many stalls of horses for his chariots did King Solomon have? . . . .

26. How many targets did King Solomon have?
. . . .

27. Who was the successor to Solomon, as king?
. . . .

28. Where did Solomon stand at the Consecration of the Temple? . . . .

29. By what route did King Solomon arrive at the middle chamber of the Temple? . . . . . .
. . . .

30. How did King Solomon celebrate the completion of the building of the Temple? . . . . . .
. . . .

31. Who was Joabert and what honors were bestowed on him? . . . .

32. Were there any Lodges in the quarries of King Solomon? . . . .

CHAPTER IV

King Solomon's Temple. The second Temple by Zernbbabel. The third Temple by Herod.

1. What is the Septuagint chronology of the building of King Solomon's Temple? . . . . .
. . . .

2. When was King Solomon's Temple dedicated?

3. About how many men worked on the building of Solomon's Temple? . . . .

4. How many years was required in the erection of King Solomon's Temple? . . . .
. . . .

5. How was the foundation of the Temple built?
. . . .

6. Who was Hiram the Builder? . . . .
. . . .

7. Did Hiram Abif survive the construction of King Solomon's Temple? . . . .

8. Do you know who Hiram Abif was other than the ceremony you recall? . . . .

9. What does Abif mean? . . . .

10. Who was Hiram, king of Tyre? . . . .
. . . .

11. What were the sole contents of the Ark of the Covenant at the dedication of the Temple?
. . . .

12. Between what two villages was the clay found which was used in molding the sacred vessels of the Temple? . . . .

13. What is a propylæum? . . . .

14. What was the cost of the building, Solomon's Temple? . . . .

15. What is the estimated cost of the priestly paraphernalia? . . . .

16. How many vessels of gold and silver were there in the Temple according to Josephus?

. . . .

17. What mosque is now located on one of the slopes of Mount Moriah? . . . .

18. What was the furniture of the Holy of Holies?

. . . .

19. Were t h e r e any bells in King Solomon's Temple? . . . .

20. What was the furniture in the Holy Place in the Temple? . . . .

21. From whom did David p u r c h a s e Mount Moriah, as the future site of the Temple? . . .

. . . .

22. How old was the Temple when destroyed by the Chaldeans? . . . .

23. What were the dimensions of the great porch of the Temple, through which the priests were admitted to the sanctuary? . . . .

. . . .

24. Why were neither hammer, axe or any iron tool used in the building of King Solomon's Temple? . . . .

25. What are the globes on the pillars of Boaz and Jachin called in the Bible? . . . .
. . . .

26. What was the peculiar construction of the "Holy of Holies"? . . . .
. . . .

27. Where does tradition give us as the ancient site of the "Sanctum Sanctorum"? . . . .
. . . .

28. Where do we hear of the "Insect Shermah"?
. . . .

29. What was Jachin? . . . .

30. Where was the adytum? . . . .

31. How large was the Holy of Holies? . . . .
. . . .

32. What were the dimensions of the great pillars called Boaz and Jachin, on the entrance to the great porch of the Temple? . . . .
. . . .

33. In whose care were these sacred vessels placed?
. . . .

34. Who returned the holy vessels of the Temple to the Jews, that had been taken away by the Babylonian king, Nebuchadnezzar? . . . .
. . . .

35. Why were the Samaritans not permitted to assist in the building of the Second Temple by Zerubbabel? . . . .

36. How many dedications of the Temple are recorded in Jewish history? . . . .

37. What is a Shekel? . . . .

CHAPTER V

Old Testament references up to the time of Moses.

1. What is the definition of the name Adam?

2. How long did Adam live?

3. How long did Methuselah live?

4. How old was Enoch at the time of his death?

5. How old was Noah at the beginning of the deluge, and how long did it rain?

6. How long did it take Noah to build the Ark?

7. How large was Noah's Ark?

8. When and where was the resting place of Noah's Ark?

9. For how long a time were Noah and his family in the Ark?

10. How many decks were there on Noah's Ark?

11. What were the dimensions of Noah's Ark?

12. How many people survived the flood by being in the Ark? . . . .

13. Who was Aaron and what was his official position? . . . .

14. Where was the Tower of Babel built? . . . .

15. Of what material was the Tower of Babel constructed? . . . .

16. How high was the Tower of Babel? . . . .

17. When was the Tower of Babel erected? . . . .

18. What did the ancients use in the construction of the Tower of Babel? . . . .

19. What was the gold covering of the Ark of the Covenant called? . . . .

20. Who were the stitchers upon the first aprons? . . . .

21. Which one of Jacob's sons, when he died, was embalmed, and placed in a coffin in Egypt? . . . .

22. Did Moses ever enter the Promised Land? . . . .

23. How many Israelites did Moses have with him in his migration from Egypt? . . . .

24. Where is Mount Sinai? . . . .

25. For what is Mount Sinai noted?

26. Who was the founder of the Hebrew mysteries?

27. At what age did Moses leave the Egyptian court?

28. Who is the reputed author of the first five books of the Bible commonly c a l l e d the Pentateuch?

29. In the building of the tabernacle what plan did Moses use?

30. What is the Decalogue?

31. What is the Pentateuch?

32. Who was the shepherd of Jethro's flock on Mt. Horeb when the angel spoke to him from out of the midst of a burning bush?

33. How many times does Moses use the plural appellation of God, in the story of the creation, showing his knowledge of the *triune* personalities of Jehovah?

34. When did the Exodus occur?

35. What was the name by which Moses was commanded to identify himself to the Jews as a messenger sent by the Lord?

CHAPTER VI

Concerning King David and some of the minor prophets.

1. Who were the "Ish Chotzeb" and the "Ish Sabbal"? . . . .

2. How did the workmen under Nehemiah build a wall? . . . .

3. Did the Biblical Hebrews have knowledge of the art of soldering? . . . .

4. Whence originated the phrase "Lion of the tribe of Judah"? . . . .

5. What is the aroba? . . . .

6. What is the definition of the word Jachin? . .
. . . .

7. What does the word Boaz mean? . . . .
. . . .

8. What was David's real name? . . . .
. . . .

9. Was King David of any assistance to Solomon in the building of the Temple? . . . .
. . . .

10. How was the shield of David shaped? . . . . . .
. . . .

11. Where was the "City of David"? . . . .
. . . .

12. Why didn't King David start the building of the Temple, when the project was so dear to him? . . . .

13. What was King David's position before he became King of Israel at Jerusalem? . . . .
. . . .

14. How did David and his son, Solomon, differ in characteristics? . . . .
. . . .

15. How far had David extended the boundary of Israel at the time of his death? . . . .
. . . .

16. Who was the first king of the ten tribes of Israel? . . . .

17. What old testament character asked, "Am I my brother's keeper?" . . . .
. . . .

18. Who was Tubal Cain? . . . .
. . . .

19. What is meant by "Lion of the Tribe of Judah"? . . . .

20. Where in the Bible do we find the story of the Gileadites and the Ephramites at the ford of the Jordan River? . . . .
. . . .

21. Who was the son of Lamech and Zillah?
. . . .

22. Who was Moloch? . . . .

23. Where are mentioned Arcturus, the star, and
     the constellations Orion and the Pleiades in
     the Old Testament? ....

24. In the Jewish and Mohammedan mythology,
     what was Azrael supposed to do? ....
     ....

CHAPTER VII

*Biblical references from the reign of Belshazzer
of Babylon down to the conquest of
Jerusalem by Alexander.*

1. Who was the king of Babylon when the mysterious handwriting appeared on the wall of his banquet hall at the time of one of his royal festivals? . . . .

2. What was the writing on the wall of his palace which his wise men could not interpret? . . . .
   . . . .

3. Who translated this inscription on the wall for Belshazzer, and what did it mean? . . . . .
   . . . .

4. For how long a period were the Jews held in captivity in Babylon and how far were they from Jerusalem? . . . .

5. When did Sargon, King of Assyria, capture Samaria and disperse the idolatrous ten tribes of Israel in fulfillment of the prophecy of Amos, "The end of my people Israel is at hand"? . . . .

6. How were the Jews treated during the Babylonian captivity? . . . .

7. What was the thickness of the walls surrounding Babylon? . . . .

8. What was the height of the walls surrounding Babylon? . . . .

9. How many of the liberated captives returned to Jerusalem under the guidance of Joshua, the High Priest and Zerubbabel at the time Cyrus gave the Jews permission to go back to their own country? . . . .

10. What is the legendary significance of the triangular chain? . . . .

11. When do the learned Jews believe the Lost Word will be found? . . . .

12. What are the names of three of Job's friends? . . . .

13. How was the Hebrew meeting or congress called? . . . .

14. What is the definition of the name Emanuel? . . . .

15. Who was Nimrod? . . . .

16. What is the modern Arabic name for the site of Nineveh? . . . .

17. Who was Nebuchadnezzar? . . . .

18. How many gates were there in the walls surrounding Babylon? . . . .

19. How long did Rehoboam, son of Solomon reign over Judea? . . . .

20. When did the Kingdom of Judah reach its zenith? . . . .

21. What king of Jerusalem was a witness to the execution of his two sons, before his eyes were put out by Nebuchadnezzar? . . . .
. . . .

22. Who was Ahashuerus? . . . .

23. What happend to Judea upon the death of Alexander? . . . .

24. When did Judas, surnamed Maccabeus, recapture Jerusalem from Antiochus? . . . .
. . . .

25. Who became King of Israel after the revolt of the northern tribes against Rehoboam, at the death of Solomon? . . . .

26. What was the practice among the ancient Hebrews in the selection of a threshing floor?
. . . .

27. What was the principal object of worship of the people of antiquity? . . . .

28. What was the principal crop of the farmer in the country round and about the Jerusalem of Biblical times? . . . .

29. Who were the custodians of scriptural truths?
. . . .

30. What were the ornaments on the robe of the High Priest? . . . .

31. Why so adorned? . . . .

CHAPTER VIII

*Various definitions. Canaan,—Old Testament
translation and form.*

1. What is the Biblical definition of the title *Rabbi?* ....

2. What is a yod? ....

3. Who were the Maccabees? ....

   ....

4. What two tribes constituted the Kingdom of Judah? ....

5. When and by whom was the Bible first divided into chapters? ....

6. What is the Septuagint? ....

7. What does the word selah, a word so frequently used at the end of a verse in the Old Testament mean? ....

8. What was a psaltery? ....

9. What was the idol most chosen by the Hebrews on one of their almost periodic defections to idolatry? ....

10. What were the boundaries of *Canaan?* ......

    ....

11. What is a shekel? ....

12. What two chapters in the Bible are similar?

    ....

13. In what book of the Bible is there no mention of God? . . . .

14. How many words in the Old Testament are there ? . . . .

15. How many books are there in the Old Testament ? . . . .

16. How many times does the word "God" occur in the Bible? . . . .

17. What is the Vulgate? . . . .

18. When was the King James or Authorized Version of the Bible published? . . . .
. . . .

19. What evidence have we of the gathering of single trades together at Jerusalem? . . . . . .
. . . .

20. Who were the Ammonites? . . . .

CHAPTER IX

New Testament data—Gethsemane—
The Essenees—Bethlehem—Herod

1. How many books and epistles are there in the New Testament? . . . .

2. How many words are there in the New Testament ? . . . .

3. In what three divisions were the occupants of the Holy Land divided, contemporary with Christ? . . . .

4. What is the Golden Gate of Jerusalem? . . . .
. . . .

5. What is the topography of Jerusalem? . . . .
. . . .

6. How did Herod become procurator of Judea?
. . . .

7. What is the date of Herod's death? . . . . . .

8. What and where is Gethsemane? . . . .
. . . .

9. What does Rabboni mean? . . . .

10. Who were the *Essenes?* . . . .

11. What Old Testament history is associated with Bethlehem? . . . .

12. How did the Christian Church in the third century come to adopt June 24th and Dec. 27th as St. John's day in summer and winter?
. . . .

13. What is a *Talith?* . . . .

4. Where in the Scriptures do we find the expression "the Lion of the Tribe of Judah"?

5. How many words are there in the Apocrypha?

6. Where is *Aceldama?*
7. Who were the Three Magi?
8. What gifts did the three wise men bring to the Infant Jesus?
9. What do the initials *I-N-R-I* mean?

0. Where was Calvary?
1. Who were the twelve Apostles?

2. To what did the Apostle John refer when he spoke of the "New Jerusalem"?

3. Which of the Apostles did the Stoics and Epicureans call a babbler at Berea?

4. Who are the Saints John?
5. What is the Eucharist?
6. About how much was the thirty pieces of silver worth, that Judas received in the betrayal of Christ?
7. After the destruction of Jerusalem by Titus what became of the Jews?
8. What is a Labarum?

CHAPTER X

Israelis. Old Jewish chronology—Weights—
Measures—Festivals

1. Will the citizens of the new state of Israel be called Israelites?. . . . .

2. Of what value has the Hebrew language to Freemasonry?. . . . .

3. What was the tessera?. . . . .

4. Did the ancient Jews have a written record of their doctrines?. . . . .

5. How did the ancient Hebrews compute time prior to the captivity?. . . . .

6. What is Armo Hebraico?. . . . .

7. What is the Hebrew Chronology as given by Dr. Zunz?. . . . .

8. When did the ecclesiastical year and the civil year begin in Hebrew Chronology?. . . . .
. . . .

9. What were the Phylacteries worn by the Hebrews? . . . .

10. What is a gonfalon?. . . . .

11. What is a cubit?. . . . .

12. What is the definition of the Hebrew, Al Shaddai? . . . .

13. What is the Talmud?. . . . .

14. What does the name Boaz mean?. . . . .

15. What was the Sanhedrim?. . . . .

16. Whose rod when dropped became a snake?

17. What is a Jesse?

18. What are the Theriog?

19. What is an omer?

20. Who were the Essenes?

21. What is the definition of Rabboni?

22. Which was the most commonly used metal in the production of household utensils, tools and weapons following the deluge?

23. How long is a span?

24. What are Jodhevavhe?

25. What was the abnet?

26. What is the Jewish festival of Purim?

27. What was the Kabbala?

28. What is the Kabbalistic name of God?

29. What was the almoner?

30. What is the Moabite Stone?

31. What was meant by the trivium?

32. What is the definition of the word "Shibboleth"?

CHAPTER XI

*First Grand Lodge of England—Operative Masonry
—Roman Collegia—The Goose and Gridiron—
The Black Death.*

1. How many Grand Lodges were there in England in the eighteenth century?

2. Are any of the four original Lodges of the first Grand Lodge of England, still in existence?

3. What happened to the Lodge which met at the "Goose and Gridiron Ale-house" in 1717?

4. What was the first code of laws adopted by the Grand Lodge of England?

5. What events during the latter years of the Middle Ages are of peculiar interest to the student of Masonic history?

6. Is there any record of the arms or insignia of the different craftsmen, prior to the formation of the Grand Lodge of 1717?

7. When did the old Operative Lodges disappear?

8. What is this period called?. . . . .

9. Why is the year 1717 an important factor in the history of Free Masonry?. . . . .
. . . .

10. What was a contributing factor to the depression in the building industry in the first quarter of the 17th century when Masonic lodges began admitting professional men and men of other non-operative vocations? . . . .
. . . .

11. When was the Prestonian system of lectures adopted by the Grand Lodge of England?. . . .
. . . .

12. What societies preceding the first Grand Lodge of England in 1717 had considerable influence in the changes and adoption of the new Rituals? . . . .

13. How many types of Gilds were there in England in the seventeenth century?. . . . .
. . . .

14. Under what names were the various operative Masons known prior to the introduction of the speculative element?. . . . .

15. Did the Grand Lodge make good progress after its organization in 1717?. . . . .
. . . .

16. What officers do the English Lodges have in addition to those which we have in this country? . . . .

17. What does "Audi, Vide, Tace" mean? . . . . . .
. . . .

18. What is the York Rite? . . . .

19. What compensation did the Operative Mason allow his apprentice? . . . .
. . . .

20. What two men are credited with contributing most to the construction of the third degree as conferred at the present time? . . . .
. . . .

21. How many degrees or Rites were fabricated in the first century after the revival in 1717 claiming to be Masonic or analogous thereto?
. . . .

22. What early record have we of non-Operatives receiving Masonic Degrees? . . . .

23. What traits were taught our ancient brethren as becoming "Gentlemen Masons"? . . . .
. . . .

24. What city in England has been called the Mecca of Masonry? . . . .

25. What period in history is generally covered in the term, Middle Ages? . . . .

26. What is the English equivalent to our calling from labor to refreshment? . . . .
. . . .

27. When did Prince Edwin summon the Masons to York? . . . .

28. What ruler in England sent soldiers to the York meeting of the Grand Lodge, to prevent their deliberations? ....

29. What is one of the customs of the English Lodges of distributing their philanthropies?

....

30. Is the alehouse, Goose and Gridiron, where the English Grand Lodge was formed, still standing? ....

31. When was the pestilence known as the Black Death in England? ....

32. How long was King Edward VII Grand Master of English Masons? ....

CHAPTER XII

Athol Masons, Ahimon Rezon—Lodge of Reconciliation,—Riding the goat.

1. Who were the Athol Masons? . . . .
   . . . .

2. Who were the "Modern" Masons? . . . .
   . . . .

3. How did this effect Masonry in America? . .
   . . . .

4. When did the reconciliation take place between the two Grand Lodges of England? . . . .
   . . . .

5. Was the same reconciliation effected in America ? . . . .

6. Was the dissention between the "Ancients" and "Moderns" in England · spread to the Colonies? . . . .

7. Who was the leading spirit in the Athol Grand Lodge? . . . .

8. When the schism between the Ancients and the Moderns occurred in 1751, did the Ancients have a large following? . . . .

9. What is the Ahiman Rezon? . . . .
   . . . .

10. What was one of the probable reasons for the popularity of the Athol Lodges following the schism? . . . .

11. When did the Athol Grand Lodge or Grand Lodge of Ancients grant its first warrant for a Lodge in the Colonies? . . . .

12. When was the union of the "Ancient" and "Modern" Grand Lodges consummated? . . . .

13. In what state is the term "Ancient Free Masons" used? . . . .

14. When was reconciliation effected between the "Ancients" or "Athol Grand Lodge" and the "Moderns" or Grand Lodge of England? . . . .

15. Who were the two leading figures in the union of the Athol Grand Lodge or "Ancients" and the Grand Lodge of England or "Moderns"? . . . .

16. What was the Lodge of Reconciliation? . . . .

17. What is a cowan? . . . .

18. What is an eavesdropper? . . . .

19. What is a hecatomb? . . . .

20. What is the source of the term "riding the goat"? . . . .

CHAPTER XIII

Manuscripts—Documents—Landmarks.

1. What is the Halliwell Manuscript? . . . .
   . . . .

2. What is the oldest Extant Masonic Warrant in existence? . . . .

3. What old manuscript indicates that Freemasonry is the *symbolic expression of a religious idea?* . . . .

4. How many of the old Manuscript Constitutions are now known as a matter of record? . . . . .

5. What is a demit? . . . .

6. What interesting fact is entered in the diary of Elias Ashmole during the period of Operative Masonry? . . . .

7. How many Landmarks are there? . . . .

8. What are the "Laws of Masonry"? . . . .
   . . . .

9. What was the pamphlet, known as Dodd's Constitutions? . . . .

10. Into how many divisions are the Landmarks grouped? . . . .

11. How many points for the Craftsman are there accompanying the Masters' articles, and what is the first one? . . . .

12. How many articles are there for the old charges for the Master? . . . .

13. What distinction is there between the land-marks and the ritual of Masonry? . . . .

14. Under what six titles are the charges compiled by James Anderson as ordered by the Duke of Montagu, the Grand Master at that time? . . . .

15. How did the "Harleian Manuscript," dated about 1600 give the last eleven of the closing words of the obligation to a candidate? . . .

16. How many original copies of the old charges prior to 1717 are still in existence? . . . .

17. Are innovations forbidden in Masonry? . . . . .

18. What old manuscript is thought to be the earliest in the use of the word accepted? . . . .

19. Where do we find the best evidence of teachings of ethics and morality in Masonry? . . . .

20. What is the Leland Manuscript? . . . .

21. Give the number of landmarks in Masonry? . . .

22. What is the Sloane Manuscript? . . . .

23. What are the "Returns of Lodges"? . . . .

24. What is the origin of the name of the Masonic Gavel? . . . .

25. What form was used originally as a seal on Masonic documents? . . . .

CHAPTER XIV

Rituals, Webb Work—Discalceation—
Circumambulation.

1. Name the three Degrees in the First Section of both the York and the Ancient Accepted Scottish Rite. . . . .

2. Why are there but three degrees in Masonry?
    . . . .

3. Who were the men engaged in the division of the ritual into three Degrees? . . . .
    . . . .

4. What is Gould's theory regarding the growth of Masonic bodies several hundred years prior to the revival in 1717? . . . .

5. During what period did the evolution of a single degree develop the present system of three degrees? . . . .

6. Why do Lodges all over the world except on special occasions meet at night? . . . .
    . . . .

7. What previously was the ruling factor concerning the time of opening of Lodges? . . . .
    . . . .

8. Whence originated this custom? . . . .
    . . . .

9. Why is the Third Degree called the Sublime Degree of a Master Mason? . . . .

10. When do we find the first mention of the Masters' degree? . . . .

11. What was the significance of the designation Apprentice, Fellowcraft and Master among the Operatives? . . . .

12. How were the Degrees of Fellowcraft and Master Mason originally conferred? . . . .

13. When were the Fellowcraft and Master Mason's degrees introduced into the work? . . . .

14. When was the Second Degree invented? . . . .

15. Define Fellow-Craft. . . . .

16. When do the best Masonic authorities think the Fellow Craft Degree was fabricated? . . . .

17. What is the earliest record we have of the second and third degrees being conferred? . . . .

18. In Operative Masonry how many years did the apprentice have to serve before he could make his "Master's Piece" to submit to his Master and Wardens of his Lodge, when he might become a Fellow and receive "the Mason Word"? . . . .

19. Is there any difference in the Entered Apprentice, Fellowcraft and Master Mason's degrees in the York and the Scottish Rite? . . . .

20. What difference is there in the obligations of an Entered Apprentice and a Fellowcraft?

21. What is the Entered Apprentice?

22. What were the degrees of Ancient Craft Masonry?

23. At what period was the Hiramic legend first introduced as part of the work in the third degree?

24. How much were the fees for degrees and dues in the first century of the revival of 1717?

25. Did the Operative Masons prior to the formation of the Grand Lodge in 1717 have three degrees of ritual?

26. What are the Degrees of the Webb or American Rite?

27. In what state does the work or ritual differ most radically from that in general use throughout the United States?

28. What is the Rite of Discalceation?

29. What is the origin of the rite of Circumambulation?

30. Was the custom of worshipping God barefooted unusual?

31. What is the Pestle and Mortar degree?

CHAPTER XV

Symbols, Emblems, Cleopatra's Needle.

1. What are the Symbolic Degrees in Masonry?

    . . . .

2. What is an emblem? . . . .

3. What is the origin of the word symbol? . . . .

    . . . .

4. What is the "Symbolism of the Temple"? . . .

    . . . .

5. Why is the Vesica Piscis held in such high
    esteem as a symbol by the Christians? . . . . . .

    . . . .

6. What was the significance of the fish, as a
    Masonic Emblem? . . . .

7. Why does the Square have such a universal
    significance as a Masonic Symbol? . . . .

    . . . .

8. Of what was the phoenix an emblem? . . . . .

    . . . .

9. What is the pomegranite? . . . .

    . . . .

10. What is probably the oldest and certainly the
    most widely distributed symbol of mankind?

    . . . .

11. What is the Swastika? . . . .

12. Among what peoples of history do we find the symbol Swastika recorded? . . . .

. . . .

13. What is the Hour Glass? . . . .

. . . .

14. What is a Broached Thurnel? . . . .

. . . .

15. What does the right hand represent Masonically? . . . .

16. Through what symbol is the virtue of industry taught to Masons? . . . .

17. What is the most ancient and distinctive badge of a Mason? . . . .

18. What is the proper material for Masonic aprons? . . . .

19. Was the apron in ancient times universally received as an emblem of truth and purity?

. . . .

20. What did the Lamb-skin represent symbolically among the ancients? . . . .

21. What is the source of the use of the symbol of the point within a circle? . . . .

. . . .

22. Of what is the acacia a symbol? . . . .

23. What is the acacia? . . . .

24. What plants were symbolic in other initiations such as the acacia is to Masonry? . . . .

. . . .

25. Of what is "Low Twelve" a symbolism? . . . . . .

. . . .

26. What is the symbolism of the circle in the Masonic Keystone? . . . .

27. What is the Masonic symbolism of the gavel and the setting maul? . . . .

28. What symbol does a Masonic Lodge represent?

. . . .

29. What do the clasped hands represent as a symbol? . . . .

30. What emblems of the builders were found on Cleopatria's needle, now in Central Park, New York City, when it was taken down in 1879 in Egypt and moved to America? . . . .

. . . .

31. What is the true symbolism in Speculative Masonry of the Trestle Board? . . . .

. . . .

32. What is the symbolism of the blazing star?

. . . .

33. What were the three symbols of Hermetic philosophy ? . . . .

CHAPTER XVI

Legends, Ceremonials, San Graal.

1. Into how many classifications does Mackey, our leading Masonic authority, divide the legends of Masonry? . . . .

2. What are the Masonic elements of consecration? . . . .

3. Why are Tasting and Smelling not mentioned in the ritual, except as making up the sacred number five? . . . .

4. What are the "Perfect Points of Entrance"? . . . .

5. Was the rite of circumambulation a ceremonial custom among other people besides the Hebrews . . . .

6. What Masonic ceremonials are usually conducted publicly? . . . .

7. What were the old Hebrew covenants from which we get the "Four Perfect Points of Entrance"? . . . .

8. Is baptism a part of the Masonic ceremonial? . . . .

9. To what does the formal procession of the candidate around the Lodge allude? . . . .

10. What are the Twelve Original Points of Freemasonry through which every candidate must
pass when taking any degree? . . . .
. . . .

11. What is the "Due Guard"? . . . .

12. What is the Pectoral? . . . .

13. How many Landmarks are there? . . . .

14. What is the Legend of the Winding Stairs? . .
. . . .

15. What is an Aphanism? . . . .
. . . .

16. What is the old Masonic tradition of Latres?
. . . .

17. How did the word free happen to become a
part of the name of the Masonic Fraternity;
that is A.F. & A.M.? . . . .
. . . .

18. What similar legend have we, among other
nations, relating to the expounding of Divine
law, similar to the account of Moses, on Mt.
Sinai? . . . .

19. What is the legend of the San Graal? . . . . . .
. . . .

20. What is the response to prayer or benediction?
. . . .

CHAPTER XVII

Jewels, Tools, Furnishings

1. How many movable jewels are there? . . . . . .
. . . .

2. What are the immovable jewels? . . . .
. . . .

3. What are the cardinal virtues? . . . .
. . . .

4. To what do the seven branches of the Golden Candlestick refer? . . . .
. . . .

5. What were the fixed lights? . . . .
6. In what Degree is the chisel a working tool?
. . . .

7. What is the significance of the Cable Tow?
. . . .

8. What is the length of your "Cable Tow"? . .
. . . .

9. Did only Freemasons make use of "marks"?
. . . .

10. What workman's metal tool swam? . . . .
. . . .

11. What is a plumb-line? . . . .
12. What is the indented Tessal? . . . .
. . . .

13. What are the three ornaments of a Lodge?

14. What is the line?

15. What is the definition of Ashlar?

16. What is the covering of a Masonic Lodge?

17. What are the furnishings of a Lodge?

18. What are the three principal supports of a Lodge?

CHAPTER XVIII

Grand Masters, Masters, Lodges, Making Masons at Sight.

1. Who was the "First Deputized Grand Master in the North American Colonies"? . . . .
    . . . .

2. How is the Grand Master addressed when presiding over the Grand Lodge? . . . .
    . . . .

3. What are the officers of a Grand Lodge? . . . .
    . . . .

4. Has the Grand Lodge founded by Henry Price July 30, 1733, maintained a continuous existence? . . . .

5. What Grand Lodge during the Colonial Wars between France and England issued traveling warrants? . . . .

6. How many Grand Lodges are there under the American flag? . . . .

7. What is the largest Grand Lodge in the United States and what is the asset value of its property? . . . .

8. Have any of the Grand Lodges given Charters to Lodges in foreign lands? . . . .
    . . . .

9. When may the Grand Honors of Masonry be given? . . . .

10. What constitutes the opening of a Lodge in "ample form"? . . . .

11. In what state does the Grand Lodge insist that one entitled to recognition as a Mason, must specifically acknowledge Gods' "inspired word" or as one authority expresses it "he may believe as he pleases so long as he believes in one true God and accepts the Holy Bible as His divine teachings and His revealed will"? . . . .

. . . .

12. To whom does the property of the Lodge belong, upon its dissolution? . . . .

13. What constitutes the Grand East? . . . .

. . . .

14. Was there any division in the Grand Lodges of the United States during the war between the states? . . . .

15. Why is it the work in each Grand Jurisdiction differs slightly in the wording? . . . .

. . . .

16. What was the Baltimore Convention? . . . .

. . . .

17. Where were the five Conventions or Congresses of Masons held in the United States? . . . .

. . . .

18. What are the rights of a Grand Master?

. . . .

19. Who only may make Masons at sight? . . . . . .
. . . .

20. What is the mode of exercising the prerogative of making a Mason at Sight? . . . .

21. What four Americans were made Masons at sight ? . . . .

22. What Grand Master had the longest tenure of office? . . . .

23. Who is the Bible-Bearer? . . . .

24. What is the origin of the wearing of collars by the Lodge officers? . . . .

25. When was the office of Deacon instituted? . . .
. . . .

26. What is the badge of office of the Deacons?
. . . .

27. What is the badge of office of the Stewards?
. . . .

28. Name the Eighth Officer of the Lodge. . . . . . .
. . . .

29. What was the origin of the title, Tyler? . . . . . .
. . . .

30. Why is it called the Tiler's oath? . . . .

31. What was one of the duties of the Tyler in colonial times? . . . .

32. Which of the Presidents have been Grand Master of his state? . . . .

33. What were "Jug Lodges"? . . . .
. . . .

CHAPTER XIX

Freemasonry, Domatic Masons, Gentleman Masons, Various definitions of Masonry.

1. What is Freemasonry?

2. What is a fine modern expression of Masonry?

3. Is Freemasonry a secret society?

4. What early Masonic leader was responsible for making the Masonic system essentially Biblical?

5. Give the definition of Masonry given in the German *Handbuch* published in 1900.

6. Is a sectarian explanation of the three Masonic degrees feasable?

7. How do we indicate Masonically the hour of mid-day or noon?

8. What do the initials A.O. mean?

9. What is a "Domatic Mason"?

10. What is considered the color of Masonry?

11. What is the first recorded use of the word Free-mason?

12. What were "Gentlemen Masons"? . . . .
. . . .

13. Give a good definition of the Moral Law. . . . .
. . . .

14. What is a Masonic dispensation? . . . .

15. What was the significance of the use of the words "it rains" among Masons? . . . .
. . . .

16. Give definition of "battery" in Masonry. . . . .
. . . .

17. Give a good definition for initiation. . . . .
. . . .

18. What was the difference between Free or Free-stone Masons and Rough Masons? . . . .
. . . .

19. Were there ever *Journeymen* in Operative Masonry? . . . .

20. What is the difference between "Letter Masons" and "Salute Masons"? . . . .

21. Why is modern Freemasonry called speculative? . . . .

22. What is an Encyclical? . . . .

23. What is a "Parrot Mason"? . . . .

24. How long was Solomon occupied in the building of the Temple? . . . .

25. Which use of the initials is proper A.F. & A.M. or F. & A.M.? . . . .

26. What are the real foundations of Masonry both material and moral? . . . .

27. What is the derivation of the word Mason? . . . .

28. What is the definition of Freemasonry? . . . .

29. What is the design of Freemasonry? . . . .

30. What is suspension? . . . .

31. What is a Mason's creed? . . . .

32. What is the real object of Freemasonry? . . . .

33. What record have we of Queen Victoria's attitude towards Masonry? . . . .

34. Can a profane prefer charges against a Mason? . . . .

CHAPTER XX

Blue Lodge, Insurance, Membership Records.

1. What two symbolic themes predominate in the first three Degrees of Masonry? . . . .
. . . .

2. Is it proper to refer to a Master Mason's Lodge as a Blue Lodge? . . . .

3. What is the principal religious qualification a Mason must have? . . . .

4. What Lodge in the days of Western pioneering was known as the "Mother of Lodges"? . . . .
. . . .

5. What is the root of the word Lodge? . . . .
. . . .

6. Has the ritual ever been uniform all over the forty-eight states? . . . .

7. Have any efforts been made in this country to form a national Grand Lodge? . . . .

8. Which is the northernmost Masonic Lodge in the U.S.A.? . . . .

9. Are there any Lodges in North America now that are members of the Grand Lodge of England? . . . .

10. What and where is the unique building erected and used for the purpose of Masonic meetings only? . . . .

11. Why is the floor of the Lodge an oblong square?

12. What is the principal link binding all Masonic Lodges everywhere?

13. Are there any insurance benefits in Masonry?

14. Can a woman become a Mason?

15. How can a Master Mason make his choice between the York and Scottish Rite degrees if he chooses to advance further?

16. What is the meaning of "brithering"?

17. What is the difference between "Esoteric and Exoteric" Masonry?

18. Which is correct usage, demit or dimit?

19. What is the definition of the name Tubal Cain?

20. What is a Lewis?

21. What is a magic square?

22. What does the Ground Floor of the Lodge represent?

23. What is an inchoate Lodge?

24. What is called a Clandestine Lodge?

25. When was the word "Clandestine" first used?

. . . .

26. What is the Masonic law in relation to "Clandestinism"? . . . .

27. When is a Lodge properly tiled? . . . .

. . . .

28. When was the business of the Lodge formerly transacted? . . . .

29. In which of the states are there some Lodges without names, using only numbers? . . . .

. . . .

30. What number constitutes a quorum in a Masonic Lodge, for the transaction of business?

. . . .

31. Whence came the custom of the Master of a Lodge wearing a hat? . . . .

32. Who presides over the Lodge when called from labor to refreshment? . . . .

33. Where is the Lodge of St. John? . . . .

. . . .

34. Is the use of any kind of decorations on a Masonic apron proper? . . . .

35. What is the meaning of "Substitute Word"?

. . . .

36. How many Lodges were there in the United States in 1948? . . . .

37. What two Lodges have the largest membership in the United States? . . . .

38. What is the present Masonic membership in the U.S.A. in the year 1948? . . . .
. . . .

39. What was the net gain in membership for the year 1948? . . . .

40. Which state has the largest membership? . . . .
. . . .

41. Which state has the smallest membership? . .
. . . .

42. Did the Lodges in Scotland admit non-Operatives to membership in the same manner as the English Lodges? . . . .

43. What was the answer of a Freemason and a great sculptor, Gutzon Borglum, to a man who asked how he carved stone into such beautiful statues? . . . .

44. Do you know the difference between a cowan and an eavesdropper? . . . .

CHAPTER XXI

The four Degrees in the Chapter.

1. What are the Capitular Degrees? . . . .
2. What is the Royal Arch? . . . .
3. When was the title Lodge replaced by the title Chapter? . . . .
4. When did the word Companion take the place of the word brother? . . . .
5. What Biblical character is the High Priest in the Chapter supposed to impersonate? . . . . . .
    . . . .
6. How many Mark Masters does tradition tell us were employed in the quarries of Zeredatha, in hewing, squaring, marking and numbering stones for the Temple? . . . .
7. What were the requirements for the initiation in the Mark Degree? . . . .
8. When was the Mark Degree first conferred?
    . . . .
9. What is the origin of the name Mark Master?
    . . . .
10. In what degree is the chisel a working tool?
    . . . .
11. Why were Masons' Marks used in the construction of all the ancient buildings? . . . . . .
    . . . .

12. When were the Chapter Degrees of "Mark" and "Most Excellent" formulated?

. . . .

13. What is the Past Master's degree?

. . . .

14. How old is the Most Excellent Master's Degree?

. . . .

15. What is the earliest record of minutes of a Royal Arch meeting?

. . . .

16. What is the earliest date of the use of the words "Royal Arch Chapter" in St. Andrews Chapter?

. . . .

17. Did the Royal Arch Chapter use the present titles for its line of officers from the beginning?

. . . .

18. When was the Royal Arch Degree originated?

. . . .

19. How was the Royal Arch Degree introduced in America?

20. What is the earliest record we have in this country of the conferring of the Royal Arch degree?

21. What is the first record of the Royal Arch Chapter being formed in America?

. . . .

22. What originally was a necessary qualification for the attainment of the Royal Arch Degree?

. . . .

23. To whom does the Masonic historian Gould, credit the formation of the Royal Arch degrees, in America? . . . .

24. What was the fee passing the Royal Arch in the eighteenth century? . . . .

25. Describe the four Royal Arch Banners. . . . .
. . . .

26. What is the appropriate color of the Royal Arch Degree? . . . . : . . .

27. How many Royal Arch Masons are there in this country? . . . .

28. Who is the Principal Sojourner? . . . .
. . . .

29. Who is the Scribe? . . . .

30. Who receives the title of Prophet in the ritual of the Royal Arch Degree? . . . .

31. What is a crow, and in what degree is it a working tool? . . . .

32. Which two of the twelve tribes of Israel, returned to Jerusalem with Zerubbabel for the re-building of the Temple? . . . .
. . . .

33. What is a convocation? . . . .

34. Who was the founder of the General Grand Chapter in the United States? . . . .
. . . .

35. Where was the first Grand Chapter organized in the United States? . . . .

36. How many states were represented at the formation of the Grand Chapter at Hartford Ct., in 1798? . . . .

37. Has any effort been made to dissolve the General Grand Chapter? . . . .

38. When did the Grand Chapter of Texas withdraw from the General Grand Chapter? . . . .

. . . .

39. How many subordinate Chapters in other countries are acting under the General Grand Chapter of the United States? . . . .

. . . .

40. What are called the Cryptic Degrees? . . . . .

. . . .

41. Were the Cryptic Degrees ever a part of the Chapter work? . . . .

42. Who was the builder of the second Temple at Jerusalem? . . . .

CHAPTER XXII

The Knights Templar Degrees.

1. What is the first printed record we have of the Degree of Order of Knight Templar being conferred? . . . .

2. Into what three distinct periods is the history of Templary in America divided? . . . .

   . . . .

3. Which is proper, Knights Templar or Knight Templars? . . . .

4. Who is the Recorder? . . . .

   . . . .

5. How many Knights Templar are there in the United States? . . . .

6. What is an accolade? . . . .

7. What are the meetings or congregations of Knights Templar called in America? . . . .

   . . . .

8. Where and when was the first Grand Encampment formed? . . . .

9. When and by whom was the Order of Knights Templars, of the Crusade era organized? . . . .

   . . . .

10. What is a "Baphomet"? . . . .

11. What is the Chamber of Reflection? . . . .

12. Who originated the Order of Knighthood called the Order of the Golden Fleece? . . . . .

13. What was the closing battle in the war of the Crusades which led the Christians to evacuate Palestine? . . . .

14. Of what is the Social Order of Beauceants composed? . . . .

15. What was the Beauseant? . . . .

16. What is the crosier? . . . .

17. What does the term "cross-legged Knight" signify? . . . .

18. What is the Order of De Molay? . . . .
. . . .

CHAPTER XXIII

Ancient Accepted Scottish Rite Masons.

1. What and where is the oldest authenticated Scottish Rite document in the Western world?

. . . .

2. To whom do Albert Pike and Dr. Mackey credit the establishement of the Bodies of Scottish Rite in America? . . . .

. . . .

3. Where and when was the first Supreme Council organized? . . . .

4. When was the Supreme Grand Council for the Northern Jurisdiction of the United States founded? . . . .

5. What is considered as the most reasonable account of the first Ancient Accepted Scottish Rite body? . . . .

6. What is the Consistory? . . . .

7. What are the Ineffable Degrees? . . . .

. . . .

8. Who are the Sublime Masons? . . . .

. . . .

9. What are the Ancient Historical and Traditional Degrees? . . . .

10. What are the Apocalyptic and Christian Degrees? . . . .

11. What are the Modern Historical, Chivalric and Philosophical Degrees? . . . .
. . . .

12. What is the motto of the Thirty-second Degree of the Ancient and Accepted Scottish Rite?
. . . .

13. What is a chasuble? . . . .

14. Who was Atossa? . . . .

15. To whom may we apply the title "Illustrious"?
. . . .

16. What is the degree of Grand Pontiff? . . . . . .
. . . .

17. What, in the higher degrees is sometimes called "Masonic Baptism"? . . . .
. . . .

18. What is a Noachite or Prussian Knight? . . . .

19. What is an allocution? . . . .

20. What is the Reformed Rite? . . . .

21. What is the Rosaic Rite? . . . .

22. What is the Grand Scotch Knight of Saint Andrew? . . . .

23. What is the probable date of the first official use of the double headed eagle and its meaning? . . . .

24. How is the Latin word Illuminati used Masonically? . . . .

CHAPTER XXIV

Eastern Star and the other female Degrees.

1. Who introduced the Order of the Eastern Star? . . . .

2. How many members in the Order of the Eastern Star in this country? . . . .

3. From what country and "rite" was the Eastern Star taken? . . . .

4. Did French Adoptive Masonry ever come to America? . . . .

5. What is meant by Androgynous Masonry? . . . .

6. Who was the author of the Eastern Star Ritual? . . . .

7. Who was the publisher of the *Manual* which gave so great a stimulus to the growth of the Eastern Star? . . . .

8. When was the Eastern Star banned from Pennsylvania? . . . .

9. What are the titles of the five degrees of the Eastern Star? . . . .

10. What is the Order of Amaranth? . . . .

11. In what state is membership in the Eastern Star forbidden to Masons? . . . .

12.   Who are Job's Daughters? . . . .

13.   What is the Order of Rainbow for Girls? . . . .

. . . .

14.   What is the Amaranth?

. . . .

15.   Who are the "Heroines of Jericho"? . . . . . .

. . . .

16.   What is the fraternity known as the Crusaders?

. . . .

17.   When was the White Shrine of Jerusalem
      formed? . . . .

CHAPTER XXV

*Masonry and the Bible—Research Lodge
—Fessler's Rite.*

1. What is the most important book a Masonic student can study? . . . .

2. In what languages was the Bible originally written? . . . .

3. Must the Bible always be placed on the altar in a Masonic Lodge all over the world? . . . .

4. Is the Holy Bible mentioned in the Constitutions of 1723? . . . .

5. When was the Bible first mentioned as a Great Light in Masonry? . . . .

6. What is the most eminent research Lodge in Masonry? . . . .

7. What is the Ars Quatour Coronatum? . . . .

8. Who is the author of the quotation from the third degree lecture, "Thus wastes man, etc."? . . . .

9. In what two languages are alpha and aleph the first letters in the alphabet? . . . .

10. What were the "Seven Wonders of the Ancient World"? . . . .

11. Is there a record of the use of the word Free Mason in literature prior to the formation of the Grand Lodge in London in 1717?

12. By what trade was architecture displaced in the fifteenth c e n t u r y as the recorder of history?

13. How many appendant modern organizations have as a requisite for admission, Masonic membership?

14. Who wrote the play in which we find the lines "To that undiscovered country from whose bourne no traveler returns"?

15. What is the Masonic Calendar?

16. How far back do the records of the Masons' Company of London run?

17. What is Fessler's Rite?

18. What were the Secret Tribunals of Westphalia or Vehmgerichte?

19. What is the "Armenbuchse"?

20. What was the earliest Masonic magazine published?

21. What is a "Lehrling"?

22. What profane record have we of Masonic operations prior to the organization of the Grand Lodge in 1717?

23. Is there any reference to the Masonic legends or Ancient Mysteries in the old classics? . . . .
. . . .

24. What are considered the finest Masonic Libraries in America? . . . .

25. Which is considered the best authority for a Mason who wishes to make a study of. Masonry? . . . .

CHAPTER XXVI

Origins of Lodges and terms, Early Constitutions.

1. Give the names of the four Lodges which formed the Grand Lodge of England at the Apple Tree Tavern in London in 1717. . . . .

   . . . .

2. Which was the largest of the four Lodges forming the first Grand Lodge? . . . .

3. Name nine of the general accepted origins of Freemasonry. . . . .

4. How old is Masonry? . . . .

5. From whence is the word Masonry derived?

   . . . .

6. What is the significance of the word "Free" in connection with "Mason"? . . . .

   . . . .

7. What is the origin of the word "Accepted" in A. F. and A. M.? . . . .

8. When was the title of "Free and Accepted Masons" first used? . . . .

9. What determines the precedency of a Lodge?

   . . . .

10. What is the origin of the word "Free" in A. F. and A. & M.? . . . .

11. When were individual names given to Lodges?

    . . . .

12. When was the first Book of Constitutions published? . . . .

13. What is the Book of Constitutions? . . . .

. . . .

14. Who wrote the first Constitution of our present order and when? . . . .

15. What is the earliest date known making reference to any such Constitution? . . . .

16. What were the Gothic Constitutions? . . . . . .

. . . .

17. What is the earliest authentic specimen of Gothic architecture in Germany? . . . .

. . . .

18. The earliest "Book of Constitutions" was the joint result of the labors of what three men?

. . . .

19. Which of the world's Lodges is credited with the exemplification of the "Purest Masonry in the World"? . . . .

20. What was the original Grand Lodge motto in 1717? . . . .

21. When did the custom of Lodges having names, become the general practice? . . . .

22. Were a grip and word used in the ceremonials of the operatives? . . . .

23. Why did the old Lodges meet "in lowest of vales and the highest of hills"? . . . .

. . . .

CHAPTER XXVII

Egyptian sources—The Mysteries—The Rosetta Stone. Cleopatra's Needle.

1. What country of ancient times was the cradle of all the Pagan mysteries? ....

2. Who was Hermes? ....

3. What did the Globe represent in the Egyptian mysteries? ....

4. Who built the Pyramid of Gizeh and for what purpose? ....

5. What was the name of the Egyptian sun-god?
   ....

6. From what people are most of our Masonic symbols taken? ....

7. Who were the sibyls? ....

8. What was Naos? ....

9. What is the clepsydra? ....

10. What was Aldebaran? ....

11. Who were the Copts? ....

12. Where is Denderah and for what is it celebrated? ....

13. What was the handled cross called and what was its symbolism? ....

14. What was the foundation of the Egyptian belief? ....

15. What is a Pharos? . . . .

16. What is Cleopatra's needle? . . . .

17. What are the dimensions of the Great Pyramid of Ghiza? . . . .

18. What is the Sphinx? . . . .

19. Where is the most celebrated Sphinx? . . . . .
. . . .

20. What are the twelve constellations? . . . .
. . . .

21. What were the ten plagues of Egypt? . . . . . .
. . . .

22. For what reason did the Egyptians use the lion as a figure of the flooding of the Nile? . . .
. . . .

23. What architectural custom is the outgrowth of that event? . . . .

24. What is alchemy? . . . .

25. By what other name was the science of alchemy called? . . . .

26. What is the Rosetta Stone? . . . .

27. Who sent the Palestinian Jews to Egypt to assist in the translation of the Septuagiut Version of the Bible? . . . .

28. Where is the Rosetta Stone at the present time?
. . . .

29. What Egyptian ruler had the Hebrew Scriptures translated into Greek? . . . .

CHAPTER XXVIII

Greek Influence—Pythagoras—Geometry and Architecture

1. What two sciences have always held a prominence in Masonic work? . . . .

. . . .

2. Who was Euclid and when was he born? . . . .

. . . .

3. Who was Pythagoras? . . . .

4. How many years did Pythagoras have to wait for initiation into the hidden mysteries of Egypt? . . . .

5. Who were the Tryonists? . . . .

6. Who were the Epicureans? . . . .

7. Who were the Stoics? . . . .

8. Who were the Magi? . . . .

9. What were the Eranoi? . . . .

10. What is the forty-seventh problem of Euclid?

. . . .

11. What was Euclid's answer to King Ptolemy when he was asked, "Can not the problem be made simpler"? . . . .

12. What was the inscription of Geometry, Plato had placed over the porch of his Academy at Athens? . . . .

13. What was the Golden Fleece? . . . .
    . . . .

14. What is the Doric order? . . . .

15. For what three orders in architecture are we
    indebted to the Greeks? . . . .

16. What is the Parthenon ?

17. Who were the Dionysian Architects? . . . . . .
    . . . .

18. To whom were the Greeks indebted for their
    inspiration in architecture? . . . .
    . . . .

19. Who was Callimachus? . . . .
    . . . .

20. What is a very well known specimen of the
    Corinthian order of architecture in the United
    States? . . . .

21. What type of column represents the West? . .
    . . . .

22. What type of column represents the South? . .
    . . . .

23. Give a celebrated specimen of the Corinthian
    type of architecture of ancient history. . . . .
    . . . .

24. What type of architecture was largely used by
    Freemasons in the middle ages and reached
    its flower in the Renaissance? . . . .
    . . . .

25. What is a pilaster? . . . .

26. What is the archetype? . . . .

27. How many forms are there in an equilateral triangle? . . . .

28. What is the basic form in geometry from which all other forms are made? . . . .
. . . .

29. What was the tetractys? . . . .

30. When was the erection of Westminster Abbey started? . . . .

CHAPTER XXIX

Roman Influences—The Collegia—The Comacines

1. What year was Rome founded? ....
....

2. What and where were the Catacombs? .....
....

3. What was the Roman Eagle? ....
....

4. To what Roman god does Tubal Cain cor-
respond? ....

5. What is the Agenda? ....

6. Of all the people of the ancient world, in profane history, which was the most advanced
and civilized in the building industry? ....
....

7. For what orders type of architecture are the
Romans famous? ....

8. Was the knowledge of fine craftsmanship wide-
ly distributed through the instrumentality of
the Roman Collegia? ....

9. What Roman commander finally destroyed
Jerusalem and burned the Temple? ....
....

10. Where do we get the original definition of the
word pontiff? ....

11. Who were the Cyclops? . . . .

12. To what order of craftsmen does Gould, the historian, credit the building of the English Cathedrals, prior to the Reformation? . . . . .

. . . .

13. What name did the Romans give to the Sea of Galilee? . . . .

14. When did the Romans first capture Jerusalem?

. . . .

15. What were the Roman Collegia? . . . .

. . . .

16. Who were the Comacine Masters? . . . .

. . . .

17. What is the abacus? . . . .

CHAPTER XXX

The Mysteries—Rosicrucians—Zoroaster
Ecc. I:1-12—Culdees.

1. What are the "arts, parts and points" of the Mysteries of Masonry? . . . .

2. What are the mystical ages in some Masonic rites? . . . .

3. What is the definition of Iconology? . . . .
. . . .

4. What is Theosophy? . . . .

5. What is the "Mystic Tie"? . . . .

6. What is the true meaning of the Lost Word?
. . . .

7. Who were the Rosicrucians? . . . .

8. Who has given the *Modern Society* of Rosicrucians its present definite form? . . . .
. . . .

9. Who were the Druids? . . . .

10. What were the three sacred colors of the Druids? . . . .

11. About when did Zoroaster proclaim his philosophy relating to the earth and the stars? . .
. . . .

12. Who were the Culdees? . . . .

13. What is the Star and Garter? . . . .
. . . .

14. What is the symbolic interpretation of the phrase from the xii chapter of Ecclesiastes, "The almond tree shall flourish."?

15. What is meant by "Or ever the Silver Cord be loosed"?

16. To what does "the keepers of the house shall tremble" refer?

17. To what does "Those that look out of the windows be darkened" refer?

18. To what does "The doors shall be shut in the streets, when the sound of the grinding is low," refer?

19. To what does "And he shall rise up at the voice of the bird," refer?

20. To what does "And all the daughters of music shall be brought low," refer?

21. To what does "They shall be afraid of that which is high," refer?

22. To what does "And fears shall be in the way," refer?

23. To what does "The grasshopper shall be a burden," refer?

24. To what does "And desire shall fail," refer?

25. To what does "Man goeth to his long home," refer?

26. To what does "The mourners go about the streets," refer? . . . .

27. To what does "The golden bowl be broken," refer? . . . .

28. To what does "The pitcher be broken at the fountain," refer? . . . .

29. To what does "The wheel broken at the cistern," refer? . . . .

30. What is theology? . . . .

31. What was the oldest and most prevalent of all ancient religions? . . . .

32. What was the name of Sun Worship? . . . . . .
. . . .

33. Name the sacred book of the Hindus. . . . . . .
. . . .

34. What is the zenith? . . . .

35. What is the Pitaka? . . . .

36. What was a Simorgh? . . . .

37. What is a Yug or Yuga? . . . .

38. What was the Tiluk? . . . .

39. What were some of the faculties of the Creator to prehistoric man? . . . .

40. What does abracadabra mean? . . . .
. . . .

41. What is the Zend-Avesta? . . . .

42. What distinguished Mason translated the Zend Avesta into English? . . . .

CHAPTER XXXI

Men of Distinction—Most of them in the Masonic Fraternity

1. Who was the most distinguished member of the craft of his time, who erected St. Paul's Cathedral in London? . . . .

2. Of what Lodge was Sir Christopher Wren a member? . . . .

3. What profane record have we that Sir Christopher Wren, the architect of St. Paul's Cathedral, was a Mason? . . . .
. . . .

4. What was the theory of Sir Christopher Wren, in which man found his inspiration for the erection of columns? . . . .
. . . .

5. The diary of Elias Ashmole is very highly thought of as a Masonic record. What other contribution has he made to the literature or history of his period? . . . .

6. Who was elected the first Grand Master of Speculative Masonry in 1717? . . . .
. . . .

7. What English nobleman gave a great stimulus to the growth of Masonry and when? . . . . . .
. . . .

8. Who was James Anderson? . . . .

9. Who was the Rev. John Theophilus Desagu-liers? . . . .

10. Who was Thomas Dunckerly? . . . .
. . . .

11. What is known of Inigo Jones of England?
. . . .

12. Who was Lawrence Dermott? . . . .
. . . .

13. What well known Masonic author was elected to membership and Master of the Lodge of Antiquity, at the same meeting? . . . .
. . . .

14. Who was John Boswell, (of Auchinleck)? . .
. . . .

15. Was the famous French writer Voltaire, a Mason? . . . .

16. Name six of the leading Masonic authorities in the earlier years of Speculative Masonry. . . . .
. . . .

17. Who was John Coustos? . . . .

18. What two celebrated Poles of revolutionary fame, who served under Washington, were Masons? . . . .

19. Who was Ludwig Greinemann? . . . .
. . . .

20. What was the best known oracle of ancient times? . . . .

21. Was John Paul Jones a Mason? . . . .

22. Who was Cagliostro? . . . .

23. What were the names of the "Three Magi"?
. . . .

24. What was "Ernest and Falk"? . . . .

25. Who was Copernicus? . . . .

26. Who and what was Mohammed? . . . .
. . . .

27. Who was the first emperor of the Holy Roman
Empire? . . . .

28. Was Tut-Ankh-Amen a Mason? . . . .

29. Who was Raymond Lully? . . . .
. . . .

30. What was the Polychronicon? . . . .
. . . .

31. Who was Chevalier Ramsey? . . . .
. . . .

32. When was Frederick the Great of Prussia made
a Mason? . . . .

33. Who are the three best known poets laureate
of Masonry? . . . .

34. Was Abraham Lincoln a Mason? . . . .

35. Was Joseph Smith, founder of the Mormon
religion, a Mason? . . . .

36. Who was Albert Pike? . . . .

37. Were either of the Roosevelts, Theodore or
Franklin Delano, Past Masters? . . . .

38. Was Mark Twain a Mason? . . . .

39. Who was Albert Gallatin Mackey? . . . .
. . . .

40. What was Thomas Smith Webb's contribution
to Masonry? . . . .

41. What Mason saved the Masonic Library of
Albert Pike during the Civil War? . . . .
. . . .

42. Was Daniel Webster a Mason? . . . .

43. Who was the Masonic "Poet Laureate" of the
United States of America? . . . .
. . . .

44. Who is rated the most erudite and scholarly
historical writer on Masonic subjects in the
United States? . . . .

45. Who was Moloch? . . . .

46. Name twelve persons of note in biblical history
represented in the Masonic Ritual. . . . .
. . . .

47. Who was Jacques De Molay? . . . .

48. What was the toast tendered to Robert Burns
the beloved Scotch poet, wherever he visited
Masonic Lodges in his later years? . . . .
. . . .

CHAPTER XXXII

Geography of Masonic interest.

1. Where is Joppa? . . . .
2. What is the tradition of the name of the port of Joppa? . . . .
3. What was the location of Ethiopia? . . . .
. . . .
4. Is the choice of Ethiopia as a place to hide regarded by Masonic historians a good one?
. . . .
5. What is the location of the land of Nod? . .
. . . .
6. What was Golgotha? . . . .
7. How long is the Euphrates River? . . . .
8. Where is Kilwinning? . . . .
. . . .
9. Where is Succoth? . . . .
10. How large is the Red Sea? . . . .
11. Where is the "terrestrial paradise"? . . . .
. . . .
12. For what is Lebanon best known? . . . .
. . . .
13. How long is the river Jordan? . . . .
14. How long is the river Tigris, which flows into the Euphrates? . . . .

15. Where was Fort Hiram? . . . .

16. What is the other geographical name for Shinar? . . . .

17. What is Kidron? . . . .

18. Where and what is Como? . . . .

19. Where is Mount Moriah? . . . .

20. Where is Tyre? . . . .

21. Where was the Latin Lodge? . . . .

22. What was the School of Alexandria? . . . .

CHAPTER XXXIII

Masonry in continental Europe and other foreign lands.

1. When was Masonry successfully introduced into Germany?..............................

2. Are there any Masonic Lodges in Italy?.....
   ....

3. What is a Compagnon?..........................

4. When did the Grand Orient of France remove the Bible from its altar and erase from its ritual all reference to Deity?................
   ....

5. When was the French Rite of Masonry established?......................................

6. What is the Elu?..............................

7. What is the name of the Grand Lodge of Switzerland?....................................

8. Who were the Maccabees?......................

9. When was a charter granted to a Cuban Lodge?
   ....

10. When was Masonry established in India?....
    ....

11. Has Masonry found a footing on the East Indian islands?......................................

12. Have Masonic Lodges been established in Japan?..

13. When was the Grand Lodge of Mexico established? ....

14. When was Masonry established in China? .. ..

●15. Is Masonry operating in South Africa? ....

16. When was Masonry established in Australasia? ....

17. What are the traitors in the third degree called in Europe? ....

18. What was known as the "Shaitan" Bungalow? . ...

19. What is the Vedas? ....

20. What is Elephanta? ....

21. In what two European countries is a belief in God not an essential requirement for membership in Masonry? ....

22. Whence originated the term "riding the goat"? ....

CHAPTER XXXIV

Various Rules and Regulations, Suspension and Expulsion.

1. What is the rule regarding rejection of an applicant for membership? . . . .

2. Why is unanimous consent required in the ballot ? . . . .

3. What is the law which excludes women from initiation into Freemasonry? . . . .

4. Can a Mason, having been acquitted by the courts of an offense with which he has been charged, be tried by his Lodge for the same offense? . . . .

5. What difference is there between a Masonic "notice" and a Masonic "summons"? . . . .

6. Who are the "Unworthy Members"? . . . . . .

7. How late a record have we of the rejection of applications for degrees of men who were not Operative Masons? . . . .

8. What amusements were forbidden to the early operative Apprentices? . . . .

9. What does the "Tongue of Good Report" mean? . . . .

10. Is "Once a Mason Always a Mason Correct"? . . . .

11. What was the fifty-second article of the Ordinances of the Fraternity of Stonemasons renewed at the Chief Lodge at Strassburg, on St. Michael's Day, 1563? . . . .

12. What types of laborers were not esteemed sufficiently honorable for admission to the stonemasons of Germany? . . . .

13. What is the law in Masonry regarding appeal? . . . .

14. What provision is made in the Grand Lodge of England regarding misconduct? . . . .

15. What are four examples of un-Masonic conduct? . . . .

16. What forms of punishment are provided for those guilty of infractions of the Masonic regulations? . . . .

17. What is the lawful age of a candidate for degrees? . . . .

18. Can a man who has lost an arm or a leg become a Mason? . . . .

19. Is there such a thing as a life membership in a Masonic Lodge? . . . .

20. What is the attitude of the Masonic Fraternity regarding intolerance? . . . .

21. What could we say of persuading a man to join the Masons? . . . .

CHAPTER XXXV

Entertainment or Fun Degrees

1. What are the entertainment or fun orders connected with Masonry? . . . .
. . . .

2. What is the Ancient Arabic Order of the Nobles of the Mystic Shrine? . . . .
. . . .

3. When was the Mystic Shrine organized? . . . . .
. . . .

4. When did the Mystic Shrine begin the building of hospitals for crippled children and how many are there now? . . . .
. . . .

5. How many crippled children have been treated in Shrine hospitals; at what total expense in building and operations? . . . .

6. What is the Grotto? . . . .

CHAPTER XXXVI

Opposition to Masonry including the Catholic Church

1. What is the earliest known governmental edict against Masonry? . . . .

2. What are the principal objections that have been urged by the opponents of Freemasonry? . . . .

3. What organization in England in 1724 openly antagonized and ridiculed Freemasonry? . . . .

4. Who were the "Scald Miserables"? . . . .

5. What resulted from the parade of the "Scald Miserables" upon the public processions of the Masons, held on feast days in London? . . . .

6. What was the attitude of Catherine the Great, Empress of Russia, towards Masonry? . . . .

7. Who was William Morgan? . . . .

8. Was William Morgan murdered by the Masons? . . . .

9. Did the Morgan episode cause a drop in Masonic membership? . . . .

10. Did the disappearance of Morgan become a political issue? . . . .

11. At the time of the Morgan excitement did the anti-Masonic people participate in national elections? . . . .

12. Has Masonry any political connection? . . . .

. . . .

13. What was John Quincy Adams' attitude towards Masonry? . . . .

14. At the time of the Morgan episode, what Lodge in western New York continued operations regardless of the public clamor? . . . .

. . . .

15. What was the only Lodge in New Jersey that never missed a single communication during the period covered by the Morgan episode?

. . . .

16. What reference is made to the Catholic Church in the Masonic Ritual or its teachings? . . . .

17. Have any of the Popes been Masons? . . . . .

. . . .

18. When Pope Clement XII issued the bull against Masonry did all the Lodges in Italy disband?

. . . .

19. Did Pope Benedict XIV ever later attack Masonry? . . . .

20. What did the future Pope Benedict tell his colleagues prior to his election? . . . .

. . . .

21. What other Pope persecuted members of one of the orders? . . . .

22. How did the invention of printing weaken the influence of the Catholic clergy prior to the Renassaince? . . . .

23. Who was one of the most prominent Roman Catholics in England who became Grand Master of the Grand Lodge of England in 1772? . . .
. . . .

24. Has a Mason ever held an official position in the Roman Catholic Church? . . . .
. . . .

25. Have Catholic clergy in recent years ever been known to publicly countenance any work of Masonry? . . . .

26. Have we any recent record of cordial relations between Knights of Columbus and any Masonic bodies? . . . .

27. Do any other Christian churches condemn Masonry? . . . .

28. Is there anything in the Masonic Ritual, lectures or teaching which can be construed as unfriendly to or critical of the Roman Catholic Church? . . . .

CHAPTER XXXVII

A few facts about Negro Lodges.

1. Why are Negro Lodges not recognized as regular in the United States? . . . .

2. How do the Masonic authorities and Grand Lodges rate the status of Negro Lodges? . . . .

3. Where did the Negro Lodges get their work?

4. Has colored Masonry ever received official recognition in this country since the formation of the Prince Hall Lodge in Boston in the eighteenth century? . . . .

5. Has there ever been any friction in the Grand Lodge on the Negro question? . . . .

6. Who was Prince Hall? . . . .

7. Was Prince Hall a slave? . . . .

8. Did Prince Hall enlist in the Continental Army in the Revolutionary War? . . . .

9. What was the date of Hall's induction into Masonry? . . . .

10. In what Lodge was Prince Hall made a Mason? . . . .

11. What became of that Lodge? . . . .
. . . .

12. Did Prince Hall and his brethren petition for
recognition to the Grand Lodge of Massa-
chusetts? . . . .

13. How was the petition received? . . . .

14. What further action was taken by the Negroes?
. . . .

15. Are American Indians eligible for membership
in Lodges in the U.S.A.? . . . .
. . . .

A'NSWERS

1. Jonathan Belcher. Born in Boston in 1681 and graduated from Harvard about 1699. During a visit to England he received his Masonic Degrees in 1704. He was governor of Massachusetts and New Hampshire for over ten years, and was a man of standing in civil and political life in his community.

2. John Moore, the King's collector at the port of Philadelphia, who in a letter to James Sandilands, Esq. of Chester, Pa., wrote under date of March 10, 1715, "Ye winter has been very long and dull and we have had no mirth or pleasure except a few evenings spent in festivity with my Masonic Brethren".

3. John Skane, merchant, who was a member of Aberdeen Lodge, Scotland, in 1670, migrated to New Jersey in 1682, and served as Deputy-Governor of the Province from 1685 to 1690.

4. A flat slab of rock found on the shore of Goat Island in Annapolis Basin of Nova Scotia by Dr. Charles T. Jackson while making a surey in 1827. On it were cut the date 1606 with the emblem of the square and compass. Different theories have been advanced as to its origin, but no definite answer has yet been found.

5. The ledger of St. John's Lodge, Philadelphia, Pa., for the year 1731.

6. Yes. Benjamin Franklin published in his own paper that several Lodges were meeting regularly in Philadelphia in 1730. As there is no record on them upon

the roll of the English Grand Lodge, they evidently met by no other authority than that of immemorial right. Franklin was initiated in 1731.

7. Dispensations and Charters were all granted from England during the early years. Later Irish and Scotch Grand Lodges granted Warrants and many of the military Lodge warrants were issued from the Grand Lodge of Ireland.

8. August 31st, 1733, by Henry Price, Provincial Grand Master, at a tavern in Boston, called the Bunch of Grapes.

9. 1720, in Boston, held in King's Chapel.

10. First Lodge in Boston, Juy 30th, 1733.

11. That of the First Lodge in Boston, December 27th, 1738.

12. Three. St. Andrews, chartered in 1756, by the Grand Lodge of Scotland; Ancient York Lodge, No. 169 of Boston, chartered prior to 1772, by the Athol Grand Lodge of England, which had but a brief existence, and the African Lodge of Boston.

13. All who participated in the raid were Masons and the entire planning was done in a Masonic Lodge-room.

14. It was the night of their stated communication and the record for that meeting states, "that the Lodge was closed until the next night, on account of the few members in attendance".

15. General Warren, who was Worshipful Master of his Lodge. He died June 17th, 1775.

16. No, he was born in Boston, son of a French Noble-

man, Rivoire de Romagneu, who after suffering financial reverses became a silversmith, and became plain Monsieur Rivoire.

17. To the Lodge of St. Andrew, which in 1764 purchased the Green Dragon Tavern or "Freemason's Arms" as a meeting place.

18. The Massachusetts Grand Lodge declared its independence early in 1777, and established itself as a Sovereign Grand Lodge, this was immediately followed by Virginia, and within a few years each state had its own Grand Lodge.

19. In the *Boston News Letter* for January 5, 1718-19.

20. By what is called prescriptive right. A sufficient number of members to open a Lodge would hold a session and confer Degrees. It was not until 1730 that there was any legal authority to constitute Lodges according to the English regulations adopted in 1717. Fanklin says there were several Lodges in the Province of Pennsylvania at that time.

21. Yes, and on June 24th, 1734, he was elected first Provincial Grand Master of Pennsylvania.

22. The Lodge of the Nine Muses, of which many literary celebrities were also members. It was in this Lodge that he participated in the initiation of Voltaire.

23. Marquis de Lafayette, whom Gen. Washington made a Mason in the Army Lodge at Valley Forge.

24. At the laying of the cornerstone of the Bunker Hill monument June 17th, 1825. At the close of the ceremony he gave his apron to Bro. Francis C. Whiston of Boston, one of the Marshals, who fifty

years later on June 17th, 1875, presented it to the Grand Lodge of Massachusetts at its quarterly Communication.

25. A Mohawk Indian who was initiated in London in 1776. While in command of some Indian troops in the British service, who were prepared to torture Captain McKinsty, an officer in the Colonial army, when he noticed the mystic appeal in the hour of danger, whereupon he interposed and saved his brother from his impending fate. He rescued McKinsty, took him to Quebec, and placed him in the hands of English Masons, who eventually returned him, uninjured to the American outposts. Years afterwards Brant visited McKinsty at his home in Greendale, N.Y.

26. Benjamin Franklin. He affiliated with the famous Lodge of the Nine Sisters (the Muses) in Paris and assisted in the initiation of Voltaire and even served as Worshipful Master.

27. Mackey says the weight of evidence is in favor of the working of Masonry, first in Philadelphia by prescriptive right, secondly in Boston by secondary constituted authority, and thirdly in Norfolk, Va., by direct charter, emanating from the Grand Lodge itself. The facsimile page of St. Johns Ledger in Philadelphia for 1731 is probably sufficient testimony to prove the validity of its claim. However each Lodge is first depending on the point of view.

28. The Headquarters of the American Revolution.

29. May 26th, 1737, at Charleston, South Carolina.

30. Yes. George Washington, Warren, Putnam, and Wayne were Masons, and it was at Valley Forge that Gen. LaFayette received his Degrees from George Washington.

31. In most of the. Colonies the "Ancients" favored the revolutionists and the "Moderns" were loyal to King George III.

32. Yes. The "Ancients" formed Provisional Grand Lodges in Massachusetts, New York, South Carolina and Virginia and Pennsylvania, where they were known as "Ancient York Lodges".

33. They charged the Moderns, as they termed them, with the introduction of innovations, whereas they in turn mutilated the Third Degree, out of which they fabricated a fourth, hitherto unknown, to the Craft.

34. In 1758, and from that time on the Lodges under the older sanction declined and gradually faded into obscurity. The last printed notice of any of them occurred in 1760.

35. Pennsylvania continues the work as it was done prior to the union of the Grand Lodges.

36. Kilwinning Crosse Lodge No. 2-237-1 dated December 1st, 1755. The name used in application for char-ter was "Kilwinnng Port Royal Crosse Lodge". They received a second charter from the Grand Lodge of Virginia, December 3rd, 1796. Becoming dormant it received a third charter December 12th, 1855, but lived ony four years. It is now operating under a fourth charter issued December 14th, 1881. It is now No. 237 and all these charters are in possession

of the present Lodge. During the Civil War, Union
troops raided the Lodge rooms and carried away
much of its belongings. Some of the articles were
restored in 1885 and 1887 which had originally come
from Scotland. The records from 1754 to 1859 were
found in an Antiquarian shop in Philadelphia in
1909. These records furnish the data given here.

37. 167. All were chartered by Grand Lodges of England,
Scotland and Ireland or subordinate Grand Lodges.

38. St. John's Grand Lodge of Massachusetts established
a Lodge at Annapolis, N.S., under date of 1740. His
Excellency Edward Cornwallis was First Master. It
is an interesting historical fact that Edward Cornwallis was uncle to the Lord Cornwallis who surrendered to General Washington at Yorktown in 1781.

39. October 24th, 1733, but no reference therein is made
to any degrees. Masons were "made" and a limited
number were "admitted". February 9th, 1736-37
the degree of Fellow Craft is first mentioned but the
language quoted would indicate that the degree had
previously been worked. Nearly four years later in
Portsmouth, New Hampshire, we read "Capt. Andrew
Tombes was made a Mason and *raised* to a Fellow-
Craft". There is considerable confusion in the
terminology.

40. It was laid September 18th, 1793, with Masonic ceremonies, conducted by the President, Brother George
Washington, who came up from Alexandria, accompanied by Alexandria Lodge, No. 39, and was joined
by Potomac Lodge, No. 9. The gavel used on that
occasion, made by one of the workmen, was presented

to General Washington; after the ceremonies it was given by him to the Worshipful Master of Potomac Lodge, No. 9, and has been in the possession of that Lodge ever since.

41. It was erected in 1784 on Lodge Alley, near Second and Chestnut Streets in Philadelphia.

42. Henry Knox of Massachusetts, Baron Von Steuben of Prussia, General Nathaniel Greene of Rhode Island, Baron DeKalb of Germany, John Sullivan and John Stark of New Hampshire, Israel Putnam of Connecticut, and General Anthony Wayne of Pennsylvania.

43. Pennsylvania. From all data available we must give Pennsylvania the preference, as having started Freemasonry in an original prescriptive organic form; working with proper officers for some indefinite period prior to June, 1731, as shown by the ledger.

44. William Hooper, Benjamin Franklin, Matthew Thornton, William Whipple, John Hancock, Philip Livingston, Thomas Nelson and many others whose Masonic records were destroyed during the war. It has been said, that, with four men out of the room, the assembly could have been open in form as a Masonic Lodge on the third degree.

45. Thirty-two of the fifty-five of the members of the convention are known to have been members of the fraternity.

46. Ten, the oldest of which was St. John's Regimental Lodge, chartered by the Provincial Grand Lodge of New York July 24th, 1775.

47.   American Union Lodge, warranted in 1776 by St. John's Grand Lodge of Massachusetts. This Lodge followed the army throughout the Revolution, and then into the Northwest Indian campaigns. It is still in existence as American Union Lodge No. 1, of Marietta, Ohio. Its war time records are preserved and make most interesting reading.

48.   Yes. Once the British during a retreat after a battle, left the emblems of their Lodge and a copy of their constitution behind. Gen. Washington returned them with an escort and a guard of honor. This is only one of a number of similar occasions.

49.   Yes. Almost every meeting was concluded with a repast, the favorite food at these suppers was "gammon" or ham, and liquor and toasts were the invariable accompaniment of every banquet.

50.   Up to 1804 there were Lodges of both English and Scotch charters. When these were merged, they ceased giving numbers, to avoid any questions of seniority.

51.   Yes. Gen Israel Putnam was about to be tortured at the stake by the Indians under French command. A French officer recognized the sign and caused his release immediately.

52.   With trifling variations they ran a little over £2. At the close of the Revolution there was a tremendous increase probably due to the depreciated Continental currency. Lodge No. 14, in Delaware received four candidates in 1780 who paid $224.00 each.

53. Yes. The public school system of New York had its beginnings in a modest experiment assisted by the Grand Lodge of that state. The Grand Lodge of Pennsylvania even maintained an adult Sunday School, in its Temple on Chestnut Street.

54. No. Since the first chartering of Lodges in Massachusetts, it has been a tradition to use only the name. Some authorities say the custom of using numbers was discarded at the time of the union of the Athol and Modern Grand Lodges, to avoid any question as to precedence.

ANSWERS

CHAPTER II

1. In Fredericksburg Lodge, Fredericksburg, Va., at the third or fourth communication after its organization, which took place Sept. 1st, 1752.

2. On Nov. 4th, 1752 in the Lodge at Fredericksburg, Va. and the records of the Lodge, still in existence, show that he paid the fee of £2-3s.

3. On March 3rd, 1753 and on Aug. 4th, following, the record shows that he was raised to the sublime degree of Master Mason.

4. Gen. George Washington.

5. In 1805 the name was changed to Alexandria-Washington Lodge No. 22.

6. Washington was buried with Masonic honors at Mt. Vernon four days after his death. With one exception, all the pallbearers were members of Lodge No. 22.

7. Warren G. Harding, who also was a Mason.

8. Alexandria Lodge No. 22 which was originally organized as Lodge No. 39 under a warrant from the Grand Lodge of Pennsylvania. In 1788 it withdrew from the jurisdiction of Pennsylvania and became first Lodge No. 22 and afterwards Alexandria Lodge No. 22 under the jurisdiction of Virginia.

9. On the spot now marked by his statue in front of the former Sub-Treasury in Wall St., New York, N.Y.

10. Robert R. Livingstone, Grand Master of F. and A. Masons and also Chancellor of the state of New York, administered the oath, where the sub-treasury formerly stood, on April 30th, 1789.

11. The Bible upon which Washington took his oath as first President of the United States April 30th, 1789.

12. St. John's Lodge No. 1, New York, N. Y.

13. No. When the Convention of the Lodges of Virginia nominated him as Grand Master of the Independent Grand Lodge of the Commonwealth, Washington declined the honor.

14. Madame Lafayette, the wife of the Marquis, who sent it from Paris to George Washington at Mt. Vernon. It is now in possession of the Washington Benevolent Society at Philadelphia.

15. At the laying of the cornerstone of the Capitol at Washington, D.C., Sept. 18th, 1793.

16. Washington College, Chestertown, Md., is the first college named for Washington, and, it is believed, the only one so named by his consent.

17. No. The cornerstone was laid in the Southeast corner.

18. The erection of the George Washington National Memorial at Alexandria, Virginia, where much of the record of Washington's Masonic affiliation and work will be preserved.

19. Thirteen. Washington, Monroe, Jackson, Polk, Buchanan, Johnson, Garfield, McKinley, Theodore Roosevelt, Taft, Harding, Franklin Roosevelt and Truman.

20. The Massachusetts Grand Lodge. It bears the following inscription:

> This urn encloses a Lock of Hair of the
> Immortal Washington.
> PRESENTED JANUARY 27, 1800
> to the MASSACHUSETTS GRAND LODGE
> by HIS amiable WIDOW
> Born Feb. 11, 1732 (old style)
> Obt. Dec. 14, 1799

ANSWERS

CHAPTER III

1. King of Israel and the central figure in the building of the Temple. He was the son of David and Bath-Sheba, and was born in the year of the world 2871. He lived fifty-eight years and died 975 B.C.

2. We are told that he was a "young and tender man;" some authorities say he was only fourteen years of age, others say he was between eighteen and twenty-five. The better authorities give his age as twenty.

3. David was a descendent of Abraham through Abraham's son, Isaac, but Bath-Sheba, the mother of Solomon was a direct descendent of Ishmael, the son whom Hagar bore unto Abraham. In this manner, two great families founded by Abraham became united in Solomon.

4. Two score or forty years. He was made king in the year 1015 B.C.

5. "Give therefore thy servant an understanding heart to judge thy people, that I may discern between good and bad; for who is able to judge this, thy so great a people."   (I Kings iii-9)

6. He began the erection of the Temple five years after he had been crowned king.

7. Second Chronicles, chapter two, verses 17 and 18.

8. Azariah.

9. A master craftsman of the tribe of Dan, who was appointed together with Bezaleel to construct the tabernacle in the wilderness, and the Ark of the Covenant. He is referred to in the Royal Arch degree.

10. The principal receiver of King Solomon's tribute and the chief overseer of the 30,000 brethren who were sent to cut timber for the Temple in the forests of Lebanon. He is said to have married a sister of Hiram, the Builder.

11. A Jebusite living in Jerusalem from whom King David purchased the threshing floor on Mount Moriah, as the site on which the future Temple was to be built.

12. Some years ago a man who had spent many years in the orient, estimated that the ancient cedars still re-

maining upon Mt. Lebanon at about four hundred. He wrote that they were in a single group of about ¾ of a mile in circumference. Many of them were almost 100 feet high and over 30 feet in circumference. Considering the slowness of a cedar's growth, this would indicate they were 1000 or more years of age.

13. On the east by the brook Kedron, on the south by the great water-sheds and reservoirs, on the west by the cities of Jebus and Milo, known in Solomon's day as Jerusalem, on the south by Zion or City of David, and the Tabernacle of Israel on the southeast.

14. He said the architecture of the Temple was of the style called Grecian. So much would seem to be a fact, whatever may be said of the legends flowing from it.

15. Gold Talent $32,500.00
Silver Talent $1,800.00
Gold Shekel 10.75
Silver Shekel 60
These are approximate figures in round numbers.

16. Yes. Gottfried Hensel, rector of Hirschberg in Germany, made a model. Rabbi Jacob Jehuda Leon was displaying one in England in 1675. Not long after, Gerhard Schott was building one in Hamburg. This was exhibited in London in 1725, eight years after the formation of the Grand Lodge of England.

17. The corner-stone. According to Oliver, Thus Solomon was enabled to level the footstone of the Temple in the fourth year of his reign.

18. In the second month of the fourth year of the reign of King Solomon, being 480 years after the exodus. In the modern calendar 1012 B.C.

19. It was finished in the eighth month of the eleventh year of the reign of King Solomon. The site was too small, so the King had huge walls built up in the valley and the space filled with earth. Josephus mentions that some of the stones in these walls were sixty feet long.

20. The Temple of Herod took thirty-six years. The Temple of Diana at Ephesus took two hundred years. St. Peter's church at Rome took one hundred and fifty-five years. St. Paul's Cathedral in London, took thirty-five years.

21. 127,000 square feet.

22. Balkis, the Queen of Sheba.

23. Because his fame was international and the story of his wisdom had spread through the orient. The biblical story is told in the tenth chapter in the first book of Kings.

24. Rabboni, the highest title of distinction among the ancient Hebrews.

25. "And Solomon had forty thousand stalls of horses for his chariots and twelve thousand horsemen." (I Kings, iv-26).

26. Two hundred targets of beaten gold; six hundred shekels of gold went to one target. (I Kings, x-16).

27. Rehoboam, his son.

28. Upon a brazen scaffold five cubits long. (II Chronicles, vi-13).

29. By a flight of winding stairs. (See I Kings, vi-8).

30. He directed that the "Ark of the Covenant" be brought from the King's house, where it had been kept by David, and deposited it with impressive ceremonies in the holy of holies.

31. According to legend, a great favorite of King Solomon; he was made provost and judge with Adoniram and later made an Elect, Perfect and Sublime Mason.

32. According to Dr. Oliver there were between seven and eight hundred. In the hundred years following the organization of the Grand Lodge of England, Dr. Oliver was the most prolific Masonic writer. However much of his work has not been substantiated by later research.

ANSWERS

CHAPTER IV

1. The foundation was begun on Monday, the second day of the month of Zif, which answers to the twenty-second day of our April, and was completed in a little over seven years, on the eighth day of the month Bul, which answers to the twenty-third of our October, six hundred years after the Exodus.

2. He dedicated it to Jehovah in the month of Tizri, 2999 years after the creation, and 1005 years before the advent of Christ. After this ceremony he stood before the altar of the Lord and offered up the beautiful prayer and invocation found in the 8th Chapter of the 1st Book of Kings.

3. According to Dr. Anderson, about 113,000, some of these men were employed in the quarries and some in the forests of Lebanon.

4. Seven years, six months and two days. The construction of the entire collection of buildings, ornaments and sculpture required a period of twenty years.

5. It was built up of large stones, ten, twenty and even forty feet long, mortised together and fastened to the side of the mountain. The cubic contents of the foundation exceeded ten million cubic feet, larger than the Great Pyramid of Cheops, which required a hundred thousand workmen over thirty years to build.

6. One of the workmen sent by Hiram King of Tyre to King Solomon. See II Chronicles ii, 13.

7. Yes. See II Chronicles, iv-11.

8. The earliest account is found in the 1st Book of Kings (vii, 13, 14) which reads:
    "And King Solomon sent and fetched Hiram out of Tyre. He was a widow's son of the tribe of Naphtali, and his father was a man of Tyre, a worker in brass, and he was filled with wisdom, and understanding, and cunning, to work all works in brass. And he came to King Solomon and wrought all his work."

9. A Hebrew word, signifying his father. The word ab or father was a title of honour "often used" says Adam Clarke, in Hebrew, to signify a master or chief operator".

10. He was a contemporary of King Solomon and assisted him in the building of the Temple. He also loaned

him one hundred and twenty talents of gold, equal in our money to about two and a half million dollars. See I Kings, v, 8, 9.

11. Two tablets of stone, on which were engraved the ten commandments.

12. Succoth and Zeredatha.

13. The court or vestibule in front of an edifice. (Also propylon).

14. About $35,000,000.00. This figure is possibly an exaggeration. Figures given by different authorities vary from five million to five billion dollars. As methods and standards of computing values on our principles were unknown at the time of the erection of the Temple, and there is such a variation as to the intrinsic money value of a talent of either gold or silver, any estimate of the cost of the building can only be a conjecture.

15. Between ten and eleven million dollars.

16. 234,000 gold and 318,000 silver.

17. The Mosque of Omar.

18. The only piece of furniture in the Most Holy Place was the Sacred Ark of the Covenant of the Lord.

19. The use of bells in the third degree is manifestly an anachronism, because bells were not invented until the fifth century.

20. Ten candlesticks of pure gold, five on each side, with lamps and scuffers. Ten tables of pure gold, five on each side, with bowls, basins, spoons and covers, a golden altar of incense, a table of shewbread. The floor was of gold set with precious stones.

21. From Ornan, the Jebusite, for which he paid six hundred shekels of gold.
22. Four hundred and thirty-five years.
23. Twenty cubits long and ten cubits broad. (I Kings, 6:3).
24. Because the stones were hewn in the quarries and all the materials pre-fabricated so perfectly that the assembly required no tinkering.
25. Pommels (II Chronicle, iv-13).
26. It was situated in the western end of the Temple, separated from the rest of the building by a heavy curtain, and enclosed on three sides by dead walls without any opening or window, it contained the sacred Ark of the Covenant, and was secluded and set apart from all intrusion, excepting the high priest, who only entered on certain solemn occasions.
27. On one part of Mount Moriah.
28. A Jewish theory, more probably legend, that the Temple was constructed by Divine methods and that the stones were squared and polished by a miraculous worm called *samis*. The worm has been designated "the Insect Sherma".
29. The name of the right hand pillar that stood at the porch of King Solomon's Temple. It is derived from two Hebrew words jah and iachin will establish. Signifying therefore, "God will establish".
30. The most secret part of the ancient Temples, where none but the priesthood were admitted.
31. It was a cube in dimensions, twenty cubits square. The two doors leading to the place were of olive wood, richly carved and overlaid with gold.

32. Each one was thirty-five cubits high and twenty-four cubits in circumference and were highly ornamented.

33. To Zerubbabel, the builder of the second Temple.

34. Cyrus the Great, who had conquered Babylon, and laid the foundation of the great Persian Empire.

35. They were originally the descendants of the ten revolted tribes of Israel, and at the building of the second Temple were an idolatrous people. Zerubbabel told them "Ye have nothing to do with us to build the house of our God".

36. Five. 1. The dedication of Solomon's Temple B.C. 1004. 2. The dedication under Hezekiah, when it was purified from the abomination of Ahaz, B.C. 726. 3. The dedication of Zerubbabel's Temple B.C. 513. 4. The dedication of the Temple when it was purified after Judas Maccabæus had driven out the Syrians, B.C. 164. 5. The dedication of Herod's Temple, B.C. 22, upon its completion.

37. In the Fourth or Mark Masters' Degree, it is said that the value of a mark is "a Jewish half-shekel of silver, or twenty-five cents in the currency of this country. The shekel of silver was a weight of great antiquity among the Jews, its value being about a half-dollar.

ANSWERS

CHAPTER V

1. From the Hebrew meaning "the ground" because he was created from the dust of the earth.

2. 930 years.

3. 969 years.

4. 365 years of age.

5. He was 600 years old and it rained for forty days and forty nights.

6. About 120 years.

7. 450 feet long, 75 feet wide and 45 feet deep. These figures are based on the biblical measure of 18 inches for a cubit.

8. Biblical scholars are pretty well agreed that it was in the spring of the year on Mt. Ararat.

9. A whole year.

10. Three. With lower, second and third stories shalt thou make it. Gen. vi-16.

11. 300 cubits long, 50 cubits wide and 30 cubits high.

12. Eight. "Noah went in, and his sons, and his wife, and his son's wives with him".

13. Brother of Moses, and first High Priest of the Mosaic Dispensation.

14. On the plains of Shinar.

15. It was composed of enormous bricks dried in the sun, each being nineteen-and-a-half feet long, fifteen feet wide and seven-and-a-half feet thick. They were cemented by slime or bitumen. Three years were occupied in making these bricks, though the greater part of mankind were employed in the work.

16. Many conjectures have been offered respecting the magnitude of this celebrated structure. Jerome says from the testimony of *ocular* demonstration, that it was four miles high, and of proportionable dimensions in bulk. It must have been of very large dimensions considering the number of people who were over forty years engaged in its erection.

17. Historians generally estimate about B.C. 1775.
18. Brick and mortar or bitumen.
19. It was called *kaphiret* from *kaphar*, "to forgive sin".
20. Adam and Eve. See Gen. III-7.
21. Joseph, his favorite son. (Gen. 50-26).
22. No. God took him up to the top of Mt. Horeb, from which point he saw it, and then died.
23. About 1,500,000, including women and children.
24. A mountain of Arabia, between the horns of the Red Sea.
25. It is the place where Moses received the two tablets of stone containing the ten commandments.
26. Moses, the lawgiver of the Jews. He was of the tribe of Levi and the brother of Miriam and Aaron.
27. When he was forty years old.
28. Moses.
29. It was patterned after the designs used by the Egyptian priesthood.
30. The Ten Commandments, or the moral law.
31. In many languages called the five books of Moses. It is the group name of the first five books of the Bible.
32. Moses. In all the systems of antiquity, fire is adopted as a symbol of Deity.
33. Thirty, according to Pierson.
34. About 1325 B.C. during the reign of Meneptah, of Egypt.
35. I am that I am, (Ex., III-14). This quotation is adopted in one of the higher degrees of the York Rite.

36. He was a brother of Moses and the first high priest under the Mosaic dispensation.

ANSWERS
CHAPTER VI

1. Literally "men of hewing", that is hewers and "Men of Burden". In I Kings (v-18) in the original Hebrew *noshesabal* Anderson says, old Canaanites who were bondsmen.

2. According to the narrative in Neh., iv-17 "Every one with one of his hands wrought in the work, and with the other hand held a weapon".

3. Yes. See Isaiah xli-7.

4. The tribe of Judah have the figure of a lion in its standard. (See also Genesis xlix-9. "Judah is a lion whelp".

5. Pledge, covenant, or agreement. From the Latin *arrhabo*. An important word in the Fourteenth Degree of the Scottish Rite. In its pure form the word "Arubbah" occurs only once in the Old Testament. (Prov. xvii-18).

6. It is derived from two Hebrew words *jah* God, and *iachin.* Signifying God will establish.

7. It is from the Hebrew, *b*, in and *oaz* signifying, in strength.

8. Kohaleth, meaning the "Preacher" (Ecc. i-1).

9. When David was about to die he charged Solomon to build the Temple upon becoming King. He gave him 10,000 talents of gold and ten times that amount of silver, which he had laid aside for that purpose.

10. Two interlaced triangles, more commonly known as the Seal of Solomon, and considered by the ancient Jews as a talisman of great efficacy.

11. Jerusalem.

12. Because he learned through the holy man Nathan that the project was not pleasing to God because David had shed so much blood.

13. He was ruler over Judah for seven years at Hebron.

14. David was simple in his tastes, frugal and temperate, possesed of great courage and deep piety; Solomon led the life of a true oriental, loving splendor, being of a haughty disposition and extravagant in his desires, less religious, but more ostentatious in his worship.

15. As far south as Egypt and north to the cities of Damascus and Hamath.

16. Jeroboam, elected king in 975 B.C. and died 954 B.C. He is the king who is known as "the man who made Israel to sin".

17. Cain, the son of Adam.

18. The son of Lamech; the first who wroght in iron and brass and the inventor of edge-tools. He is the Vulcan of the pagans.

19. This phrase when used in the Masonic ritual, refers in its original interpretation to Christ, Him who "brought life and immortality to light".

20. In the Book of Judges, Chapter 12, first seven verses.

21. Tubal Cain. The pioneer craftsman in metals.

22. The deity of the Ammonites.

23. In the Book of Job (ix-9), considered by many biblical scholars to be the oldest book in the Bible.

24. It means in Jewish "help from God". It was the name of the angel who ministered to the dying and helped separate the soul from the body.

ANSWERS

CHAPTER VII

1. Belshazzar, the son of Sargon, who was slain by the Medes and the Persians, under Cyrus.

2. *"Mene, Mene, Tekel, Upharsin"*.

3. The prophet Daniel, "You have been weighed in the balance and have been found wanting".

4. They were in captivity for seventy-two years and were removed four hundred and seventy-five miles almost due east from Jerusalem.

5. 722 B.C. Henchforth the identity of the Kingdom of Israel is lost in the labyrinth of history.

6. They were not subjected to the rigors of slavery. They were treated more like colonists than slaves, were permitted to retain much of their personal property, and even to purchase lands and erect homes. Some of them were advanced to offices of dignity and power in the royal palace.

7. 87 feet.

8. 350 feet.

9. 42,360, and their servants.

10. When the Jews were taken captives to Babylon, they were bound by triangular chains which to them was

an insult, because to a Jew the triangle or delta was a symbol of the Deity.

11. When the Messiah returns to redeem the Jewish people.

12. Bildad the Shuhite, Eliphaz the Temanite and Zophar the Naamathite.

13. By the blasts from two silver trumpets.

14. God with us.

15. He was the son of Cush. In the Old Constitutions referred to as one of the founders of Masonry, and in the Scriptures as the architect of many cities. He was the grandson of Ham, and is supposed to have been the founder of Babylon, the first king and the first conqueror. Legends quote him as employing 60,000 men at the building of Ninevah.

16. Kouyunjik.

17. A king of Bablyon, who in the eleventh year of the reign of Zedekiah, King of Judah, captured Jerusalem after a seige of about twelve months. The city was destroyed and most of the citizens taken as captives to Babylon.

18. There were twenty-five gates on each side made of solid brass. There were also two hundred and fifty towers placed on the walls to afford additional protection.

19. He became king at the age of forty-one and reigned seventeen years.

20. During the reign of King Uzziah. Under Ahaz it became tributary to Assyria, but Hezekiah rebelled and aroused the wrath of Sennacherib, whose army carried away many of the inhabitants.

21.   King Zedekiah, who afterwards was carried as a captive in chains to Babylon.

22.   A king of Persia who succeeded Cyrus. In profane history called Zerxes. We read of him in the book of Esther, who became his wife.

23.   It was annexed to Egypt by Ptolemy Soter who appeared before Jerusalem one Sabbath day 320 B.C. and entered the city without resistance as he knew the Jews did not fight on the Sabbath.

24.   In 166 B.C. he routed the forces of Antiochus, and Jerusalem was again in Jewish hands. The Temple was dedicated anew and the interior refurnished. The feasts and sacrifices of dedication lasted eight days and is to this day celebrated under the name of "Hannukah", known as the Festival of Light.

25.   Jeroboam who had been an exile at the Egyptian court of Shasanq.

26.   They selected circular spots of hard ground for the purpose of threshing their grain. After they had been properly prepared for the purpose, they became a permanent possession. One of these, the property of Ornan the Jebusite, was on Mount Moriah.

27.   The Sun.

28.   The cultivation of vineyards and raising of grapes.

29.   The priesthood.

30.   "A golden bell and a pomegranate, a golden bell and a pomegranate upon the hem of the robe round about." (Exodus, xxviii-34).

31.   "That he might be heard when he went into the Temple and when he came therefrom". The assump-

tion is that when he is heard, he will be seen by all men.

ANSWERS

CHAPTER VIII

1. A teacher and interpreter of the law. It was a title of great honor.

2. A Hebrew letter phonetically equivalent to i or y. In symbolic Masonry the yod has been replaced by the letter G, but in the higher degrees it is retained, and within a triangle is the symbol of the Deity.

3. An heroic family, whose patriotism and valor form a bright picture in the Jewish annals. The name is generally supposed to be derived from the letters M.C.B.I.—which were inscribed upon their banners, being the initials of the Hebrew sentence, which translated reads, *"Who is like unto Thee among the gods, O Jehovah"*.

4. The tribes of Benjamin and Judah. Known as the Davidian dynasty.

5. In 1250 A.D. by Cardinal Hugo de Sancto Caro. The division into verses as we find the arrangement today was made about 1550 A.D., by Robert Stevens, a printer of Paris. In 1557 the first versified New Testament and in 1560 the entire Bible was first published in this form.

6. A translation of the Old Testament into Greek, used at the present time by the Greek Catholic Churches.

7. A pause or musical note.

8. A stringed musical instrument used by the ancient Hebrews.

9. Baal or Bel or Belus. Chief divinity representing the sun among the Phoenicians.

10. Low country. Original boundaries were Mt. Lebanon, Arabia, the Jordan, and at some points the Mediterranean. At the coming of Christ it was divided in five provinces: Judea, Samaria, Galilee, Perea and Idumea, being 180 miles long, and 75 miles wide.

11. A weight among the Hebrews, of which there were two kinds, the king's shekel and that of the sanctuary. The latter being double the value of the former. The shekel was not a coin, but a definite weight of gold or silver. The common shekel alluded to in the Mark Degree, was worth about half a dollar.

12. Chapter 19 of II Kings and Chapter 37 of Isiah are alike.

13. The Book of Esther.

14. 592,439.

15. 39.

16. 4,370 times.

17. A Latin version of the Scriptures in use in the Roman Catholic Church, made originally by St. Jerome.

18. In 1611. It has been well said that Shakespeare and the King James version will preserve the English language for all time.

19. Mention of The Bakers' Street (in Jeremiah, xxxvii-21).

20. Descendants of Lot, and the perennial enemy of the ancient Hebrews.

ANSWERS

CHAPTER IX

1. 27.

2. 181,253.

3. Essenes, Pharisees and Sadducees.

4. So called from its proximity to the site of the Temple, the doors of which are said to be covered with gold. It faces the road to Bethany from which Christ made His triumphal entry. The Turks walled it up upon hearing the tradition that through this gate a conqueror would wrest Jerusalem from them.

5. It is built on the crest of four hills and is at an average elevation of 2500 feet above sea level. The Mosque of Omar which stands on the site of Solomon's Temple is the most conspicious building in the city. Being less than fifty miles from the Dead Sea, which is 1300 feet below sea level, furnishes a good idea of the nature of the country.

6. Julius Caesar was friendly towards the Jews. He appointed Antipater procurator of Judea in 47 B.C., who was poisoned by a political rival in 43 B.C., whereupon his son Herod succeeded to the office. After he had subdued a rebellion, he inaugurated a system of great cruelty, even strangling three of his sons to death.

7. It is generally placed at 4 B.C. He was succeeded by his son Archelaus, who received the title of ethnarch from Augustus. Because of his cruelty he was banished to Gaul.

8. An olive garden, about half an acre of ground on the west side of Mt. Olive commanding a full view of Jerusalem.

9. This word may be translated as signifying most excellent master. The word appears once as applied to Christ in the New Testament, when "Mary turned herself and saith unto him, 'Rabboni'," which is to say, Master.

10. At the time of the advent of Christ, there were three religious sects in Judea—the Pharisees, the Sadducees, and the Essenes, and to one of these sects every Jew was compelled to unite himself. Jesus is supposed, by many writers, to have been an Essene.

11. It was here that Jacob lost his beloved wife, Rachel. Later we read about it in connection with Boaz and Ruth. Still later it is mentioned as the boyhood home of David. It is about five miles from Jerusalem and has a present population of less than five thousand souls, chiefly Christian.

12. Having failed to win pagans from celebrating these two dates of the summer and winter solstices, the Church by a wise diplomacy gave these dates new names and a place on the sacred calendar.

13. An oblong shawl made of wool or camels' hair worn over the head or shoulders by the Hebrews. It was the garment worn by Jesus in which we are told in Matt. ix-20 that "A woman came behind him and touched the hem of his garment".

14. It is found in the Apocalypse.

15. 152,185.

16. Translated, "Field of blood". A small piece of land for the burial of strangers, just without the walls of Jerusalem, south of Mt. Zion. Originally called "potters field", because it furnished much of the clay for the potters' wares.

17. The "Wise Men of the East" who came to Jerusalem, bringing gifts to the infant Jesus. The traditional names of the three are Melchior the Hindu, offering gold, Gaspar the Athenian, who offers frankincense, and Balthazar the Egyption who tenders Myrrh.

18. Gold, Frankincense and Myrrh.

19. The initials of the Latin sentence which was placed upon the cross, *Jesus Nazarenus Rex Judæorum,* which translated reads "Jesus of Nazareth, King of the Jews".

20. It is a small hill or eminence, situated due west from Mount Moriah. In modern times it has been greatly reduced by excavations made in it for the construction of the Church of the Holy Sepulcher.

21. Simon Peter and his brother Andrew; James and John, the sons of Zebedec; Philip and Bartholomew; Thomas the doubter and Matthew the tax-gatherer; James the son of Alphagus, and Lebaeus, whose surname was Thaddeus, Simon the Canaanite and Judas Iscariot who betrayed him.

22. The symbolic name of the Christian Church. (Rev. xxi, 2-21: iii, 12).

23. The Apostle Paul.

24. St. John the Baptist, whose festival falls on June 24th, and St. John the Evangelist whose festival occurs on December 27th.

25.   The sacrament of the Lord's Supper.

26.   About seventeen dollars.

27.   The Jews ceased to exist as a nation. They were absorbed with other races into the great empire of Rome. The religious beliefs of the Jews have enabled them to withstand absorption into the nations of the world, and they exist today as a distinct race, with a continuous history of three thousand years amongst people who recognize them as the pioneers of civil and religious freedom, and the torchbearers of a Monotheism that has shown with unfailing splendor in the darkest ages of history.

28.   A monogram of the name of Christ, formed by the first two letters of that name in Greek. Legend says it appeared in the sky at noonday to the Emperor Constantine.

ANSWERS

CHAPTER X

1.   No, its citizens will be called Israelis. The provisional government has stated that Israelites was a name of Bible times. This is a modern state.

2.   Because of the definitive nature of the alphabet, making it a key to many words used in Masonry.

3.   Literally the "token of the guest". It was an ancient custom when an alliance of friendship was established between two people, to take a small piece of stone, bone, ivory or even wood, and dividing it into two parts, each person inscribed his name on his half. They then exchanged the pieces, each one

promising to retain the part as a perpetual token of friendship.

4. They did not. For generations the traditions and revelations were transmitted orally by the priesthood.

5. The year always has been a source of dispute among scholars as to its duration, beginning and end. Some think that to the one hundred and sixtieth year of Enoch, that mankind reckoned only by weeks and that the Angel Uriel revealed to Enoch the use of months, years, the revolution of the stars and the returns of the seasons. Some people made their year consist of one month, others three, others six and so on. Some made a year of winter, another of summer. Some used lunar months, others solar, and with some each equinox began a different year. But when Moses led the Israelites out of Egypt, he retained the Egyptian year.

6. "In the Hebrew year."

7. 3988 B.C., Creation.
    2332 B.C., Flood.
    2040 B.C., Abraham born.
    1575 B.C., Moses born.
    1495 B.C., Exodus.
    1051 B.C., David acknowledged king.
    1004 B.C., First Temple built.
    586 B.C., First Temple destroyed.
    536 B.C., Cyrus' Decree.
    516 B.C., Second Temple completed.
    330 B.C., Alexander conquers Palestine.

8. The ecclesiastical year commenced 1st Nisan, March,

but the civil reckoning begins 1st Tishri, September, which is New Year's Day.

9. Ornaments called *tephillin* worn on the forehead and arm, consisting of leather boxes. They were bound together by long leather straps.

10. An ecclesiastical banner.

11. A measure of length, originally denoting the distance from the elbow to the extremity of the middle finger or the fourth part of a well proportioned man's stature. The Hebrew cubit according to most authorities was eighteen inches. By this measure the dimensions of the various parts of the temple were computed.

12. Almighty God.

13. The Talmud, which is a Hebrew word, signifying *doctrine*, is a collection of treatises written by the priests and wise men and embodying the civil and canonical laws of the Jews.

14. Literally, fleetness, strength.

15. The highest judicial tribunal among the Jews, consisting of seventy-two persons besides the High Priest.

16. Aaron's rod. When he picked it up the snake became a rod again.

17. A large candlestick of metal, with many sconces, hanging from the ceiling, and symbolically referring to the Branch of Jesse.

18. The 613 precepts into which the Jews divided all the Mosaic law. Thus, numerically the Hebrew letters express 613.

19. A Hebrew measure.

20. According to legend it is a sect among the Jews, supposed by Masonic writers to have been the descendants of the Freemasons of the Temple, and through whom the order was propogated to modern times.

21. Literally, *my master*. The word occurs once, as applied to Christ, in the New Testament. (John xx-16).

22. Copper. The ancients later learned the secrets of tempering copper, now a lost art.

23. The space from the thumb to the end of the little finger when extended. Nine inches.

24. Hebrew letters spelling Jehovah.

25. A band or apron made of fine linen and worn by the Jewish priesthood. It was borrowed from the Egyptians. This probably was the apron which some regarded as a Masonic insignia on some of the mummies of the Pharaos.

26. A celebration to commemorate the deliverance of the Jews in Persia from the destruction threatened by Haman. It was instituted by Mordecai, the father of Esther, and observed on the fourteenth and fifteenth of the month Adar, the sixth of the civil and the twelfth of the sacred year.

27. The mystical philosophy or theosophy of the Jews is called the Kabbala. Its teachings embrace certain mysical interpretations of Scriptures and metaphysical speculations concerning the Deity, man and spiritual things.

28. Achmetha.

29.   A dispenser of alms.

30.   A stone of black basalt rounded at the top about two by four feet. It is now in the Museum of the Louvre, Paris. It was found at Dibau, in the land of Moab in 1868. It is dedicated to Chemosh, the principal god of Moab, by Mesha, the king, who defeated the Israelites about 875 B.C. The stone is inscribed with thirty-four lines of inscription in Phoenician characters. The text was completed from paper "squeezes" or matrices taken before the original was broken. The covenant name of God occurs in the inscription.

31.   The three liberal arts—grammar, logic and rhetoric classified in medieval schools of the lower group of liberal arts.

32.   The word has two meanings in Hebrew. First, an ear of corn; and secondly a stream of water.

Additional data as to Ancient Chronology may be in order. The Egyptian Calendar was composed in 4241 B.C. which would imply a Dynastic period at least as far back as 4500 B.C. Khufu, under whose reign the pyramid of Giza was built, ruled in 2689 B.C. A total eclipse of the sun, 763 B.C., has been of great assistance in comparative computations. Uzziah ruled over Judea 751 B.C. The first Olympiad of the Greeks was 776 B.C. These dates are taken from the historical section of Merriam's Webster whose research staff is probably the best authority that can be found.   —THE PUBLISHERS.

ANSWERS

CHAPTER XI

1. Four. The original Grand Lodge organized in 1717 at the Apple Tree Tavern, Charles Street, Covent Garden, London. The Grand Lodge of All England at York, 1725. Dormant in a few years, revived in 1761, but no trace after 1792. The Grand Lodge of England, south of the river Trent, established in 1779, also at York. The only real rival, constituted July 17, 1751 at the Turk's Head Tavern, Greek Street, Soho, London, as the Grand Lodge of England according to the Old Constitutions, called "Ancients" and also spoken of as "Athol Masons".

2. The Lodge of Antiquity, No. 2, is the oldest Lodge in England, and one of the four which particiated in February, 1717, in the meeting at the Apple Tree Tavern. At that time this Lodge met at an alehouse, with the sign "Goose and Gridiron" in St. Paul's Church yard.

3. When the Grand Lodge was formed it assumed the precedency as No. 1, which it retained until the union of the two Grand Lodges in 1813, when in casting lots, it lost its primitive rank and became No. 2, which number it has ever since retained. In 1770 it adopted the title of the Lodge of Antiquity, which it has continued to use ever since.

4. The Charges of a Free Mason added to the first edition of the Book of Constitutions by Dr. Anderson, published in 1723.

5. The diffusion throughout Europe of the Roman Colleges of Artificers, the establishment of the archi-

tectural school at Como, the rise of the gilds, the organizations of the building corporations of Germany and the company of Freemasons of England.

6. Robert Freke Gould, in the third volume of his "History of Freemasonry" gives us a splendid copy of Stonemasons, Bricklayers and others, arms in colors, from Masons of Cologne in 1396 down to a banner in possession of York Lodge in 1776.

7. About the year 1723. By that time Speculative Masonry had become the whole element of the fraternity.

8. The period of "Transition".

9. Because during that year, due to the lack of building operations, changes were made in the rules admitting men of all professions and vocations. This marks the beginning of speculative or philosophic Masonry as we know it today.

10. The Reformation. The building of great cathedrals practically came to a standstill, throwing many fine artisans out of employment.

11. In 1772. Between the period of the Revival and 1772 there had been at least seven revisions. Dr. Desaguliers and Thomas Dunckerley were both largely instrumental in most of these revisions. Preston's "Ilustrations of Masonry", published in 1772, went through twelve editions in forty years.

12. The Ancient Mysteries; The Roman Collegia; The Medieval Guilds; The French Companionage; The German Stein-Metzen, and the old British Craft Lodges.

13. Three. The Religious Gilds, the Merchant Gild and Craft Gilds. The first representing the Church, the second the twelve great livery companies in London and the trade unions of today are nothing but Craft Gilds under another name.

14. Traveling Freemasons, in Italy, Mestrice des Macons in Gaul, Steinmetzen in Germany, Guilds in England and Companies in Scotland.

15. Yes. In June, 1721, twelve Lodges were represented by their Masters and Wardens, in September of the same year, Anderson reports the presence of representatives of sixteen Lodges, in March, 1722, it had increased to twenty-four and in April, 1723 the number had increased to thirty.

16. In the York Rite as practised in England, the additional officers are, a Director of Ceremonies, a Chaplain and an Inner Guard.

17. "Hear, see, and be silent", a motto frequently found in Masonic Medals. It was adopted as the motto of the Grand Lodge of England in 1813.

18. This is the oldest of all the rites, and consisted originally of only three degrees. 1, Entered Apprentice; 2, Fellow-Craft; 3, Master Mason. The Rite in its purity does not now exist anywhere. The nearest approach to it is the St. John's Masonry of Scotland.

19. Food, drink and lodging and other necessities, an apron and a new pair of shoes annually.

20. Rev. James Anderson, D.D. and Rev. John T. Desaguliers, L.L.D. The material for the degree dates back to the legendary period.

21. Over three thousand.

22. Elias Ashmole, the Antiquary, states in his diary, that he and Col. Mainwaring were initiated in a Lodge at Warrington in 1646, and he records the admission of several other non-operatives in 1682 at a Lodge held in London.

23. Good-fellowship, morality and secrecy.

24. York. The record of minutes of Lodges in the city of York are the oldest in the country.

25. The better historians extend the date of the liberation of Rome in 493 A.D. by Theodoric to the fall of Constantinople in 1453 A.D., followed by the discovery of America in 1492.

26. Calling off.

27. 926 A.D.

28. Queen Elizabeth.

29. The awarding of annuities to old members, or dependents of deceased brethren.

30. No, it was demolished about 1894.

31. In the fourteenth century. It reached England August 1348 and lasted until Michaelmas 1349. Half of the population succumbed leaving England with barely two million people. Following this the power of regulating the crafts and trades seems to have been completely in the hands of the municipalities.

32. For twenty-seven years. When as Prince of Wales, he was Grand Master from 1874 to 1901, at which time he became king upon the death of his mother, Queen Victoria. He was succeeded by his brother the Duke of Connaught.

ANSWERS

CHAPTER XII

1. The Masons who, in 1752, seceded from the Grand Lodge of England and established themselves under the name of Ancient Masons, who in 1776 elected the Duke of Athol their Grand Master, an office which he held until 1813, when the union of the two Grand Lodges took place.

2. The "Ancients" gave that name to the supporters of the original Grand Lodge of England which was formed in 1717.

3. There was a constant lack of harmony between the Lodges which under warrants from the Grand Lodge of "Ancients" and those which received theirs from the regular or "Moderns".

4. In 1813 A.D.

5. Yes. The two Grand Lodges of South Carolina were the last to unite in 1817 and the differences between the "Ancients" and "Moderns" was abolished.

6. The "Antient" work as it was spelled was introduced into Pennsylvania in 1757, the first Lodge chartered in 1758. Pennsylvania work is to this day that of "Antient" Grand Lodge, differing in many details from that of any other American Grand Lodge.

7. Laurence Dermott, who was its secretary for over thirty years. In 1756 he published their first book of laws, called *Ahiman Rezon*, or *Help to a Brother*.

8. The Ancients were fortunate in having Laurence Dermott, a fighting Irishman, on their rolls, and he was a big factor in the success of their movement. In

1771, when the Duke of Athol became Grand Master, the Ancients had almost two hundred Lodges on their rolls.

9. This is the name of the Book of Constitutions, which was used by the Ancient Division of Freemasons, which separated in 1739 from the Grand Lodge of England. The "true Ahiman Rezon" was compiled in 1772 by Laurence Dermott, Deputy Grand Master of that body.

10. The adoption of a fourth Degree by the Grand Lodge of Ancients gave to that body a popularity which it probably would not otherwise have obtained. This Degree is now known to the fraternity as the Royal Arch.

11. In 1758, in Pennsylvania.

12. Dec. 17th, 1813, at Freemason's Hall, London. The articles of union were signed by the two Grand Masters and six commissioners, and the seals of both Grand Lodges were affixed. Upon the nomination of the Duke of Sussex by the Duke of Kent, he was unanimously elected and placed on the throne.

13. In South Carolina since 1817. There had been a reconciliation effected between the Athol and Modern Lodges in 1808, but for only a brief period. However, in 1817 a new union was effected which has been permanent.

14. Movements toward a reconciliation were inaugurated toward the close of the 18th century, and finally, in 1813, the Athol Grand Lodge was forever dissolved by a fusion of the two contending bodies in England

into the now existing body under the title of the "United Grand Lodge of England".

15. Two sons of King George III, one of whom headed the "Moderns" and the other the "Ancients". They arranged articles of Union between the two Grand Lodges, which were ratified in each of those bodies, December 1, 1813, in the Freemason's Hall, London.

16. When the two contending Grand Lodges of England, known as the "Ancients" and the "Moderns" resolved in 1813, to put an end to all differences, it was provided in the fifth article of union for a Lodge of Reconcilation. Its purpose being to visit Lodges in both jurisdictions to instruct the officers, in order to establish a uniformity of ritual. It was constituted December 27th, 1813, and when its duties had been fulfilled, it ceased to exist by its own limitation in 1816.

17. One of the profane. This purely Masonic term is derived from the Greek kuon, a dog. In the early ages of the church, infidels and unbaptized profane were called "dogs". See Matt. xii. 6, "Give not that which is holy unto the dogs".

18. A listener. A name taken from the punishment, according to Dr. Oliver, to be inflicted to a detected cowan, and which was "To be placed under the eaves of a house in rainy weather, till the water runs in at his shoulders and out at his heels".

19. A sacrifice of a hundred oxen.

20. Dr. Oliver stated the English commonly thought that Freemasons "raised the devil" in their Lodges, so

riding the goat an alleged practice of witchcraft, was transferred to the Masons. The idiom remains up to the present day.

ANSWERS

CHAPTER XIII

1. The oldest Masonic document extant, known as the Regius poem; it is not only Christian but definitely Catholic. It is dated about 1390.

2. One "by the Right Worshipful and Right Honorable Lord Kingston, Grand Master of all the Lodges of Free Masons, in 1731", signed Tho. Griffith, Secretary.

3. The Sloane Manuscript No. 3329 in the British Museum.

4. There are now seventy copies (or forms) that have not only been traced, but transcribed, but to these must be added nine printed versions (some of which are fragments of unknown originals).

5. It is a certificate of withdrawal of membership. It relieves the member from all pecuniary contributions and debars him from pecuniary relief, but does not cancel his Masonic obligation.

6. "1646, October 16, 4:30 P.M.—I was made a Free Mason at Warrington, in Lancashire, with Col. Henry Mainwaring, of Karingham in Cheshire. The diary also gives "the names of those that were then of the Lodge".

7. Twenty-five. Until the year 1858 no effort had been made to give them a comprehensible form, until

Mackey in that year published an article in *the American Quarterly Review of Masonry* on "The Foundation of Masonic Laws" which contained a distinct enumeration of the Landmarks, which has since been generally adopted by the fraternity.

8. They came under three classifications:
The Landmarks.
General Laws adopted prior to 1721.
Local Laws. These are the regulations which since 1721 have been enacted by the Grand Lodge, and are in force only in those jurisdictions which have adopted them.

9. A pamphlet of twenty pages in quarto entitled, "The beginning and the first foundation of the Most Worthy Craft of Masonry, etc. By a deceased brother, for the benefit of his widow. Printed in London, 1739 for Mrs. Dodd, at the Peacock without Temple Bar. Price, sixpence".

10. Into four.
Usages that Mark the Masonic from the Outer World.
Usages that Mark the Degrees of Masonry.
Usages that Mark the Various Ceremonies.
Usages that Mark Official Powers and Duties and Private Rights and Duties.

11. Fifteen. The first one is, The worthy Craftsman must love well God and the holy church, the Master he is with and his Fellows also.

12. Fifteen.

13. There is a slight difference in the ritual in every country and in our country in the different states, but the landmarks are always the same everywhere.

14.   1.   Concerning God and religion.

       2.   Of civil magistrates, supreme and subordinate.

       3.   Of Lodges.

       4.   Of Masters, Wardens, Fellows and Apprentices.

       5.   Of management of the Craft in working.

       6.   Of behavior under different circumstances and in various conditions.

15.   "So help me God, and the holy contents of this book".

16.   About thirty. Seven of these are in the British Museum. Five in the custody of York Lodge, No. 236. One in possession of the Grand Lodge of Canada and the remaining Ms. distributed throughout the British Isles.

17.   The installation ceremony specifically charges "it is not in the power of any man or body of men to make innovations in the body of Masonry.

18.   The Harleian Constitution of 1670 stipulates in the twenty-sixth article that "no person shall be *accepted* a Mason unless he shall have a Lodge of five Freemasons" and the following article provides "no person shall be *accepted* a Freemason but such as are of able body, honest parentage", etc.

19.   In the ancient charges which accompanied by the landmarks are the foundation of Masonry.

20.   An old Masonic document first published in the *Gentleman's Magazine* for 1753, Page 417, claiming to be a reprint of an earlier publication printed in Frankfort in 1748. It claims to be a series of questions propounded by Henry VI, and the replies given by Masons.

21. There are twenty-five according to Dr. A. G. Mackey, who is probably our best Masonic authority. Some other sources give different figures from four to sixty.

22. There are three copies of the Old Constitutions which bear this name, but the most interesting and valuable is the Ms. 3329 in the British Museum. It differs materially from the others as it is a description of the ritual of the Society of Free Operative Masons at the period when it was written.

23. Every Lodge is required to make an annual statement to the Grand Lodge of the names of its members, the number of admissions, demissions, expulsions or rejections that have taken place within the year. A tax is levied for each member based on this statement, which is called a *return*.

24. It borrows its name from its shape, being that of the *gable* or *gavel* end of a house.

25. Many old Masonic diplomas and charters are still in existence, where the seal consists of a circular tinbox filled with wax, on which the seal is impressed, the box being attached by a ribbon to the parchment. But now the seal is placed generally on a piece of circular paper.

ANSWERS

CHAPTER XIV

1. The Symbolic Degrees of Entered Apprentices, Fellow Craft and Master Mason. These are not only the basic, but the oldest Degrees in Masonry.

2. The Latin poet Virgil is quoted as saying "God delights in odd numbers". Everywhere among the ancients, three was deemed most sacred of numbers. There are in all degrees three principal officers, three supports, three greater and three lesser lights, three movable and three immovable jewels, three pripcipal tenets, three orders in architecture, and everywhere the number three is a prominent symbol.

3. Dr. Anderson and Dr. Desaguliers were the pioneers and improvement in the lectures were made by Hutchinson. About the same period Dunckerly made many additions and subtractions. The fourth attempt to improve the lectures was by William Preston, whose work found great favor among the more scholarly members of the fraternity. Finally Thomas Smith Webb, made many changes in the work and the lectures, which is now standard in the United States, except in Pennsylvania.

4. "As far as I can gather", the upper ten, "so to speak, among the building trades gathered themselves together in more regular and elaborately constituted bodies about the close of the fourteenth and beginning of the fiftheenth centuries, in both Germany and England, and at the same time began, in the latter country, to be called Freemasons".

5. Gould tells that from 1730 to 1738 candidates were admitted into Masonry according to the old system as well as the new, and that until the publication of the Constitution of 1738, there is not a scrap of evidence from which we may infer that the three degrees of Masonry were practised with the sanction

(or recognition) of the earliest of Grand Lodges, either express or implied.

6. In this selection of the hours of night and darkness for initiation, the usual coincidence will be found in the ceremonies of Freemasonry and those of the Ancient Mysteries. This practise was almost universal from the Druids of Britain and Gaul to the Mystics of Persia and India.

7. The opening was regulated by the seasons of the moon.

8. In order that all Lodges when feasible should open and work during similar periods to signify the unity and universality of Masonry.

9. Because of the exalted lessons that it teaches of God and of a future life.

10. In the Regulations of 1720.

11. The titles were granted not because of any ceremony or degree work, but on account of the length of service and skill manifested in the workmans' handicraft.

12. They were conferred only in the Grand Lodge, but this was found too inconvenient and it was decreed that a Master with his Wardens and a competent number of the Lodge assembled in due form can make Masters and Fellows at discretion.

13. Masonic historians are agreed that some time between 1723 and 1730 the second and third degrees were evolved, and in this evolution of degrees, ritualism and symbolism were developed, resulting in the philosophical Freemasonry of our time.

14.   In 1719. Its ritual had been completed but the
       Masters of the Lodges had not yet become so well
       acquainted with its forms and ceremonies as to be
       capable of conducting an initiation.

15.   Compagnon. The second degree of Ancient Craft
       Masonry. It is particularly devoted to science. In
       the degree of Entered Apprentice, every emblem-
       atical ceremony is directed to the lustration of the
       heart; in that of Fellow Craft, to the enlargement
       of the mind.

16.   About 1719. Bro. Lyon, in his *History of the Lodge
       of Edinburgh* cites the minutes of the Lodge of Dun-
       blane under the date of December 27th, 1720, when
       an "Entered Prentiss" was passed to a "Fellow of
       Craft".

17.   Mackey states that we have authentic documentary
       evidence of the "General Regulations" published in
       1723, that two Degrees had been superimposed on
       the original one. Later interpretation would indicate
       the third Degree was fabricated between 1723 and
       1738.

18.   Seven years.

19.   No. The York Rite has sovereign control everywhere
       over the three basic degrees.

20.   The obligation in the Entered Apprentice Degree
       stresses largely the necessity for secrecy; while in
       the Fellowcraft Degree, secrecy is enjoined upon the
       brother, he also assumes duties toward his fellows,
       and takes upon himself sacred vows not given to
       an Entered Apprentice.

21. The first degree in Masonry, and tho it supplies no historical knowledge, it is replete with information on the internal structure of the order, and remarkable, too, for the beauty of the morality which it inculcates.

22. At the union of the two Grand Lodges of England it was stated that "pure Ancient Craft Masonry consisted of three degrees and no more, viz: those of the Entered Apprentice, the Fellow Craft, and the Master Mason, including the Supreme Order of the Holy Royal Arch".

23. As the historian Gould says, "the progress of the degree is to a great extent veiled in obscurity", but the by-laws of London Lodge of about 1731 and the constitution of a Country Lodge May 18th, 1733, would indicate the conferring of the third degree.

24. In 1760 the fee for initiation and passing was about £1 1s.; raising 5s; quarterage 6s. Customarily those present paid something, usually a shilling; visitors from other Lodges 18 pence, unattached brethren, two shillings.

25. There is no record that Freemasonry before that date consisted of more than one degree.

26. 1. Entered Apprentice.
2. Fellow Craft.
3. Master Mason.
4. Mark Master.
5. Past Master.
6. Most Excellent Master.
6. Royal Arch.
8. Royal Master.

      9. Select Master.

     10. Illustrious Knight of the Red Cross.

     11. Knight Templar.

     12. Knight of Malta.

27. The work in Pennsylvania differs materially from the American Rite as taught by Webb.

28. The ceremony of removing the shoes, as a token of respect, whenever we are on or about to approach holy ground. It is referred to in Exodus iii, 5 when the angel of the Lord said to Moses, "Draw not nigh hither; put off they shoes from off thy feet, for the place whereon thou standest is holy ground". It is taken from the Latin *Discalceatus*, unshod or bare foot.

29. To prehistoric man the sun seemed to move from east to west by way of the south, so early man circled his altars on which burned the fire (which was his god) from east to west, by way of the south.

30. On the contrary in ancient times and in many lands to this day, it is well nigh universal.

31. A farcical side degree of horseplay to which none but physicians were eligible. Had some vogue along the middle of the nineteenth century in the mid-west, but is now obsolete.

ANSWERS

CHAPTER XV

1. The first three degrees, Entered Apprentice, Fellowcraft and Master Mason.

2. An occult representation of something unknown or concealed by a sign that is known. In all the ancient mysteries the mode of instruction adopted was by emblems.

3. Symbol is from the Greek verb which signifies "to compare one thing with another."

4. To a Master Mason the Temple of Solomon is a symbol of this life; to the Royal Arch Mason the Temple of Zerubbabel is the symbol of the future life. The former the search for the truth, and to the latter, the symbol of the discovery of truth.

5. Because the fish among primitive Christians was a symbol of Jesus. The Pisces in the Zodiac constellation is represented by a fish.

6. The five letters of the Greek word meaning fish are the first letters of the five words Jesus Christ, God's Son, Savior. Many regret its discontinuance as an ornament.

7. Because the ninety-degree angle is not only a right angle, but it is *the* right angle—the only angle which is "right" for stones which form a wall, a building or a cathedral. Any other angle is incorrect, Masonically.

8. It was an emblem of immortality.

9. A symbol of plenty, for which it is well adapted by its swelling and seed-abounding fruit.

10. The Swastika.

11. An ancient ornament still used as a symbol of good luck, consisting of a Greek cross with the ends of the arms bent at right angles, all in the same direction.

12. On the bricks of the Chaldeans, among the ruins of Troy, the vases of ancient Cyprus, the panels of Egypt, on the stone tablets of the Hittites, the pottery of the Etruscans, the cave temples of India, the Roman altars, the Runic monuments of Britain, in Thibet, China, Korea, Mexico, Peru, and the pre-historic burial grounds of North America.

13. An emblem in the third degree, reminding us, by the quick passage of the sands, of the transitory nature of human life.

14. In the lectures in the early part of the eighteenth century, the Immovable Jewels of a Lodge are said to be "the Tarsel Board, Rough Ashlar and Broached Thurnel". This last Jewel was a cubical stone with a pyramidal apex.

15. Filedity.

16. The Bee Hive.

17. The Masonic Apron.

18. Leather. Usually a lambskin.

19. Yes. The Israelites when preparing for their flight from Egypt were enjoined to eat the Passover with *their loins girded.* Job is commanded to gird up his loins like a man. Samuel when received into the ministry, was girded with a linen ephod. David upon his recovery of the Ark, danced before it, invested with an apron, Elijah the Tishite and John the Baptist, were both girded with aprons of white leather.

20. Dr. Oliver says it "appears in ancient times, to have been an honorary badge of distinction". In the Jew-

ish economy none but the superior orders of the priesthood were permitted to so adorn themselves."

21. It is from the Egyptian and is a symbolic sign for the sun and the god Osiris.

22. The immortality of the soul.

23. The ancient name of a plant, most of whose species are evergreen, and six of which, at least are natives of the East. It is the *mimosa nilotica* of Linnæus and grew abundantly in the vicinity of Jerusalem.

24. The ivy in the mysteries of Dionysius, the myrtle in those of Ceres, the erica or heath in the Osirian, the mistletoe in the Celtic and the lotus in those of Egypt and India.

25. Midnight. Low twelve in Masonic symbolism is an unpropitious hour.

26. In the obsolete lectures of the old English system, it was said, "the circle has ever been considered symbolical of the Deity".

27. The gavel is a symbol of order and decorum; the setting maul of death by violence.

28. The Temple of King Solomon.

29. Fidelity and trust. Horapollo says in Egypt it was the symbol of the builder. The origin of the sign is lost in antiquity.

30. The rough Cube and polished Cube in pure white limestone, the Square cut in syenite, an iron Trowel, a lead Plummet, the arc of a Circle, a stone Trestle-board and the Masters' Mark.

31. As the Operative Mason follows the plans laid down on the Trestle Board of the architect in building his

edifice, so should the Speculative Mason in obedience to the rules and precepts of the Grand Architect of the Universe erect that spiritual temple, that
house not made with hands, eternal in the heavens.

32.   The concurrent testimony of ancient religions indicate that the star was the symbol of God.

33.   Mercury, salt and sulphur.

ANSWERS

CHAPTER XVI

1.   Three. 1. The Mythical legend. 2, The Philosophical
legend. 3, The Historical legend.

2.   Corn, wine and oil. In processions, the corn alone
is carried in a golden pitcher, the wine and oil are
placed in silver vessels, and this is to remind us that
the first, as a necessity and the "staff of life" is more
worthy of honour than the others.

3.   Preston says, "Smelling and tasting are inseparably
connected; and it is by the unnatural kind of life
which men commonly lead in society that these senses
are rendered less fit to perform their natural duties".

4.   The Gutteral (refers to the entrance upon the penal
responsibilities; the Pectoral to the entrance into the
Lodge; the Manual, to the entrance on the Covenant;
and the Pedal, to the entrance on the instructions in
the northeast.

5.   Yes. It was practised by the Greeks, Romans,
Hindoos and other races. Virgil describes Corynoeus
as purifying his companions at the obseques of
Misenus by passing three times around them while

aspersing them with lustral water. The procession was always in such form that the right hand was nearer the altar.

6. Burials of deceased brethren, the laying of corner stones of public edifices and the dedications of Masonic Halls. The installation of officers is frequently conducted in public in America, with only a slight variation in the ceremonial.

7. Abraham, in obedience to Divine command, took a heifer, a she goat and a ram, "and divided them in the midst, and laid each piece one against another". (Gen. 15, 10).

8. Not in this country. Confusion is sometimes caused because of a ceremony in the higher degrees, properly called *lustration*.

9. In imitation to the course of the sun, from east to west. The candidate must always have the altar on his right side during the procession.

10. By the decree of the Grand Lodge these no longer are a part of the ritual, but Oliver gives these as part of the ceremony prior to 1813. 1, *The opening of the Lodge;* 2, the *preparation* of the candidate; 3, the *report* of the Senior Deacon; 4, the *entrance* of the candidate; 5, the *prayer;* 6, the *circumambulation;* 7, the *advancing* to the altar; 8, the *obligation;* 9, the *entrusting* of the candidate; 10, the *investiture* of the lambskin; 11, the *ceremony of the northeast corner;* 12, *closing of the Lodge.*

11. A mode of recognition which derives its name from its object, which is to duly guard the person using it in reference to his obligation. It is an Americanism

of comparatively recent origin, being unknown to the English and continental systems. In some old rituals dated 1757 however the expression is used, but in reference to what is now called the sign.

12. Pectoral is from the Latin, *pectus*, "belonging to the breast". The heart has always been considered the seat of courage, hence the symbolic relation to the virtue of fortitude.

13. Twenty-five. But it is uncertain that there are no universal Landmarks. Each Grand Lodge is a law unto itself and determines what its Landmarks are.

14. The story of the "Winding Stairs" in the second degree is purely mythological and has no base other than the allusion in the 1st Book of Kings (vi-8) and its only value is derived from symbolism taught in its legend.

15. In the ancient legends, the death or disappearance of some heroic god. The concealment of this body by the murderers was called the aphanism.

16. The legend is derived from Josephus. The old *Constitutions* said the children of Lamech knew that God would take vengeance for sin, by fire or water, so they wrote of the sciences on pillars of marble that would not burn and *latres* which would float. The word *later* is Latin for brick.

17. It arose from the fact that during the period of Operative Masonry that the members were exempted by several papal bulls, from laws which applied to ordinary laborers, as well as burdens imposed upon the working classes in England as well as on the continent.

18. That of Zoroaster, the Persian; Manu, the Hindoo; Minos, the Cretan; Lycurgus, the Spartan, and Numa, the Roman.

19. It is represented as the emerald dish from which Christ partook of his last supper. It is reputed that Joseph of Arimathea further sanctified it by receiving into it the blood from the five wounds of Jesus on the cross, and afterwards carried it to England, from whence it disappeared, due to the sins of the people and was long lost. When Merlin established the Knights of the Round Table, he told them that the San Graal would be discovered by one of them, but that only he could see it, who was without sin. "The quest of the San Graal" became the most celebrated myth of the legends of King Arthur.

20. "So mote it be, Amen", which should always be audibly pronounced by all the Brethren.

ANSWERS

CHAPTER XVII

1. Three. The Rough Ashlar, the Perfect Ashlar and the Trestle Board.

2. Plumb, square and level.

3. Temperance, fortitude, prudence and justice.

4. In Jewish symbolism they were supposed by some to refer to the seven planets, and by others to the seventh day or Sabbath.

5. In the old lectures of the eighteenth century, the *fixed lights* were the three windows always supposed to be in the East, South and West. Their uses were,

according to the Ritual "to light men to, at and from their work". In the modern lectures they have been omitted and their place supplied by the *lesser lights*.

6. In the Mark Masters' Degree. In the English Ritual it is also a working tool of an Entered Apprentice.

7. This was called "cable rope" in the old rituals. Cable Taw propably is from the German, "Kabel Tau", is symbolic of the cord binding the new born infant to its mother, and the tie by which the initiate is attached to his Mother Lodge.

8. The old writers define the length of a "Cable Tow" to be three miles for an Entered Apprentice. But this expression is really symbolic, and, as it was defined by the Baltimore Convention in 1842, means the scope of a man's reasonable ability.

9. No, they were in use by practically all of the building craftsmen.

10. The Axe, caused to swim by Elisha. See (II Kings vi-6).

11. A line to which a piece of lead is attached to cause it to hang perpendicularly. A working tool of a Fellowcraft.

12. The tesselated border, one of the three principal ornaments.

13. The Mosaic Pavement, the Indented Tessel and the Blazing Star.

14. One of the working tools of a Fellowcraft.

15. "Free stone as it comes out of the quarry", *Bailey*. In Speculative Masonry, we adopt the Ashlar in two different states, as symbols in the Apprentices De-

gree. The Rough Ashlar, in its rude and unpolished condition, is emblematic of man in his natural state —ignorant, uncultivated and vicious, but when education has expanded his intellect, restraining his passions and purifying his life, he is represented by the Perfect Ashlar, smoothed and squared and fitted for its place in the building.

16. We are told in the lectures that our ancient brethren met in a high hill or a low vale, hence the covering must have been the overhanging vault of heaven. So in the symbolism of Masonry, the *covering of the Lodge* is said to be "a clouded canopy or starry-decked heaven.

17. The Holy Bible, Square and Compasses with the Charter from the Grand Lodge.

18. Beauty to adorn it, Strength to support it, and Wisdom to contrive it.

ANSWERS

CHAPTER XVIII

1. Daniel Coxe in 1730. However there is no record of his having officiated as such. He was a member of Lodge No. 8 in London, at the Devil Tavern within Temple Bar.

2. Most Worshipful (except Pennsylvania where the Ancient title Right Worshipful is used). All officers below Grand Master are addressed Right Worshipful.

3. Grand Master, Deputy Grand Master, Senior Grand Warden, Junior Grand Warden, Grand Treasurer and Grand Secretary. Two each Grand Deacons and

Grand Stewards, a Grand Marshal, Grand Pursui-
vant, Grand Sword-Bearer and Grand Tiler.

4. It has. The same is true of the First Lodge in Boston,
now St. John's Lodge. These two bodies have weath-
ered the vicissitudes of over two hundred and fifteen
years, and are therefore entitled to precedence as the
oldest Masonic organizations in America.

5. St. John's Grand Lodge issued two warrants. One in
1738 and one in 1756 to the troops in the Crown
Point expedition.

6. 51. One in each state, 1 in District of Columbia, 1
in Puerto Rico and 1 in the Philippines. Now that
the Philippines have their independence, it is probably more proper to say 50, but 51 is the latest
published statistics in 1948.

7. New York has a membership of 282,210. Property
valuation $13,270,081.10. Pennsylvania has a mem-
bership of 210,347 but a property valuation of
$22,285,950.75. Close of year 1947.

8. Yes. Massachusetts Grand Lodge maintains Lodges
in Canal Zone, Manchuria, China and Chili. Grand
Lodge of New York has chartered Lodges in Lebanon
and Syria. Record is of year 1948.

9. They are practised by the Craft on only four occasions: When a Masonic Hall is to be consecrated, a
new Lodge to be constituted, a Master-elect to be
installed, or a Grand Master or his deputy to be
received on an official visit.

10. When the Grand Master is present at the opening or
the closing of the Grand Lodge. All ceremony per-

formed by the Grand Master is said to be done "in ample form."

11. Tennessee.

12. As the Lodge owes its existence and all its rights and prerogatives to the Grand Lodge from whom it received its Charter or Warrant, it is a principle of Masonic Law that when such a Lodge ceases to exist, either by withdrawal or surrender of its Charter, all of its property reverts to the Grand Lodge. Should the Lodge be restored, by a revival of its Charter, its property should be returned, because the Grand Lodge held it only as a trustee.

13. The city in which the Grand Lodge or other governing Masonic Body, is situated. A document issued from the Grand Lodge of Massachusetts, would be dated from the "Grand East" of Boston. It is in constant use in America and continental Europe, but only rarely in the British Isles.

14. No. The Grand Chapter of Texas surrendered its membership in the National Grand Chapter which action has never been rescinded.

15. Efforts have been made at numerous times beginning during the war of the Revolution in 1779 to a meeting in 1855 to form one national Grand Lodge, without success. As long as we have different Grand Lodges, a variation in the work is inevitable.

16. A Masonic Congress which met in the city of Baltimore, May 8th, 1843. It consisted of delegates from thirteen states and the District of Columbia, for the purpose of establishing a uniformity in the work. It continued in session for nine days in an effort to

perfect the ritual, and form a national Grand Lodge to meet every three years. Too much bitterness entered into the controversy however, and it is doubtful that a national Grand Lodge will ever be established.

17. In Washington, D.C., in 1822. In Baltimore, Md., in 1843 and 1847. In Lexington, Ky., in 1853 and the last one of record in Chicago, in 1859, it being a volunteer assemblage.

18. He is the presiding officer of the Symbolic Degrees in his jurisdiction. He of course presides over the Grand Lodge. He can visit Lodges, examine their records as often as he chooses. He grants dispensations for the creation of new Lodges. He can make Masons at sight.

19. Grand Masters. The prerogative of the Grand Master to make Masons at sight, is described as the eighth landmark of the Order. It is but right to say that this doctrine is not universally received as established law by the Craft.

20. The Grand Master summons to his assistance not less than six other Masons, convenes a Lodge, and without any previous probation, but *on sight* of the candidate, confers the degrees upon him, after which he dissolves the Lodge and dismisses the brethren.

21. John Wanamaker, at Philadelphia, Pa.; Charles W. Fairbanks, at Indianapolis, Ind.; Rear-Admiral Winfield Scott Schley, at Washington, D.C.; and William Howard Taft, as President-elect, at Cincinnati, Ohio, February 18, 1909, by the Grand Master of Ohio.

22. The Duke of Sussex, who at his death in 1843, had been Grand Master for over thirty years.

23. In Masonic processions the oldest Master Mason present is generally selected to carry the open Bible, Square and Compasses on a cushion before the Chaplain. The "Grand Bible-Bearer" is an officer of the Grand Lodge of Scotland.

24. The use of the collar in Masonry as an official decoration, is of a very old date. The custom is derived from the practices of heraldry. It was an article of investiture of city and state officers as well as knights.

25. About 1800 A.D. They were to relieve the Wardens of a portion of the duties previously performed by them. The Athol Lodges began having deacons in the line of officers upon the adoption of the Constitution of 1751, compiled by Pratt.

26. The Senior Deacon carries a rod and wears as a jewel, of a square and compass with the sun in the center; the Junior Deacon also has a rod, and has a somewhat similar jewel excepting that the square and compass has a moon in the center.

27. They carry a rod and a jewel of their office is the cornucopia, which is the symbol of plenty.

28. The Tiler.

29. He was called Tiler or Tyler because the man who put on the roof or tiles (tiler) completed the building secure from intrusion, so the officer who guarded the door, by analogy, was named Tiler.

30. It was general given in the Tiler's room and previously administered by him.

31. To visit every member of the Lodge and personally summon him to attend each meeting.

32. Andrew Jackson, who had been Grand Master of Tennessee, and our present chief executive, Harry S. Truman, who has been Grand Master of Missouri.

33. A contemptuous title, given during the anti-Masonic excitement following the Morgan episode, given to certain groups of swindlers who professed to confer Masonic degrees on men gullible enough to be victims. They derived their instructions from the so-called expositions of Morgan. The customary fee was a jug of whiskey.

ANSWERS
CHAPTER XIX

1. Many definitions have been given, but the best, possibly is, "Freemasonry is a system of morality, veiled in allegory, and illustrated by symbols." This is so often quoted, it is difficult to give its origin.

2. Freemasonry is not a Lodge, it is not a Ritual but a plan for the living of the life and a belief in the fatherhood of God and the brotherhood of man.

3. Literally it is not, but an association of men with secrets. The society, its membership and insignia are well known. Music is a secret from the mute, Mathematics are a secret from the ignorant, Philosophy is a secret from the unscholarly mind. So Freemasonry is a secret from the uninitiated.

4. Rev. George Oliver, D.D. He was born November 5, 1782 and died March 3, 1867. He was the most prolific Masonic scholar of his time.

5. "Masonry is the activity of closely united men who, employing symbolical forms borrowed principally from the Mason's trade and from architecture, work for the welfare of mankind, striving morally to ennoble themselves and others, and thereby to bring about a universal league of mankind, which they aspire to exhibit even now on a small scale."

6. Hardly. While it teaches the principles of Christianity, its legends and historical drama are all taken from the pre-Christian era. Many of the higher degrees are based on incidents of the Christian era, but the three symbolic degrees refer in no way to New Testament history.

7. High Twelve.

8. Year of the order. The date used in documents connected with Masonic Templarism. It refers to the establishment of the Order of Knights Templar in 1118 A.D.

9. At one time particularly in Scotland Operative Masons were called "Domatic," while the Speculative Masons were known as "Geomatic." The derivation of the two terms is unknown.

10. Blue. To the Mason it is a symbol of universal friendship and benevolence, because, as it is the color of the vault of heaven, which embraces the earth, we are thus reminded that in the breast of every brother, these virtues should be equally extensive. It is therefore the only color, except white, which should be used in a Master's Lodge.

11. In the Statute 25 Edward I (1350) entitled *"Le Statuts d'Artificers et servants"* which fixes the rate

of wages viz: "Item, Carpenters, Masons and Tilers
and other workmen on houses, shall take no other
wages for their work, but as they used to do before
the year 1346; that is to say, a master carpenter
3 den., and another (namely a joiner) 2 den., a
Master Free-Mason 4 den., and other masons 3 den.,
and their servants 1 den., a Tiler 3 den., and their
knaves 1 den." etc.

12. In some of the lectures of the eighteenth century
this title is used as equivalent to Speculative Free-
mason. Thus they had the following catechism:
"Q. What do you learn by being a Gentleman
Mason?"
"A. Secrecy, Morality, and Good Fellowship."
"Q. What do you learn by being an Operative
Mason?"
"A. Hew, Square, Mould stone, lay a level, and raise
a Perpendicular."
Hence we see that Gentleman Mason was in con-
trast with Operative Mason.

13. The will of God, relating to human actions, grounded on the moral differences of things; and because
discoverable by natural light, obligatory upon all
mankind.

14. Permission to do that which, without such permission, is forbidden by the constitutions and usages
of the order, and is granted only by authority of
the Grand Master or his deputy.

15. Among English Masons in the middle of the last
century it was the custom among the members when
discussing Masonic subjects, to announce the ap-

pearance of a profane, by the warning expression, "it rains."

16. A given number of blows by the officers, or by the hands of the Brethren, as a mark of approbation or reverence, and at times accompanied by the acclamation. A practice of the higher degrees of Masonry.

17. "Initiation is an analogy of man's advent from prenatal darkness into the light of human fellowship, moral truth, and spiritual faith." From the Latin *initium;* a beginning, a birth, a coming into being.

18. The first knew how to draw plans and lay out work. The latter were setters and layers. The quotation is given from Wyclifs' Bible of 1382. I Chron. xxii, 15. "Many craftise men, Masouns and leyers."

19. A Mason, who having served his apprenticeship, began to work for himself, was then called a journeyman, but he was required in a reasonable period (in Scotland it was two years) to join a Lodge when he was said to have passed a Fellow Craft. Thus, in the minutes of St. Mary's Chapel Lodge of Edinburgh, on the 27th of December 1689, it was declared that "No Master shall employ a person who has not been passed a Fellow Craft in two years after the expiring of his apprenticeship;" and the names of several journeymen are given who had not complied with the law.

20. This was a distinctive difference in the Stone-Masons in Germany in the Middle Ages. The Salute Masons had signs, words and other methods of recognition, while the Letter Masons were identified only by documentary evidence.

21. To denote the differences between the Speculative and the original Operative art.

22. A circular, sent to many places or persons. They are sometimes issued by Grand Lodges or Grand Masters to members in the jurisdiction. The word is not in common use.

23. One who commits to memory questions and answers of the cathetical lectures and the formulaes of the ritual only.

24. Seven years. The construction of the collateral addition covered thirteen years, the entire task consuming about twenty years.

25. They are about equally divided in this country. The practice was inherited from the great schism, the MODERNS using the former and the ANCIENTS the latter.

26. The real foundation of Masonry is the deep need and aspiration of man, his creative impulse, his love of light and his instinctive faith that the mind of man is akin to the Mind that made it.

27. The search for the etymology of the word *Mason* has given rise to numerous theories, many of them absurd. Dr. Murray thought that the word was from the root of Latin "maceria" (a wall), but we prefer the better root of Medieval Latin *Maconner*, to build or *Maconetus* a builder.

28. Dr. Oliver in his "Historical Landmarks of Freemasonry" declares it to be "a system of morality, by the practice of which its members may advance their spiritual interest. It is not a religion, but it is a handmaiden to religion."

29. It is neither charity nor the cultivation of the social graces, both of which are merely incidental to its organization; but it is the search after truth, and that truth is the unity of God and the immortality of the soul.

30. A Masonic punishment depriving a member of its privileges. It is of two kinds, definite and indefinite, but the effect of the penalty during the period of its existence is the same.

31. First, a belief in God, secondly, a belief in the eternal life.

32. The real object of Freemasonry, in a philosophical and religious sense, is the search for truth.

33. In 1882 Queen Victoria became Chief Patroness of the Royal Masonic Institution for Girls. Six years later £51,500 was raised in a single evening by the Grand Master for its maintenance at the Centenary Festival of that Institution.

34. No, the charges must be made by a member of the Lodge, but the information can be given to a Master Mason and he in turn can file the charges against the accused through the Junior Warden.

ANSWERS

CHAPTER XX

1. One is the search for light and the other is the labor of building.

2. Yes, it is a Symbolic Lodge, in which the first three degrees of Masonry are conferred, and it is so called from the color of its decorations.

3. It is required of every candidate for initiation that
    he believe in God as a supreme power, and in a
    future life.

4. Western Star Lodge No. 107, at Kaskaskia, on the
    Mississippi in what is now the state of Illinois. It
    was chartered by the Grand Lodge of Pennsylvania
    in 1805. Due to conditions of travel in those days
    the dispensation did not reach Kaskaskia until
    December 1806.

5. It comes from the Sanskrit *loga*, which in the sacred
    language of the Ganges, signifies world, of which
    every Lodge is a representation. To what we call
    Lodge the Persians gave the name of *Jehan*, whence
    by corruption, comes our expression, *a Lodge of
    St. John*.

6. No. And the adoption of a uniform ritual through
    all the forty-eight states will in all probability never
    occur.

7. Yes. Ever since the formation of the thirteen col-
    onies, efforts have been made to form a General
    Grand Lodge without success, but it is doubltful that
    we will ever have a supreme Grand Lodge in this
    country.

8. The Lodge in Fairbanks, Alaska.

9. Yes. St. Paul's No. 374, Montreal constituted 1770.
    Royal Standard No. 398, Halifax constituted 1829.
    St. George's No. 440, Montreal constituted 1829.
    All are under the authority of the United Grand
    Lodge of England. There are also fourteen Lodges on
    the island of Newfoundland on the English Register

and an additional number of Lodges in the British West Indies.

10. There are a number of buildings for the exclusive use of Masonic gatherings, but probably the most unusual one is one in the little village of Woodbury, Conn., built on top of a cliff, fifty feet in height. It is patterned architecturally from the Parthenon at Athens. It was constructed for and has been owned and occupied by King Solomon's Lodge since 1839. The Temple of Tuscan Lodge, St. Louis, Mo., is probably the most sumptious Lodge Room of any single Lodge in the United States, if not in the world.

11. Because it is half as wide as it is long. Patterned after the Ark of the Covenant, Moses had made for the children of Israel on their journey to the promised land.

12. Lawful authority. No Lodge can be formed and work without this essential element.

13. No. The "Low Twelve" clubs are Masonic only in membership, but aside from that fact, have nothing to do with Masonry.

14. According to Masonic law, No. However in France and many Latin American countries women have been made Masons. The Hon. Mrs. Aldworth was initiated in Doneraile, Ireland, in 1734.
Another authenticated case is that of Mrs. Beanton, who died in Norwich, England, in 1802 at the age of 85. Both of these women had acquired Masonic secrets surreptitiously and were compelled to submit to initiation.

15. This is a matter purely of individual taste, they are both beautiful and instructive. An orthodox Jew is hardly consistent were he to take the York Rite just as a good Roman Catholic would not petition for Masonic degrees at all.

16. The Scotch word for Masonic initiation.

17. That secret portion of Masonry which is known only to the initiates is esoteric as distinguished from exoteric or monitorial. The words are from the Greek and were first used by Pythagoras who divided his classes according to the degree of knowledge they had attained.

18. Mackey and Webster both give it demit. This subject is treated exhaustively by Mackey in his Masonic Jurisprudence, book III, chapter III, sect. vi.

19. The English Masons and through them the French, have derived Tubal Cain from the Hebrew, *tebel*, earth, and *kanah*, to acquire possession. This interpretation has not been introduced into this country.

20. The son of a Mason, in England, was called a Lewis. Only a Lewis was admitted under the age of twenty-one but he was eligible for membership at eighteen. Term obsolete in this country, though some authorities think that may account for the admission of Washington when he was only twenty years of age.

21. A magic square is a series of numbers arranged in an equal number of cells constituting a square figure, the enumeration of all these columns, vertically, horizontally and diagonally, will give the same sum.

22. Mount Moriah, on which the Temple of Solomon was built. It was remarkable for three events re-

corded in the Scripture. It was here that Abraham prepared to offer up his beloved son Isaac; it was here that David, when his people were afflicted with a pestilence made peace-offerings and burnt offerings to appease the wrath of God; it was here that Solomon, upon completion of the Temple, dedicated that magnificent edifice to the service of Jehovah. The Kabalists delight to invest it with still more solemn associations, and declare it was the spot where Adam was born and Abel slain.

23. From the Latin, *inchoatus*, unfinished, incomplete. Lodges working under the dispensation of the Grand Master, because they do not possess all the prerogatives of a Lodge working under a warrant of constitution from a Grand Lodge.

24. A body of Masons uniting in a Lodge without the consent of the Grand Lodge; or even if legally constituted to continue to work after its charter has been revoked.

25. In a note by Noorthouck on page 239 in his edition of the *Book of Constitutions* published in 1784.

26. Regular Masons are forbidden to converse with clandestine Masons on Masonic matters.

27. A Lodge is said to be tiled when the necessary precautions have been taken to prevent the approach of unauthorized persons.

28. Prior to 1717 all business was transacted in the first or Entered Apprentice degree.

29. There are twelve Lodges in the Pennsylvania Jurisdiction that have numbers only.

30. The Old Constitutions and Regulations are silent on this subject, and authorities consequently differ. However it is generally accepted that as seven Masons are sufficient to open a Lodge and carry on business, other than initiation, that number would constitute a quorum.

31. Removal of the hat in the presence of superiors in all Christian nations has been a mark of respect. The oriental uncovers his feet when he enters a place of worship. The converse of this is also true. To keep the head covered while all around are uncovered, is a mark of superiority of rank or station.

32. The Junior Warden.

33. The Masonic tradition is that the primitive or mother Lodge was held at Jerusalem and dedicated to St. John, first the Baptist, then the Evangelist, and finally to both.

34. No. All extraneous ornaments and devices are in bad taste, and detract from the symbolic character of the investiture.

35. It is a symbol of the unsuccessful search after Divine Truth and the attainment in this life, of which the first Temple is a type.

36. 15,389. Several states and also Porto Rico have not reported later than 1947.

37. Albert Pike Lodge No. 303 Wichita, Kan., 4,358. Ivanhoe Lodge No. 446 Kansas City, Mo., 2,950.

38. 3,284,068.

39. 181,993.

40. New York, 1,036 Lodges; 271,905 members in 1948.

41. Nevada, 20 Lodges; 3,937 members in 1948.

42. Yes. As early as 1600 we have a record of admission of non-professionals into the Lodge of Edinburgh. Before 1650, noblemen, baronets, physicians and advocates are recorded in the minutes as receiving Degrees.

43. "It is very simple. I merely knock away with hammer and chisel the stone I do not need and the statue is there—*it was there all the time*".

44. Cowan, a purely Masonic term technically means an intruder whereas eavesdropper signifies an unauthorized listener. The word came to England from the Scotch Operatives as a term of contempt.

ANSWERS

CHAPTER XXI

1. The Degrees conferred under the charter of an American Royal Arch Chapter, which are Mark Master, Past Master, Most Excellent Master, and Royal Arch Mason.

2. More properly called the Holy Royal Arch, it is the seventh degree in the York Rite. The ritual relates largely to the Biblical story following King Solomon about seventy years.

3. April 29th, 1768, in England.

4. It was first used in England in 1778.

5. Joshua, the High Priest of the Jews when they returned from the Babylonian exile.

6. 80,000.

7. The record states that it could only be conferred on one having previously received the degree of Fellowcraft and Master.

8. The earliest record of the Mark Degree being conferred bears the date of January 7th, 1778.

9. Its origin is veiled in obscurity, but it sprang into existence in the earlier period of Speculative Masonry. It was customary for the operative to select a Mark, to be placed on every piece of work wrought by them, in order that a check could be made by the Overseer, and to facilitate the payment of wages.

10. In the Chapter Degree of Mark Master. It symbolizes the effect of education on the human mind.

11. To indicate which artisan had done the work.

12. The early records of the Chapter do not show any recognition of preparatory Degrees. The "Most Excellent" was first conferred on April 17th, 1807 and the "Mark" on July 20th, 1818. They were not even then obligatory, but appear to have been taken or not, at the choice of the candidate.

13. It is the second in the series of the Chapter, hence arose the terms, Actual Past Master and Virtual Past Master, the latter meaning one who had received the degree in the Chapter but had not been elected or served as Master of a Lodge. A Virtual Past Master is not recognized in the Grand Lodge as a Past Master.

14. St. Andrew's Chapter, Boston, Mass., conferred this degree from 1769 to 1797. The Chapter degrees can date their birth from 1723 to 1760.

15. The records of York Chapter, June 12th, 1765.

16. In the Secretary's record of the minutes of the meeting of January 30th, 1794.

17. No. The records of St. Andrew's Chapter in Boston, instituted August 28th, 1769, show the three highest officers as Master, Senior Warden and Junior Warden. The same titles were used in the election April 17th, 1770. Due to the difficulties preceding and during the Revolution, no further election was recorded until October 21st, 1790. The earliest record of the titles of High Priest, King and Scribe occur April 1st, 1789, in St. Andrew's Chapter.

18. The early history of this Degree is lost in obscurity, but in the opinion of the late Bro. W. J. Hughan its origin may be ascribed to the fourth decade of the eighteenth century. Mention of it occurs in the account of the meeting of a Lodge (No. 21) at Youghal, in Ireland, in 1743, when the members walked in a procession and the Master was preceded by "the Royal Arch carried by two excellent Masons".

19. The first Degrees were conferred by Lodges under the authority of Lodge warrants or in Chapters apurtenant to a Lodge. This was the procedure of the "Ancients" and while it was not approved by the "Moderns", it is now well established that they did likewise prior to 1765, when a Grand Chapter was formed.

20. December 22nd, 1753, when it was conferred under a Lodge charter in Fredericksburg, Va. It was conferred into New York and Pennsylvania about the same time by a military Lodge.

21. A Chapter of Royal Arch Masons was established in Philadelphia in 1758, working under the Masters' Warrant of Lodge No. 3. The minutes of this Chapter, Jerusalem Chapter No. 3, are in existence as far back as 1767, and they mention prior minutes.

22. Originally an indispensable qualification for the Degree was that the candidate should be a Past Master. As the restriction to those only who had presided for twelve months over a Symbolic Lodge, circumscribed the candidates within a very narrow limit, the ceremony of passing the chair was invented, by which the candidate became a "Virtual Past Master" in contradistinction to an "Actual Past Master".

23. "While Webb retained the names of the Degrees and probably the leading ideas of the ritual, he revised, amplified and made more dramatic the 'work' of every one; in that sense he is the author of the American system of Royal Arch Masonry." That verbal and other slight changes were made, and will continue to be made, goes without saying; but otherwise the work remains substantially as Webb taught it in 1797".

24. According to Goulds' History it was five guineas.

25. An eagle, on a blue banner representing the tribe of Dan. A man, on a purple banner representing the tribe of Reuben. An ox, on a scarlet banner representing the tribe of Ephraim, and a lion on a white banner representing the tribe of Judah. The last being borne by the Royal Arch Captain, and the other

three by the Grand Masters of the first, second and third veils.

26. Red, scarlet or crimson, for it is called by each of these names and it is said symbolically to represent the ardor and zeal, which should actuate all who are in possession of that sublime portion of Masonry.

27. Approximately 600,000.

28. An officer in the Royal Arch Chapter whose duties are similar to those of a Senior Deacon in a Symbolic Lodge.

29. The Scribe is the third officer in a Royal Arch Chapter and is the representative of Haggai.

30. Haggai, who in the American Rite of the Royal Arch is called the Scribe, in the English system receives the title of *prophet*, and hence in the order of precedence, he is placed above the High Priest.

31. An iron bar used to raise heavy articles. It is a working tool of a Royal Arch Mason, and symbolically teaches him to raise his thoughts above the corrupting influence of worldly mindedness.

32. The tribes of Judah and Benjamin.

33. An assemblage of Royal Arch Masons.

34. Thomas Smith Webb. He was the son of English parents who had come to this country several years prior to his birth which was Oct. 13th, 1771. He received the primary Degrees in Keene, New Hampshire in 1792. After moving to Albany, N.Y., he became active in the Chapter of Royal Arch and Commandery of the Temple. In 1797 he published his first Freemason's Monitor. While using Preston's

work as a model, he changed the arrangement of the lectures to make them more "agreeable to the present mode of working". His influence over Masonry is to be ascribed almost wholly to his personal contact with them and also his oral teachings. He seems though to be the author of a Masonic system now universally practiced in the United States. He died in Cleveland, Ohio, July 6th, 1819.

35.   In Hartford, Conn., in 1798.
The one formed in Pennsylvania in 1795 was merely an instrument of the Grand Lodge, who alone could sanction the holding of a Chapter.

36.   Only four, Massachusetts, Rhode Island, Connecticut and New York.

37.   At the annual convocation of the Grand Chapter in Lexington, Ky., September 5th, 1825, resolutions were adopted to address letters to the other Grand Chapters on the propriety of dissolving the General Grand Chapter. The memorial was issued and is found in the proceedings of the General Grand Chapter on September 4th of the following year. After due discussion and deliberation that body by a vote of 47 to 2, refused to comply with the resolution as presented and the Grand Chapter of Kentucky appeared to be contented with the decision.

38.   In the first year of the war between the states. On June 17th, 1861, the Grand Chapter of Texas adopted the following resolution:
Resolved, that all connection between this Grand Chapter and the General Grand Chapter of the

United States, is dissolved and forever annihilated by the separation of our State from that government.

39. Ten; King Cyrus No. 1, Valparaiso, Chile; Luzon No. 1, Manila, P.I. Island No. 1, Havana, Cuba; Santa Fe No. 2, Isle of Pines; Canal Zone No. 1, Ancon; Cristobel No. 2, Panama; City of Mexico No. 1, Mexico; D.F. Tampico No. 2, Tampico; and Monterey No. 3, Monterey, N.L.; Keystone No. 1, Shanghai, China.

40. The Degrees of Royal and Select Master. Some modern Ritualists have added the Degree of Superexcellent Master, now, often conferred in a Cryptic Council, but its legend has no connection with the crypt or secret vault.

41. No. Several attempts have been made to have the Degrees of Royal and Select Master incorporated as preparatory steps in the Capitular system, the last effort having been made in 1870, which like the others, failed of adoption.

42. Zerubbabel, who with the High Priest Joshua and Haggai the Scribe led the Jews back to Jerusalem. The second Temple was completed 515 B.C.

ANSWERS

CHAPTER XXII

1. The Lodge, styled St. Andrews Royal Arch Lodge, held its first recorded meeting August 28th, 1769, in Mason's Hall, Boston, and the record of that meeting contains the first account of the conferring of the Order of Knight Templar that has not yet been discovered in manuscript or print.

2. Three. First, between the years 1769-1816 covering the date prior to the organization of the Grand Encampment; second, 1816-1856 the period of General Grand Encampment; and third 1856 to the Grand Commanderies, and since the adoption of the present constitution.

3. Knights Templar is the form now adopted, from the authority of the Constitution of the Grand Commandery of the United States.

4. An officer in the Commandery of Knights Templar and a Council of Royal and Select Masters, equivalent to a Secretary in a blue Lodge.

5. Last reports available give a membership of 272,019.

6. An embrace on the conferring of Knighthood.

7. Commanderies, the national meetings every three years is called Grand Commandery. When three or more Commanderies are instituted in a state, they may unite and form a Grand Commandery.

8. Massachusetts and Pennsylvania both lay claim to this distinction. The Grand Encampment of Massachusetts and Rhode Island was formed May 6, 1805. Pennsylvania held her first Grand Encampment May 12th, 1797, composed of delegates from Nos. 1 and 2 of Philadelphia, No. 3 of Harrisburg, and No. 4 of Carlisle. The claim of Massachusetts is predicated on the fact that Sir Henry Fowle, a member, fabricated the ritual which for years was standard in all the bodies, both Grand and Subordinate, within the United States.

9. In the year 1118 by Hugo de Payens, Godfrey de St. Aldemar, and seven other knights whose names history has not preserved. They took the vows of poverty,

chastity and obedience in the presence of the Patriarch of Jerusalem.

10. An imaginary idol or symbol, which the Knights Templars were accused of using in their mystic rites.

11. The preparation room in which the candidate remains until he is introduced in the degree of Knights Templar.

12. It was established in 1429 A.D. by the Duke of Burgundy in Flanders, and was in high repute as an Order of Knighthood.

13. The fall of Acre in 1292 A.D. under the vigorous assault of the Sultan Mansour. The Templars, after a brief stay on the island of Cyprus, retired to their different Preceptories in Europe.

14. Its membership is confined to the immediate female kin of the Knights Templar.

15. The vexillum belli, or war banner of the ancient Templars. It was also the war-cry of the Ancient Templars.

16. The staff of the Prelate.

17. The custom of interring a Knight Templar with one leg crossing over the other. This posture is assumed in an allusion to the position of Jesus while upon the Cross.

8. A juvenile Lodge called Chapters to which the sons of Masons between sixteen and twenty-one are eligible. It was founded in 1919 at Kansas City, by Frank S. Land. It comprises two Degrees and its ritual is based on the martyrdom of Jacques De Molay, March 11th, 1313. There are about a thousand Chapters and over 100,000 members.

ANSWERS

CHAPTER XXIII

1. One relating to the Provincial Grand Lodge in the West Indies, warranted by the Grand Lodge of Pennsylvania in the year 1802. An original Scottish Rite Certificate issued to Ossonde Verriere, a planter in St. Domingo, dated October 26th, 1764, signed by no less a dignitary than Stephen Morin, which is without doubt the most ancient authenticated Scottish Rite document known, at least on this side of the Atlantic.

2. To Stephen Morin. He in turn appointed M. M. Hayes a Deputy Inspector General for North America, who appointed Isaac da Costa a Deputy for South Carolina, and through him the Sublime Degrees were disseminated among the Masons of the United States.

3. It was formed in Charleston, S.C., May 31st, 1801, by John Mitchell, Emanuel De La Motte, Abraham Alexander, Major T. B. Bowen and Israel Delidien. This was a transformation of the former "Rite of Perfection" or Ancient and Accepted Rite. The Grand Council Headquarters were moved to Washington, D.C. in 1870.

4. August 5th, 1813, by the Most Illustrious Brother E. De La Motte, "Special Deputy Representative" and others from the said Supreme Grand Council at Charleston, S.C.

5. Chevalier de Bonneville formed a chapter of twenty-five Degrees of the so-called High-Degrees in the College of Jesuits of Clermont, in Paris in 1754. The

adherents of the House of Stuart had made the college of Clermont their asylum, they being mostly Scotchmen. One of these Degrees being the "Scottish Master", the new body organized in Charleston, S.C., in 1801, gave the name of Scottish Rite to these Degrees, which name ever since that time has characterized the Rite all over the world. The name previously given to these Degrees was the "Rite of Perfection", or the Ancient and Accepted Rite; while some authorities have a different version, Mackey is usually the most reliable.

6. The meetings of members of the Thirty-Second Degree or Sublime Princes of the Royal Secret in the Ancient and Accepted Scottish Rite.

7. The eleven degrees conferred in the Lodge of Perfection, 4th to 14th inclusive. Secret Master, Perfect Master, Intimate Secretary, Provost and Judge, Intendant of the Building, Master Elect of Nine, Master Elect of Fifteen, Sublime Master Elected, Grand Master Architect, Master of the Ninth Arch and Grand Elect Mason.

8. The initiates into the Fourteenth Degree of the Ancient Accepted Rite are so called. The form, "Grand, Elect, Perfect, and Sublime Mason" is the term generally employed.

9. The two Degrees conferred in a Council, Princes of Jerusalem 15th and 16th, Knight of the East or Sword and Prince of Jerusalem.

10. The two Degrees conferred in a Chapter of Rose Croix de H-R-D-M 17th and 18th, Knight of the East and West and Knight of the Rose Croix de H-R-D-M.

They are founded on the revelations of St. John, whose symbols and machinery of initiation are derived from that work.

11.   19° Grand Pontiff
      20° Master ad Vitam
      21° Patriarch Noachite
      22° Prince of Libanus
      23° Chief of the Tabernacle
      24° Prince of the Tabernacle
      25° Knight of the Brazen Serpent
      26° Prince of Mercy
      27° Commander of the Temple
      28° Knight of the Sun
      29° Knight of St. Andrew
      30° Grand Elect Kadosh or Knight of the White and Black Eagle
      31° Grand Inspector Inquisitor Commander
      32° Sublime Prince of the Royal Secret
      Conferred in a Consistory, Sublime Princes of the Royal Secret, 32°.

OFFICIAL GRADES

33° Sovereign Grand Inspector General
Conferred only by the SUPREME COUNCIL, 33°, and upon those who may be elected to receive it by that high body which assembles yearly.

12.   Spes mea in Deo est, which translated means "My hope is in God".

13.   The outer dress which is worn by the priest at the altar service, and is an imitation of the old Roman

toga. It is used in the ceremonial of the Rose Croix Degree.

14. The daughter of King Cyrus of Persia and the mother of Xerxes. Referred to in the sixteenth degree of the Scottish Rite.

15. To all those who have taken the Ancient and Accepted Scottish Rite Thirty-Second or Thirty-Third Degrees.

16. The 19th Degree of the Ancient Scotch Rite, and is occupied in an examination of the Apocalyptic mysteries of the New Jerusalem.

17. The wearing of white gloves, it is nothing else, but the symbolizing, by a ceremony, the doctrine of clean hands as the sign of a pure heart.

18. The 21st Degree of the Ancient Scotch Rite, called by its possessors not a degree, but "the very Ancient Order of Noachites".

19. An address of the presiding officer of a Supreme Council of Ancient Accepted Scottish Rite, is sometimes so called. The word's origin is from the Roman practice of generals addressing their troops, called allocutions.

20. A Rite established in 1782 by a convention of Masons under the presidency of the Duke of Brunswick who was elected Grand Master. It spread rapidly thru Germany, France, Italy and Switzerland, its supreme body being situated at Zurich. The Rite consisted of five degrees.

21. A Rite instituted in Germany by M. Rosa, a Lutheran clergyman. It was at first very popular, but was superseded by the Strict Observant Rite of Baron Hunde.

22. The 29th Degree of the Ancient and Accepted Scotch Rite founded on a legend of the Chevalier Ramsey.

23. In 1758, when the Council of Emperors of the East and West was established in Paris. It had reference to the double jurisdiction which this council claimed.

24. It signifies *the enlightened*, often applied in Latin diplomas as an appelation of honor in Masonry.

On page 245 will be found a brief synopsis of all the Scottish Rite Degrees from the fourth to the 33rd Degree inclusive. This synopsis was prepared for the Henry L. Palmer Class of the Wisconsin Consistory and will be found both instructive and interesting.

ANSWERS

CHAPTER XXIV

1. Robert Morris in 1855.

2. 376,543.

3. From France, where it was known as "Adoptive Masonry". In 1744, the Grand Orient of France called it the "Rite of Adoption".

4. No, though modifications of the Degree were conferred at the close of the eighteenth century.

5. The five degrees of the Eastern Star. It is claimed that Josephine when the wife of Napoleon, as First Consul patronised the "Loges d'Adoption", the original French order, from which the Eastern Star originated.

6. Robert Morris, one of the "poet laureates" of Masonry. He had received his Masonic Degrees in Oxford, Miss., and while sick in 1850, he had done considerable reading of the Holy Scriptures, from which he received his inspiration. He chose five female characters, upon whose virtues he elaborted in so interesting and dramatic a manner, that today there are over twelve thousand chapters and nearly two million members throughout the world in its membership.

7. Robert Macoy, of New York, in 1866, the year Morris started off on a trip to the Holy Land.

8. In 1921. R.W. Grand Master John S. Sell issued an edict in 1921 forbidding members of the Masonic Fraternity in Pennsylvania to join the Eastern Star and compelling those who already were members to resign. The edict has never been revoked.

9. Jephthah's daughter, Ruth, Esther, Martha and Electa.

10. Until 1921 it was an adjunct of the Eastern Star. Like the Eastern Star its membership is limited to Masons and female relatives. The name is taken from a Greek flower, signifying a blossom that never withers, symbolically representing immortality.

11. Pennsylvania. Membership in the Eastern Star is also banned in England.

12. A feminine order composed of girls between thirteen and twenty who are related to Master Masons. It was founded in 1922 by Mrs. Ethel T. Wead Mick of Cleveland. The scheme of its ritual has particular

reference to Job 42:15, in the Old Testament. The Daughters meet in Bethels, which now number over three hundred with a membership of about 60,000.

13. This is another feminine order for girls of Masonic kinship which is international in scope, even as far as Australia. It started in 1921 in McAlester, Oklahoma. There are over 750 groups of girls between thirteen and eighteen.

14. A Royal and Exalted Degree in the Rite of Adoption. It is a female degree and it is claimed to have been created by Christina, Queen of Sweden, in 1658, to honor an attendant at her court, the beautiful Lady Amaranta. For some time it was very popular in Europe. The Eastern Star is the basis of the Degrees.

15. This is another Ladies' appendant degree, claimed to be the oldest of all Female Degrees. The Degree is founded on the friendship existing between Ruth and Naomi. They operate in courts with ten officers and confer three Degrees. Not conferred in a Lodge, but usually at the house of some Royal Arch Mason. It can not be conferred by any Mason on his own wife.

16. A feminine auxiliary of the Knights Templar. Its ceremonial is composed of a narrative of the mother of Constantine the Great and her pilgrimage to the Holy Land.

17. It was incorporated in Illinois June 10th, 1895 and at the present time it has an enrollment of over four hundred Shrines and 130,000 members in the United States, Canada and Europe. This is another organiz-

ation for the gentler sex. In their ceremonies they call themselves sojourners.

ANSWERS

CHAPTER XXV

1. The Bible.

2. Hebrew, Chaldian and Greek. Christ spoke the Aramaic tongue, but the New Testament was written in Greek, and Abraham originally came from Chaldea.

3. The Ancient Landmark requirement provides that a *"Volume of the Sacred Law be open upon the Masonic Altar whenever the Lodge is open"*. A Lodge entirely Jewish may choose to use only the Old Testament; in Turkey and Iran the Koran would be used and the Brahmin would use the Vedas. In the far east some Lodges frequently have several sacred books upon the altar.

4. No. Not even in the article on "God and Religion". It is mentioned in some footnotes by Dr. Anderson.

5. About 1760, but the first of the Old Charges, published in 1723, reads as follows:
   "A Mason is obliged by his tenure to obey the moral law; and if he rightly understands the art, he will never be a stupid atheist, nor an irreligious libertine".

6. Quatuor Coronatum, No. 2076.

7. It is the name under which the transactions of the Lodge Quatuor Coronatum, No. 2076, London, the

premier literary Lodge of the world, are published in annual volumes, beginning with 1888.

8. William Shakespeare in one of his historical plays.

9. The Greek and the Hebrew.

10. The Egyptian Pyramids and Sphinx; the Hanging Gardens of Babylon; the Temple of Diana at Ephesus; the Statue of Jupiter Olympus; Mausolus' Tomb; the Pharos at Alexandria, and the Colossus of Rhodes.

11. Yes. A William Boude, a bachelor of divinity, was the author of a book found by a W. J. Williams in the British Museum, printed in 1524, entitled "Ars Quatuor Coronatorum" in which the words Apprentices and Free Masons are both used.

12. By the invention of printing. Next to the introduction of the alphabet, by far the greatest invention in history.

13. Between forty and fifty.

14. William Shakespeare in the first scene of the third act of the tragedy, Hamlet.

15. Masons in America and England date from the creation of the world, calling it "Anno Lucis", which they abbreviate A.L., signifying, *in the year of light.* Thus with them the year 1850 is A.:L.: 5850.

16. From 1620. The historian Condor gives its establishment as 1220 or possibly earlier.

17. Probably the most abstrusely learned and philosophical of all the rites. It was formerly practised by the Grand Lodge at Berlin. It consisted of nine degrees taken from Swedish and French chapters.

18. They were secret criminal courts in the Middle Ages. Their historical existence is confined to the fourteenth and fifteenth centuries. At first their trials were conducted with impartiality, but later their administration became corrupt, a change which finally led to its decay.

19. The poor box. The name given by German Masons to the box in which collections of money are made at a Table-Lodge for the relief of poor brethren and their families.

20. Der Freymaurer, published at Leipsic, Germany, in 1738.

21. German for Entered Apprentice.

22. A Dr. Plott, in his "Natural History of Staffordshire", printed in 1686, states that "persons of most eminent quality did not disdain to be of the fellowship".

23. In the sixth book of Virgil's immortal epic, Aeneid, he is supposed to have described the ceremony of initiation into the Ancient Mysteries.

24. The Grand·Lodge Library of Iowa at Cedar Rapids, and the Libraries of the Grand Lodge of Massachusetts and Pennsylvania.

25. Mackey's "Enclyclopedia of Freemasonry". It is a great Masonic Library. It is published in two volumes.

ANSWERS

CHAPTER XXVI

1. 1. At the Goose and Gridiron Alehouse at St. Paul's Churchyard.

2. At the Crown Alehouse in Parker's Lane near Drury Lane.

3. At the Apple Tree Tavern in Charles Street, Covent Garden.

4. At the Rummer and Grapes Tavern in Channel Row, Westminster.

2.   The one meeting at the Rummer and Grapes Tavern. It had seventy members, mostly Speculative. It had the highest type of membership, including Dr. Anderson and Dr. Desaguliers, who were both so influential in the organization of the Grand Lodge and its ritual.

3.   1. To the traditions of the patriarchs. 2. To the Ancient Mysteries. 3. To the building of Solomon's Temple. 4. To the Roman Collegia. 5. To the Comacines. 6. To the traveling Masons. 7. To the Rosicrucians. 8. To James the Pretender. 9. To Dr. Anderson and Dr. Desaguliers.

4.   It is well known that Speculative Masonry is the offspring of the Operative art. These Operative Masons go further back than recorded history, but Masonic historians give its age as over 4000 B.C., but Masonry, as we know it today dates from the union of Lodges in London in 1717.

5.   According to Mackey from the Latin "*Maconner*, to build or *Maconetus*, a builder."

6.   It originally signified that the persons so called were free of the company or gild of incorporated Masons. Those Operative Masons who were not thus free of the gild, were not permitted to work with those who

were. The term seems to have been first used in the tenth century, when traveling Freemasons were incorporated by the Roman Pontiff.

7. The period of transition from Operative to Speculative. Masonry was an age when learning was difficult to acquire. Many men desirous to improve their mental status sought admission to the fraternity, and a place was made for them by taking them in as "Accepted Masons". The roll of the Lodge of Aberdeen in 1670, shows that out of forty-nine names, thirty-nine were those of Accepted Masons.

8. It was first used by Dr. Anderson in the second edition of the Book of Constitutions, published in 1738, the title of which is "The History and Constitutions of the Most Ancient and Honourable Fraternity of Free and Accepted Masons."

9. The sequence of its number. The rule of precedency was adopted December 27th, 1727.

10. The ancient Roman *Collegia* of Architects was the last to feel the ban of the Roman Emperors. These members were *free* a fact more important than the name implies. Roman sarcophigi show carvings of square, compasses, level and plumb. The free builders who continued the spirit level of the craftsmen ever maintained freedom from bondage as an essential to membership.

11. Towards the close of the eighteenth century in England, but in Scotland at a much earlier period. There we find St. Mary's Chapel, Kilwinning, Aberdeen, etc. Lodges in continental Europe as well as America usually had distinctive names.

12. It was compiled by Dr. Anderson previously but not published until 1723.

13. It is the book in which is contained the rules and regulations of the order, giving the duties of officers and the rights of members, and the ceremonial details for different occasions.

14. Rev. James Anderson in 1722. It was revised in 1738. It is usually called the 1723 Constitution because it was published that year, but it was approved in 1722.

15. During the reign of Edward IV which stated that Prince Edwin had assembled the Masons at York in 926. They goverened the craft for some years under the name of "Gothic Constitutions" until 1721, when the Duke of Montagu ordered Brother James Anderson to digest them in a better method.

16. Those regulations of the craft, which were adopted In 926, at the assembly in York, under Prince Edwin, and to which additions were made from time to time. Several copies of them were in existence at the revival of Masonry in 1717 and in 1721 were digested and codified by Dr. Anderson and published a few years later.

17. St. Elizabeth's Cathedral at Marburg, in 1235 A.D.

18. The "Book of Constitutions," submitted on January 17th, 1723 was the joint production of Payne, who compiled the regulations; Desaguliers, who wrote the preface, and Anderson, who digested the entire subject matter.

19. St. John's Lodge of the Grand Lodge of Scotland.

20. "In the Lord is all our trust."

21. In England, Lodges do not appear to have received distinctive names before the latter part of the eighteenth century. Up to that period, the Lodges were distinguished simply by their numbers. Thus, in the first edition of the Book of Constitutions, published in 1723, we find a list of twenty Lodges registered by their numbers, from "No. 1 to No. 20 inclusive."

22. The best Masonic historians question their use in connection with the ritual in any manner.

23. In the Old York lectures was the following passage: "The better to see and observe all that might ascend and descend and in case a cowan should appear, the Tiler might give timely notice."

ANSWERS

CHAPTER XXVII

1. At one time Egypt was in possession of all the learning and religion that was to be found in the world. It extended to other nations the influence of its sacred rites and esoteric doctrines.

2. Whether a man or a myth no one knows, but he was a great figure in the Egyptian Mysteries, and was called the Father of Wisdom.

3. It was a symbol of the Supreme Being. Among the early Mexicans it represented Universal power.

4. Khufu, for the study of the stars.

5. Amen Ra.

6. From the Egyptians, who formed the world's oldest civilization.

7. Egyptian priestesses who were supposed to have supernatural knowledge.

8. The ark of the Egyptian gods. In its proportions unlike the Ark of the Covenant. The Egyptian gods were reputed to be concealed in the interior of the Naos of the sacred barks, behind hermetically closed doors.

9. A device for measuring time by a graduated flow of water thru an aperture in its mechanism, or a water clock.

10. A star of the first magnitude.

11. Natives of Egypt. Descendants of Ham, one of Noah's three sons.

12. A ruined town of upper Egypt. Its Temple is of great interest because of its astronomical allusions on the ceiling of the main portico. The temple dates from the period of Cleopatra.

13. Crux Ansata, meaning the cross with a handle. It was used by the Egyptians, and was a symbol of immortality.

14. Eternal life.

15. A lighthouse.

16. A famous obelisk, now in Central Park, New York, the gift to our nation from Ismail, Khedive of Egypt in 1878. Originally it stood near the temple of the Egyptian Sun-god at Heliopolis, dating back 1500 B.C. It was examined by the Grand Lodge of New

York and its emblems pronounced to be unmistakably Masonic.

17. Its base is 761 feet 8 inches on each side and it is 485 feet high. It was built of large stones, none less than thirty feet long and five feet square, quarried at a great distance, transported hundreds of miles, crossing the river Nile, and raised to their lofty position in the structure by methods unknown to the engineers of today.

18. A fabulous monster, to which the ancients give the face of a woman and the body of a lion. It is found in great abundance on Egyptian monuments. As a symbol of mystery it has been adopted as a Masonic emblem.

19. Near Thebes, in Egypt.

20. Aries, Cancer, Gemini, Capricornus, Aquarius, Leo, Libra, Pisces, Scorpio, Sagittarius, Taurus and Virgo.

21. 1. The river turned into blood. 2. Frogs came on land. 3. Dust became lice. 4. Swarms of flies. 5. A fatal infection among the cattle. 6. Boils. 7. Hail. 8. Locusts. 9. Darkness. 10. Death of the first born.

22. Because the seasonal flooding of the Nile occured when the sun was passing through the constellation of Leo.

23. The use of a lion's mouth as a waterspout on fountains, reservoirs, cisterns, etc.

24. A so-called division of chemistry, treating of the art of transmutation of baser metals into gold.

25. The Hermetic Philosophy, because it is said to have been first taught by Hermes Trismegistus in Egypt.

26. The stone is a slab of black basalt, found in 1790 among ruins near the Rosetta mouth of the Nile and is now in the British Museum. The inscription on it is a decree of the Egyptian priests at Memphis, in honor of Ptolemy V., Epiphanes, in recognition of the benefits conferred by him upon his people. The inscription is first in hieroglyphics, or the writing of the priests; second, in demotic, or the writing of the people; and third in Greek. This stone furnished the first clue to decipherment of the Egyptian hieroglyphics on monuments and was of tremendous value to historical research.

27. Eleazar, the high priest.

28. It is in the British Museum.

29. Ptolemy II. The Ptolemys were Macedonian Greeks, descended from the rulers of the Alexandrian conquest.

ANSWERS

CHAPTER XXVIII

1. Geometry and Astronomy. The study of the latter being well nigh impossible without a knowledge of the former.

2. Euclid was a famous geometrician and was born in the year of the world 3650 or about 300 B.C. He was of Macedonian-Greek ancestry and was born in Alexandria Egypt.

3. One of the most celebrated of the Greek philosophers. Born 586 B.C. at Samos, and tradition says he died of starvation 506 B.C. He was educated as an athlete,

winning a prize in wrestling, which he subsequently abandoned and devoted himself to the study of philosophy. He is regarded as the inventor of the problem known as the 47th problem of Euclid. Students flocked to him from Europe, Asia and Egypt.

4. Twenty years, so cautious were they of candidates, especially of foreigners.

5. Those Pythagoreans who abstained from animal food.

6. An Athenian school of philosophers followers of Epicurus, who were mistakenly accused of self indulgence in the extreme. The facts are, that Epicurus taught his pupils, that the best in and of everything in life was that for which they should strive.

7. Disciples of the Greek philosopher Zeno, who taught that a man should be governed by reason, subdue passion and be indifferent to pleasure or pain.

8. The ancient Greek historians so termed the hereditary priests among the Medes and the Persians.

9. Associations among the ancient Greeks whose purpose was to aid and assist the distressed and needy members. It was sustained by voluntary contributions.

10. "In any right angled triangle, the square which is described upon the side subtending the right angle, is equal to the squares described upon the sides which contain the right angle". Mackey tells us it is sometimes called the "Carpenters' theorem".

11. "There is no royal road to geometry".

12. "Let no one who is ignorant of geometry enter my doors".

13. According to Greek mythology it was a fleece of gold

secreted in a sacred grove, guarded by a dragon. In the middle ages it was one of the most important symbols of the Hermetic philosophers.

14. The oldest and most original of the three Grecian orders. The distinguishing characteristics of this order is the want of a base.

15. Doric, Ionic and Corinthian.

16. The Greek temple, now in ruins, on the Acropolis at Athens, which was built in honor of Athena (Minerva). It is the finest example of Greek architecture extant.

17. A fraternity of builders established in Asia Minor about 1000 B.C. by the priests of Bacchus. They are said to have continued their existence to the time of the Crusades, when they passed over to Europe and became merged with the Traveling Freemasons.

18. From the great builders in Egypt.

19. A noted Greek artist and architect. He is known as the original designer of the Corinthian Column.

20. Our national Capitol, housing the congress at Washington, D.C.

21. The Doric.

22. The Corinthian, because it is said to be a pillar of beauty.

23. The Pantheon at Rome is considered the finest building extant, of the ancient type of Corinthian architecture.

24. The Gothic, in which they were complete masters.

25. A square column or pillar inserted partly in a wall.

26. The principal type, figure, pattern or example whereby and whereon the thing is formed.

27. There is only one equilateral triangle.

28. The triangle.

29. A Greek word, literally meaning four. It was composed of ten dots arranged in a triangular form of four rows.

30. In 1221, and the building of the London Bridge forty-five years earlier in 1176.

ANSWERS
CHAPTER XXIX

1. About 753 B.C.

2. Subterranean sepulchers in Rome, much used in addition to burial places as a refuge for the early Christians to escape persecution.

3. The Eagle, to the Romans, was the ensign of imperial power.

4. Vulcan.

5. A Latin word meaning "things to be done".

6. The people of Etruria, a region of Italy, between the Arno and the Tiber.

7. The Tuscan and Composite.

8. Yes. The histodian Marcianus tells us that the Roman Collegia flourished in fifty-nine cities.

9. Titus in A.D. 70, a few days before the Feast of the Passover. He tried to save the edifice, but a Roman soldier had thrown a burning piece of wood into the building and Titus was forced to withdraw from the

sanctuary on account of the smoke and flames.

10. From a corporation of bridge makers and tenders in Rome called *pontifices*, considered a sacred task by the early Romans. Probably from Ponta, Latin for bridge.

11. A fabled race of giants on the island of Sicily, having but one eye in the middle of the forehead.

12. To the Roman Collegia.

13. They called it the Sea of Tiberius. It is seven miles wide and thirteen miles long. It is 682 feet below the level of the Mediterranean Sea. The water is very clear and abounds in fish. The best known city of the New Testament era on its shores is Capernaum.

14. In the year 66 B.C. under Pompey. He entered the Temple, but left the treasures untouched.

15. Associations of men engaged in similar pursuits, and prior to the decline of Rome they became so powerful the Emperors endeavored to abolish the right of free association. The *"Collegia"* of architects or builders was the last to be broken up, when they fled from Rome.

16. When the Roman *Collegia* of architects fled Rome many of them settled on an island called "Isola Comacina" in beautiful Lake Como in northern Italy. What once was only a tradition of the connection between the ancient craftsmen, *the "Collegia"* and the ancient guilds, is now shown by many citations from records, to be an established fact.

17. Beads or balls strung upon rods or wires, used for arithmetical computations.

ANSWERS

CHAPTER XXX

1. *Arts* means the knowledge, or things made known; *parts*, the degrees into which Masonry is divided, and *points*, the rules and usages.

2. Three, five and seven years for the Entered Apprentice, Fellowcraft and Master Mason respectively.

3. The science which teaches the doctrine of images and symbolic representations, and is somewhat collateral with Masonry.

4. A mystic cult, which seeks a closer union with the Divine, by a higher spiritual development. Annie Besant was its best known apostle, up to the time of her death.

5. That sacred and inviolate band which unites men of the most discordant opinions into one band of brothers, and Freemasons because they alone are under the influence of this tie, or enjoy its benefits, are called "Brethren of the Mystic Tie".

6. The word must be conceived to be the symbol of *Divine Truth;* and all its modifications—the loss, the substitution, and the recovery—are but component parts of the mythical symbol which represents a search after truth.

7. Their founder, John Valentin Andrea, was born in Wurtemburg in 1586 and died in 1654. He was a man of high ideals, untiring, studious and of a philanthropic nature. He wrote a romantic story of a Christian Rosencreutz, whom he said was born in 1378 and died in 1484 at the age of 106. To this

man he gave all the attributes of faith, hope and charity, with a mission in life, to raise the moral and spiritual level of mankind to a higher plane. His efforts in his native Germany were less fruitful of results than in England and France, where he found many influential supporters.

8.   Robert Wentworth Little in England in 1866.

9.   An order whose rites were practised in Britain and Gaul, though brought to a higher standard of perfection in the former country, where the isle of Anglesea was considered as their chief seat. According to Caesar, it was unlawful to commit their ceremony to writing, *"Neque fas esse existimant, ea literis mandare"*.

10. White, the symbol of light, Blue, of truth, and Green, of hope. The aspirant for degrees was robed in these colors.

11. Authorities vary. Some Greek writers say 1800 B.C. Aristotle says 6000 years before Plato and Albert Pike accepts that estimate.

12. They were the officiating clergy of the Cathedral of St. Peters at York in 936, and their prayers were invoked by King Athelstan in that year on behalf of himself and his expedition against the Scotch. According to legend, Athelstan was "the mightiest warrior" who ever sat upon the throne of Saxon England, and "he loved Masons well", but his son Edwin loved them better still, and procured from the king a charter to hold an assembly of Masons at York every year.

13. This order was and still is considered the highest decoration that can be bestowed on a subject by a sovereign of Great Britain.

14. It refers to the white flower of that tree and the allegorical significance is to old age, when the hair of the head shall become gray.

15. In this beautiful description of the body of man suffering the infirmities of old age we find those words followed by "or the golden bowl be broken". Dr. Clarke's explanations of these metaphors thus, "the silver cord is the spiritual marrow, the golden bowl is the brain", and so on.

16. The keepers of the house are the arms, shoulders and hands, the trembling comes with the feebleness of old age.

17. The windows are the eyes. Failing sight is a trait common to old age.

18. The doors are the lips, the streets are the mouth by which nourishment enters, and the sound of the grinding is the human voice. In old age when the teeth are lost, mumbling is a very common attribute.

19. The bird is the crowing cock. In old age mankind is more restless in his slumbers, and early rising is a habit with many.

20. The daughters of music are the ears. The voice loses its strength and hearing becomes less acute in the aged.

21. In the declining years men fear to scale the heights which in their prime they ascended with ease and alacrity.

22. Timidity is a common fault of older people. They are filled with apprehension at the first sign of danger.

23. To the weaknesses of old age, even the weight of so small a thing as a grasshopper, is a burden.

24. The appetites and desires of youth cease in the declining years.

25. Literally to his grave. As the poet puts it, "To that undiscovered country from whose bourne no traveler returns".

26. To the oriental custom of having official mourners, who make public lamentations for the dead. It is even practised by the orthodox Jews very frequently in this country in 1949.

27. The brain is called the golden bowl, from its yellow color. Death prevents its further functioning.

28. The pitcher is the great vein which carries the blood to the ventricle of the heart, here called the fountain.

29. The wheel represents the aorta or great artery which receives the blood from the left ventricle of the heart or cistern and distributes it through the body. When this ceases "The dust shall return to the earth as it was, and the spirit shall return unto God who gave it".

30. The science that treats of the existence, nature and attributes of God and man's relations to God.

31. Sun-worship.

32. Sabaism.

33. The Vedas.

34. The point in the heavens which is vertical to the spectator.

35. Literally, basket. The Bible of Bhuddhism containing 116 volumes. The canon was fixed about 240 B.C. and commands a following of more than one-third of the human race.

36. A monstrous griffin, guardian of Persian mysteries.

37. One of the ages according to Hindu mythology, into which the Hindus divide the duration or existence of the world.

38. The sacred impress made upon the forehead of the Brahman, like unto the Tau to the Hebrew, or the cross to the Christian.

39. Thunder was His voice, lightning was His weapon, wind was His breath, and fire was His presence.

40. It formerly was worn as an amulet against certain diseases; it was to be written on a piece of parchment in triangular form arranged in eleven lines, the first being Abracadabra and the last the letter A or in reverse. At some times a form of incantation.

41. The scriptures of the Zoroastrian religion containing the doctrines of Zoroaster. *Avesta* means the sacred text and *zend* the commentary.

42. Albert Pike.

ANSWERS

CHAPTER XXXI

1. Christopher Wren, who was knighted for this splendid achievement.

2. Elmes records that Sir Christopher Wren was a Master of St. Paul's Lodge, which during the building of the Cathedral of St. Paul's, met at the "Goose and Gridiron" in St. Paul's Church-yard, and is now the Lodge of Antiquity.

3. The British Journal of March 9th, 1723, gave the news item that *"the corpse of that worthy Free Mason Sir Christopher Wren, Knight, was interred under the Dome of St. Paul's Cathedral on March 5th."*

4. His delight in the spirit of worship found in the groves of the forest.

5. His "History of the Order of the Garter" is considered authoritive and it is regretted that he never was able to undertake the "History of Masonry" which he contemplated writing.

6. Anthony Sayer, gentleman.

7. The Duke of Montagu, upon his election to the office of Grand Master in 1721, the same year that the old Constitution of the Craft was revised. His standing and prestige before the country acted as a magnet to men of broader scholarship and mental attainments.

8. James Anderson, D.D., the compiler of the Book of Constitutions, was a native of Scotland, but for many years of his life, a resident of London, and the minister of the Scotch Presbyterian Church in Swallow Street, Picadilly, London.

9. Called the Father of Modern Speculative Masonry. He was born in Rochelle, France, March 12, 1683, the son of a French Protestant clergyman. The family moved to England as refugees on the revoca-

tion of the Edict of Nantes. While he was a clergyman he was more distinguished in science than in theology, and was an intimate friend of Sir Isaac Newton. He was Grand Master in 1720, and in collaboration with Dr. Anderson he compiled the early form of Masonic lectures, following the organization of the Grand Lodge in 1717.

10. Born 1724 in London and died 1795. He constructed a code of lectures, revised the ritual and gathered all the ancient formulas for the Grand Lodge of England. He reconstructed the Royal Arch of Dermott, and through his influence some of the ritual of the Third Degree was transferred to the fourth.

11. He became general superintendent of royal buildings in 1607 and at the same period was head of the Masonic order in England. It was he who instituted quarterly gathering instead of the old annual assemblies. This was prior to the introduction of Speculative Masonry.

12. He was Grand Secretary of the Ancients following the schism of 1751. He was a man of marked ability and published a book of constitutions which he called "Ahiman Rezon". He also caused the formation of Army Lodges which added great influence to the Ancients. He was Deputy Grand Master in 1739.

13. William Preston, on June 15th, 1774. He was a very scholarly man and his work on the lectures was a very valuable contribution in the formation of the Ritual in the eighteenth century.

14. A Scotch laird of the family of the biographer of Dr. Johnson. His presence in the Lodge of Edinburgh

in June, 1600, is the earliest authentic instance of a person being a member of the fraternity who was not an architect or a builder by profession.

15. He was initiated in the Lodge of the Nine Sisters, at Paris, February 7, 1778, in the presence of Benjamin Franklin and others distinguished in Masonry.

16. Rev. James Anderson, 1680-1739; Rev. Dr. John Theophilus Desaguliers, 1683-1744; William Hutchinson, 1732-1814; William Preston, 1742-1818; Rev. George Oliver, 1782-1867, and Laurence Dermott, 1720-1791, who for thirty years was Secretary of the Athol Grand Lodge and their great leader.

17. A Freemason, born in Switzerland, who emigrated with his father to England in 1716, and became a naturalized subject. In 1743, as a journeyman lapidary, he moved to Lisbon, Portugal, where he bought and sold precious stones. A female servant who knew of the Masonic gatherings in the home of Coustus disclosed the facts to her confessor accusing Coustus and brethren of shocking crimes. He was then arrested on false charges and suffered imprisonment and persecution, until released upon demand of the British minister as a subject of the King of England. He was ordered to leave the country which he happily obeyed, and upon his return to London he published a 400 page, octavo volume on his experiences. The book was reprinted in Birmingham in 1790.

18. Thaddeus Kosciusko and Casimir Pulaski.

19. A Dominican monk who while preaching a course of Lenten sermons at Aix-la-Chapelle in 1779, tried

to prove that the Jews who crucified Christ were Freemasons; that Pilate and Herod were Wardens in a Masonic Lodge, and that Judas Iscariot became a Mason just prior to the betrayal. To subdue the excitement, the authorities ordered him to refrain from stirring up the mob or they would prohibit him from the collection of alms in their territories.

20. The oracle at Delphi, who neither spoke nor kept silence, but made his revelations by signs.

21. Yes, born John Paul, son of a Scotch gardener, was born July 6, 1747 in Arbigland, parish of Kirkbean, stewartry of Kirkcudbright, Scotland. He was initiated November 27, 1770 in St. Bernard's Lodge No. 122 A.F. & A.M. of Kilwinning. He was a lifelong active Mason, and we have a record of his Masonic activities in the Colonies, England and France.

22. The greatest Masonic swindler of all time. The story of his life was published in London in 1787. His real name was Joseph Balsamo, born in 1743 in Palermo. He died in a fit of apoplexy in 1795. He invented what he called "Egyptian Masonry".

23. Melchior the Hindu with offerings of gold; Gasper the Greek, who offers frankincense, and Balthazar the Egyptian, with a long spreading beard, who tenders myrrh. The story is graphically told in Lew Wallaces' book "Ben Hur".

24. A series of talks, written by Gottlieb Ephraim Lessing first published in 1778 in German. Findel says "that it is one of the best things ever written about Masonry".

25. A great Polish astronomer, who asserted that the
    sun is the center of planetary space, and that the
    daily rotation of the earth on its axis accounts for
    the apparent revolution of the stars.

26. He was a camel driver and eventually became the
    founder of the Mohammedan religion.

27. Charlemagne, who was crowned emperor in Rome
    in the year 800 A.D. by Pope Leo III.

28. When Lord Carnarvan's party opened the saropha-
    gus of King Tut, January 3, 1924, they found after
    the unwrapping of many layers of material, what has
    been described as a Masonic apron. Many authori-
    ties are agreed that Masonry was practiced in Egypt
    during the time of the Pharaohs.

29. A famous chemist and philosopher, born about 1234.
    His researches resulted in the improvement in the
    methods of rectifying spirits and refining silver. He
    was an eminent Rosicrucian.

30. Ranulf Higden, a monk from Chester, about 1350
    wrote a Latin chronicle, under this title, which was
    translated into English in 1387 and published by
    William Caxton in 1482 under the same name. Many
    of the old Masonic legends come to us from this
    source.

31. He was a scholarly writer early in the eighteenth
    century. It is supposed that he was made a Mason in
    England in 1730. While visiting the Archbishop of
    Cambrai he was converted to Catholicism, but later
    his Masonic writings were publicly burned by the
    Pope at Rome. His lectures ascribing the origin of
    Masonry to the Knights of the Crusades, won him

considerable standing with the aristocracy, and by many it is thought to have been the inspiration for the fabrication and production of the higher Degrees, notably the Scottish Rite.

32. He was initiated at Brunswick, August 14th, 1738.

33. Robert Burns of Scotland. Robert Morris of Mississippi. Fay Hempstead of Arkansas.

34. No.

35. It is very probable. His successor, Brigham Young, had the design of the Morman Temple in Salt Lake City patterned after Solomon's Temple.

36. He was Sov. G. Commander of the Southern Supreme Council A.A. Scottish Rite, elected in 1859 and an honorary member of almost every Supreme Council in the world. Also considered one of the best authorities in Masonic history and literature. He is usually credited with having composed the ritual of the 33rd Degree.

37. No. Theodore was raised April 24th, 1901 in Matinecock Lodge No. 806, Oyster Bay, N.Y. Pentalpha Lodge No. 23, Washington, D.C. made him an honorary member April 4th, 1904.
Franklin Delano Roosevelt was raised in Holland Lodge No. 8, New York City, November 28th, 1911. He took the Scottish Rite Degrees in Albany, Feb. 28th, 1929. He attended Architect Lodge No. 519, New York City, Feb. 17th, 1933, when he raised his son Elliott to the Sublime Degree, at which time he made an eloquent address on Masonic principles and his faith in the Americanism of the fraternity.

38. Yes. He was a member of Polar Star Lodge No. 79, in Missouri.

39. A profound and lucid historian and writer in all departments of Masonry, unequalled by any man of his period. Born in Charleston, S.C., March 12th, 1807, died in Old Point Comfort, Va., June 20th, 1881. He ranks with Gould as one of the best Masonic historians.

40. His "Freemasons' Monitor", first published in 1797.

41. The Union officer, Thomas H. Benton; Grand Master of the Grand Lodge of Iowa, when the troops under his command attacked Little Rock, he threw a guard about the house of Albert Pike, the Confederate General, to protect his Masonic Library.

42. Very improbable. During the excitement connected with the Morgan disappearance, he favored the prohibition of the oaths of secrecy by legislative enactment.

43. Robert Morris.

44. Dr. Albert G. Mackey.

45. The fire-god of the ancient Phoenicians and Ammonites, to whom human sacrifices were offered.

46. Aaron, Eleazar, Joshua, Jephtha, Moses, Solomon, Adonirum, Hiram, King of Tyre, Hiram Abif, Zerubbabel, Aholiab, Bezaleel.

47. The famous Grand Master of the Knights Templar at the time of their suppression by Pope Clement V. He was elected Grand Master in 1297 and suffered martyrdom on March 18th, 1314, with the three principal dignitaries of the order. Fifty-four Knights

had suffered the same fate three years previously.

48. "Caledonia, and Caledonias' bard, Brother Burns".

ANSWERS

CHAPTER XXXII

1. A town of Palestine about forty miles west of Jerusalem. This was the port to which the King of Tyre sent his ships with materials for King Solomon's Temple.

2. It is said that the city was founded by Japhet the son of Noah, and from him to have taken the name of Japho afterwards Joppa, and now in modern times Jaffa.

3. A tract of country to the south of Egypt and watered by the Upper Nile.

4. No. The selection of Ethiopia as a refuge by the ritualist, seems to be inappropriate, when we consider the character of that country in the age of Solomon.

5. The mysterious land of which Cain journeyed after killing Abel. See Gen. iv.-16.

6. A Hebrew word, signifying "a skull". It was the name given by the Jews to Mount Calvary, where Christ was crucified.

7. About 1700 miles long.

8. An obscure little village in Scotland which claims to be the birthplace of Scotch Masonry.

9. A town of Judea, 34 miles northeast of Jerusalem, near which Hiram Abif cast the sacred vessels of the Temple.

10.   It is about 1400 miles long and about 150 miles wide.

11.   The Vale of Cashmire, in India, has often been called the "terrestrial paradise". The story of this district has been immortalized by Thomas Moore in his poem Lalla Rookh.

12.   For its cedars, which King Hiram had cut, hewn and sent to King Solomon to use in the building of the Temple.

13.   It is about 135 miles long, rising on the southern slope of Mt. Herman about 1700 feet above the sea. It passes through the Sea of Galilee and empties into the Dead Sea 1300 feet below sea level. It has many rapids and falls, the water being sweet and clear. The Hebrews called it Yarden, the descender.

14.   1150 miles.

15.   An earthwork erected on October 3rd, 1814, at Fox Point, Rhode Island, by the Grand Lodge with about two hundred and thirty Masons participating. Thomas Smith Webb, Grand Master, authorized his Deputy, Senior Grand Warden to work on the defenses. It consisted of a breastwork four hundred and thirty feet long, ten feet wide, and five feet high.

16.   Babylonia, in its fullest extent.

17.   A brook near the Mount of Olives, meaning turbid water.

18.   A city in Lombardy in northern Italy, also a lake of that name. It was the seat of the Comacines or Traveling Freemasons during the Middle Ages.

19.   Overlooking Jerusalem. It is 14½ miles from the River Jordan, 15 miles from the Salt Sea and 41 miles from the Mediterranean.

20. A city of Phœmicia, ninety-three miles north of Jerusalem on the east coast of the Mediterranean Sea, and the source of many fine artisans sent by King Hiram to King Solomon.

21. A physician named Brown organized the Roman Eagle Lodge at Edinburgh, the whole work of which was conducted in the Latin language.

22. A school of philosophy founded by Alexander in Egypt in B.C. 333, from which was derived the system of symbols and allegories, which lay at the bottom of Masonic philosophy.

ANSWERS

CHAPTER XXXIII

1. Preston tells us that in 1733 a charter was granted by the Grand Lodge of England to eleven German Masons in Hamburg. In 1738 another Lodge was established in Brunswick, under authority of the Grand Lodge of Scotland.

2. Not very many. Lord Charles Sackville organized one in Florence in 1733, and others were established in Leghorn, Turin, Genoa and the other principal cities. Due to the enmity of the papacy their meetings are held with great secrecy, and the brief tenure of Mussolini made the progress of the craft even more difficult.

3. A French term for Fellow-Craft.

4. In 1877, and for doing it was disfellowshiped by nearly every Grand Lodge in the world.

5. 1786 A.D.

6. This, which may be translated "Elected Mason", is the fourth degree of the French rite. It is occupied in the details of the detection and punishment of certain traitors, who just before the completion of the Temple were guilty of a heinous crime.

7. Alpina.

8. A heroic family whose patriotism and valor form bright pictures in Jewish annals. The name is derived from the letters M.C.B.I., which were inscribed upon their banners, being the initials of the Hebrew sentence, "Mi Camocha, Baalim, Jehovah". *Who is like unto Thee among the gods, O Jehovah.*

9. On Dec. 17th, 1804, the Grand Lodge of Pennsylvania chartered at Havana "Le Temple des Vertus Theologoles, No. 103, Joseph Cerneau being the first Master. Later the Grand Lodge of Louisiana and South Carolina granted warrants.

10. The Grand Lodge of England authorized George Pomfret "to open a new Lodge in Bengal" in 1728. This Lodge was established in 1730 by Captain Ralph Farwinter, the successor to Pomfret, as "Provisional Grand Master of India".

11. Yes. An English Lodge at Bencoolen, Sumatra, 1765, on Java by the Grand Lodge of Holland in 1769, another English Lodge at Elopura in North Borneo in 1885.

12. Yes. The Grand Lodge of England chartered a Lodge in Yokohama in 1865, where a Masonic Hall was erected in 1869.

13. 1825 A.D.

14. Amity Lodge, No. 407, was constituted in 1767 under an English warrant and Elizabeth in 1768, both at Canton, under a Swedish dispensation. Both came to an end in 1812, but at the close of the nineteenth century there were thirteen English, one American and four Scotch Lodges in Hong Kong and the Chinese treaty ports.

15. Prior to the acquisition of Cape Colony by Great Britain, two Dutch Lodges had been erected at Cape Town in 1772 and 1802, respectively. Later the Grand Lodge of England as well as the Athol Masons established a number of Lodges.

16. The Lodge of Social and Military Virtues, No. 227, on the roll of the Grand Lodge of Ireland, was organized in 1752 in New South Wales, and after many vicissitudes was at work in the same at Sydney in 1816. At one time there were eighty-six regular Lodges in Australia working under English, Scotch and Irish jurisdictions.

17. In continental Europe they are called *assassins*. The English and American Masons have adopted the more homely appellation of ruffians.

18. In India in fairly modern times, a meeting place for Lodges was called a Shaitan Bungalow. The superstition was that the evil spirit was a factor in secret orders.

19. The most ancient of the religious writings of the Indian Aryans written in Sanskrit. It is a sacred canon to the Hindus, being to them what the Koran is to the Moslem and the Bible is to the Christians.

20. The cavern of Elephanta in Hindustan is the most ancient temple in the world. It was the principal place for the celebration of the mysteries of India.

21. France and Belgium, but they do not forbid such a faith.

22. This is an extremely ancient superstition. The Greeks and Romans portrayed Pan in horns, hoof and shaggy hide. The early Christians substituted Satan for Pan and in the Middle Ages the Devil appeared "riding on a goat".

ANSWERS

CHAPTER XXXIV

1. Under the English Constitution three black balls must exclude a candidate; but the by-laws of a Lodge may enact that one or two shall do so. (Rule 190). In America one black ball will reject a candidate, and he can apply in no other Lodge for admission unless the first Lodge to which he has applied, waives jurisdiction.

2. During the revival of Masonry in 1718 to secure a membership of good character, the sixth of the General Regulations provided that no man could be admitted without the unanimous consent of all the members present.

3. In the charges compiled by Anderson and Desaguliers and published in 1723, the rule denying membership to women was explicit. This is accented more forcibly by the obligation taken in the final degree.

4. Yes. This is well covered in the Proceedings of the G.L. Texas, Vol. II, P 273.

   "An acquittal by a jury, while it may, and should, have its influence on deciding on the course to be pursued, yet has no binding force in Masonry. We decide our own rules, and our views of the facts".

5. A notice or notification is just what the name implies and demands neither obedience or action. A summons however is an order and comes under the province of his obligation. To ignore a summons may be cause for reprimand or discipline.

6. Those whose lives and characters reflect no credit on the Institution, whose hearts are untouched by the influence of brotherly love. They are in the Temple, but not of it. As Dr. Oliver says: "Freemasonry is not answerable for the misdeeds of an individual brother."

7. April 24th, 1786, two petitions were rejected in Domatic Lodge, No. 177, London, because the applicants were not Operative Masons.

8. Not to frequent taverns or drinking places, cards and dice, or other illegal gambling games.

9. It is the equivalent in Masonic technical language to being of good character and having a good reputation. It is required that the candidate for initiation should be one out of whom no tongue speaks evil. The phrase is an old one, and is found in the earliest rituals of the last century.

10. No. A man comes into Masonry of his own free will and accord and goes out in the same manner and is

no way obliged to continue his membership for any period of time. Once demitted, suspended or expelled a man is no longer a Mason.

11. "And in future, in no Lodge, no matter for what cause, shall any one be beaten without the knowledge and consent of the workmaster. And there shall not be in any employment or elsewhere, anything be judged or heard by either masters or fellows, without the superior workmaster's knowledge and consent in the judgement of the penalty".

12. Bath attendant, barber, gravedigger, trumpeter, herdsman, watchman, headsman, etc. Article 60 also provided that he must be born in wedlock and that his progenitors must be freeman for at least two generations.

13. The Master is supreme in his Lodge, so far as the Lodge is concerned. He is amenable for his conduct in the government of the Lodge, not to its members, but to the Grand Lodge alone. Similar rules are the same in both the Chapter and the Commandery.

14. "If any brother behaves in such a manner as to disturb the harmony of the Lodge, he shall be thrice formally admonished by the Master; and if he persists in his irregular conduct, he shall be punished according to the by-laws of that particular Lodge, or the case may be reported to higher Masonic authority".

15. Failure to pay Lodge dues. Persuading a man to petition for Masonic degrees. Divulging secrets of Lodge or Ritual to non-members. Criminal conviction.

16. 1. Censure; 2, Reprimand; 3, Exclusion; 4, Suspension, definite or indefinite; 5, Expulsion.

17. Lawful age is not settled by any universal law or landmark. The Ancient Regulations provide that he must be of "mature and discreet age". There is some variation today in different countries. The Grand Lodge of Switzerland fixes the age at twenty-one, Prussia, twenty-five, France, Ireland and America, twenty-one, England, with some exceptions, twenty-one.

18. No. Exceptions have been made where the applicant has received a special dispensation from the Grand Master.

19. Yes. In Illinois a man becomes a life member when he has been a dues paying member for 50 years. Some Grand Lodges sell Life Memberships, remitting to the local Lodges the income therefrom.

20. Intolerance is the arch enemy of Freemasonry. Toleration is one of the chief foundation stones of the fraternity, and Universality and Brotherly Love are ever taught.

21. It violates his specific instructions and is considered un-Masonic.

ANSWERS
CHAPTER XXXV

1. The Grotto for Master Masons and the Mystic Shrine for Knights Templar and 32nd Degree Masons, and the White Shrine for the ladies.

2. It is the principle Fun Degree affiliated with the Masonic fraternity. It is non-Masonic in its ritual but

its membership is confined to Knights Templar and 32nd Degree Masons. Its principal benevolence is hospitals for the care and possible cure for crippled children of any race or faith.

3. Wm. J. Florence, the actor, on a tour to the near East in 1870, met the Sultan in Cairo, Egypt. The Sultan, who was head of a society after which the Shrine was patterned, was intrigued by Florence's wit and charm and had him inducted into the order. Florence upon his return to America had the ritual translated into English, and with a Dr. Walter M. Fleming, he became a co-founder of the Mystic Shrine. Membership from its inception was confined to either Knights Templar or Scottish Rite Masons, to insure a "select class of men to compose its membership."

4. In 1922 and at the present date, 1948, it is operating 16 hospitals.

5. Over 100,000 children at a total cost of over $45,000,000.

6. An organization similar to the Shrine, of no connection with Masonry, excepting that qualification for membership. It is the playground of Blue Lodge Masons as membership in the higher Degrees is not a necessary qualification. It is known as the "Mystic Order of Veiled Prophets of the Enchanted Realm." Its main concern is to forget your troubles and have a hilarious time. It started in Hamilton, N.Y., in 1899 and has over 150 Grottoes and about 90,000 members.

ANSWERS

CHAPTER XXXVI

1. A law passed in England under Henry VI, of England, forbidding Masons to confederate in chapters and congregations. This law however was never enforced.

2. They may be enumerated under six heads: 1. Its *secrecy*. 2. The *exclusiveness* of its charity. 3. Its admission of *unworthy members*. 4. Its administration of *unlawful oaths*. 5. Its claim to be a *religion*. 6. Its *puerility* as a system of instruction.

3. The Gormogons. No Mason could join, until he had first been degraded and then renounced his Masonic affiliation. It was ridiculous in its pretentions and claimed descent from an ancient society in China. It had a very brief existence.

4. In the eighteenth century Masonic parades were very great occasions and a group of enemies and critics of the fraternity formed a loose organization to satirize these affairs. The first one elicited considerable laughter but the more sober minded of the populace frowned on the exhibition and in a few years they were discontinued.

5. It finally resulted in their discontinuance. These mock parades were instituted in 1741 for purpose of ridicule and in consequence the processions were discontinued in 1747.

6. In 1762 she issued an edict prohibiting all meetings in her dominions. But later, better sentiment prevailing she revoked the order and invited Masons

to re-establish their Lodges and constitute new ones. This rule was in effect until her death in 1796, when the persecution of the order was renewed by her successor.

7. William Morgan was born in Virginia in 1776 where he learned the trade of stone mason. His brewery in Canada was destroyed by fire in 1821, when he went to Batavia, N.Y., where he visited Wells Lodge as a visitor. He was rejected by a new chapter being organized there. With a publisher named Miller he concocted a scheme to divulge Masonic secrets. He disappeared in September 1826, but there has never been any evidence that the Masons had anything to do with his disappearance.

8. Most improbable. Every Mason takes a solemn oath of secrecy, but in none of the Degrees, either of the York or Scottish Rite, does his vow require him to lift the hand of Cain against an erring brother who betrays his trust. DeWitt Clinton, Governor of the State of New York, offered a large reward for the apprehension of the guilty person or persons. Thurlow Weed, the New York politician of unsavory recollection, had his men try to palm off the corpse of a man found on the shore of Lake Ontario as Morgan, saying "it is good enough for Morgan until after election". He created nauseating publicity on the subject for political purposes, but years of patient search, in spite of all sorts of affidavits, have failed to prove a case against the Fraternity. A Baptist preacher named David Bernard was guilty in the same degree as Morgan about the same time, but the

election was over and the matter failed to have any but local publicity.

9. Yes. In New York with more than 500 Lodges and 20,000 members only 52 Lodges with 1,500 members remained in 1832. In New Jersey 33 out of 41 Lodges went out of existence. Not one of 19 Rhode Island Lodges relinquished its charter, but they lost two-thirds of their members. In Maine the Grand Lodge never failed to hold its annual communication but on one occasion not a single Lodge was represented. In Illinois, the Grand Lodge and all subordinate Lodges ceased to exist. In Vermont the Grand Lodge barely kept alive with biennial sessions of Grand Officers alone.

10. Yes. Gov. Clinton of New York was a prominent Mason and Thurlow Weed, his opponent, charged the fraternity with felonious actions to such a degree that Morgan's disappearance became a national issue.

11. Yes. In 1832, they nominated William Wirt of Maryland· and Amos Ellmaker for President and Vice-President. This ticket received the entire electoral votes of the state of Vermont. By 1836 the anti-Masonic excitement was definitely passing away.

12. No, but there was an anti-Masonic political party formed after the Morgan episode, but it had a brief existence. In the presidential election of 1832 it carried one state but was officially dead in 1833.

13. He hated the Institution and was the author of the well known pamphlet on the subject of the "Abduction of Morgan."

14. Olive Branch, No. 39 at Le Roy, never ceased its meetings, although located in the immediate neighborhood of the place where the whole difficulty originated, and is considered as the preserver of Masonry in western New York during all those years of persecution.

15. Trenton Lodge, No. 5.

16. None whatever. Incidentally, Myron C. Taylor, personal representative of the President of the United States, to His Holiness the Pope, has been a member of Humanity Lodge No. 406, Lyons, N.Y., since Oct. 13th, 1897, and has been honored as such, by the Grand Lodge of New York in his official capacity as envoy of the Vatican.

17. Pope Pius IX was reputed to have been a Mason, as was Pope Benedict XIV who was said to have affiliated while a plain priest in his native Bologna. He was elected Pope August 16th, 1740, when sixty-five years old.

18. No. Many Lodges continued operations secretly and called themselves Xerophagists; those who live without drinking.

19. Yes. May 18, 1751, he issued the second Bull directed against Masonry confirming that issued in 1738 by his predecessor Clement XII.

20. "If you want as a Pope a saint, select Gatti; if you want a politician, select Aldovrandi; if you want a good fellow elect me." And this they did.

21. Pope Clement V, who associated with Philip IV of France persecuted the Knights Templar. He as-

sisted in the overthrowing of the order. He was one of the earliest opponents of Templarism.

22. It facilitated the speedy dissemination of religious literature, particularly the Bible. The Church was no longer the unquestioned interpreter of Divine teachings and revelations. The importance of Cathedral architecture waned as a teacher of the people, and with it the importance of the operative stone mason as a craftsman.

23. Lord Petre who as late as November 24th, 1791, was present at the Grand Lodge meeting. The papal bull of 1738 had not been published in England, hence was not effective in that country.

24. On Jan. 1st, 1771, Pierre Gamelin, a Mason and man of high standing, was elected a warden in the Notre Dame Church in Montreal. He was asked by the parish priest not to "frequent Lodges while occupying the office of warden."

25. At the laying of the cornerstone of the Montreal Freemasons Hospital, Mr. Charles Duquette, mayor, was the orator of the day and the cornerstone was blessed according to Roman Catholic rites by Mgr. Gerald McShane, parish priest of the Irish Congregation of St. Patrick.

26. New Brunswick Knights of Columbus made a donation of $500.00 to the Montreal Shrine Hospital for crippled children. As 65% of the hospitalized children were of the Catholic faith and were of course non-paying patients, it was a splendid tribute to the truth of the Apostle Paul's statement that "the greatest of these is Charity.

27. One of the Synods of the Lutheran Church in the
United States, bans membership in any secret fraternity and though Masonry is not specifically in-
dicated the general opinion is that the ban is aimed
at Masonry.

28. No. Unless it would be in the 33rd degree and that
would be a fantastic supposition. The Southern
Jurisdiction of the A. A. S. R. has taken issue with
the Pope on the Public School question, but that is
all of which we have any record.

ANSWERS

CHAPTER XXXVII

1. Because they are operating under Grand Lodges
which in turn are operating from Lodges whose
charters lapsed many years ago.

2. They consider the assumption of authority by the
Negro Grand Lodges as illegal Masonically, and
therefore consider the entire organization clandestine.

3. Prince Hall and thirteen other Negroes were made
Masons in a military Lodge in the British Army in
Boston, on March 6th, 1775. They were granted
a charter from the Grand Lodge of England on
Sept. 20th, 1784, though not received until 1787.
It bore the name of African Lodge, No. 429, and
was situated in Boston, Mass. After the death of
Hall it became dormant. Later it was revived, but
under what process of Masonic law is unknown.
June 18th, 1827, they issued a protocol declaring
they were free and independent of any Lodge from

this day. They assumed the name of "Prince Hall Grand Lodge" and issued charters to subordinate Lodges of Negroes in the United States where they are represented in thirty-eight states where they have Grand Lodge organizations as well as in Canada and Liberia.

4. Only by the Grand Lodge of Washington in 1898 in a resolution presented at their Grand Lodge meeting that year. This action was annulled the following year after protests from all the other Grand Lodges in the country.

5. Yes. About 1908 the Grand Lodge of Mississippi discontinued "Fraternal Correspondence" with the Grand Lodge of New Jersey, and Oklahoma followed suit, because it had had affiliations with a colored Lodge for forty years. The Grand Lodge of New Jersey expressed regret, and it was generally agreed that the Negro Lodge would pine away from lack of support.

6. He was the son of an English leather merchant, whose wife was a free Negro woman of French descent. He settled in Boston in the middle of the eighteenth century.

7. No, his status was that of a "free" Negro.

8. Yes; he served in the companies of Captains Benjamin Dillingham and Joshua Welboro, and afterwards in Thacker's Regiment.

9. March 6th, 1775.

10. In a Military Lodge working under the Grand Lodge of Ireland. It was attached to one of the regiments in the Continental Army under General Gage.

11.   It moved to New York State and is reputed to have taken part in the first Grand Lodge of Masons in that state.

12.   Yes. They petitioned Provincial Grand Master Joseph Warren for Masonic recognition.

13.   Favorably, but before official action could be taken, Warren was killed at the Battle of Bunker Hill.

14.   The claim is made that further petitions were made in 1779 in Massachusetts and in 1868; and that in 1857 Negroes petitioned a Massachusetts Lodge for Degrees, but all were ignored or denied. Later petitions for recognition in New York were also denied, because their Lodges were considered clandestine. The Grand Lodge of Washington took friendly action toward the colored people about 1898, but when such action caused friction in their own ranks and throughout the entire country, their action regarding the colored brethren was rescinded; and at the present time there is no fraternal relationship with the Negro Lodges. This in spite of the fact that no Masonic writer of standing has seen fit to criticize the Ritual, work or fundamentals of the Negro Lodges and Mackey in his history treats of it at length, with no criticism excepting the technical question of its charter.

15.   Yes. At one time they were not so considered, but for some years there was a full blooded Indian, who was a physician by profession, very active in the degree work in Chicago and an exceedingly competent worker in the third Degree.

CHAPTER XXXVIII

Synopsis of the Scottish Rite Degrees (4th to 33rd)—in narrative form.

The Ineffable Degrees 4th to the 14th inclusive, are conferred in a Lodge of Perfection, and pertain to KING SOLOMON'S TEMPLE. They have reference to all the events in detail, in connection with the completion and dedication of King Solomon's Temple, and can be classified as follows: the 4th and 5th concern the tribute due to the memory of the third Grand Master of the Temple. The 6th, 7th and 8th relate the filling of the vacancy caused by the demise of the Architect of the Temple, in recording the plans agreed upon by King Solomon and King Hiram of Tyre, the auditing of the accounts and compensation of the laborers, the adjustment of disputes, and the resumption of the Temple construction. The 9th and 10th Degrees relate to the faithful dispensation of justice, which never sleeps.

The 11th Degree relates to the rewards to the true and faithful for bringing the offenders to the bar of justice and the equitable collection and distribution of the revenues of the realm. The 12th relates to the science of architecture, the use of all the devices and tools and their symbolical morals. It also treats of geometry and astronomy and the lessons we may derive from the study of the starry firmament. The 13th treats of the fortunate discovery of that which had been lost, (but) unknown to the discoverers; and the 14th, the final preparation of the mind, heart and body by consecration to the service of the Craft, and receipt with the fullest and most ample explanations of the great treasure and reward on the completion of the Temple.

THE SECOND TEMPLE DEGREES are the 15th and 16th Degrees and are conferred in a Council of Princes

of Jerusalem. The story of these two Degrees is based on
the history of the reigns of two Persian kings, Cyrus and
Darius; the destruction and pillage of the Temple of
Solomon and the city of Jerusalem by Nebuchadnezzar;
the Jewish captivity, the royal decrees of these kings
permitting the rebuilding of the Temple by Zerubbabel,
the return of the holy vessels and the restoration to the
Jews of their freedom. It also tells of the opposition of
the Samaritans who were an idolotrous people. All this
symbolizing the difficulty of regaining, when once lost, the
freedom of a people. It teaches the lessons of fortitude
under the most severe afflictions and trials.

THE SPIRITUAL TEMPLE DEGREES are the 17th
and 18th, and are conferred in a Chapter of the Rose Croix.

The 17th Degree portrays the life and history of St.
John the Baptist and his fate like the Master Builder of
the Temple, who fell a Martyr to the principle of integrity;
also the history and lessons taught by St. John the Beloved
Disciple. The 18th Degree portrays the history of Him
who came to redeem mankind. Its great lessons expound
the principles of Toleration, Humanity and Fraternity.

THE HISTORICAL, PHILOSOPHIC, AND CHIV-
ALRIC DEGREES comprise the degrees from the 19th to
the 32nd, inclusive, and are conferred in a consistory.

The 19th Degree relates to the Apocalyptic vision of
St. John the Evangelist and the hoped for millenium,
when there shall be a perfect union of mankind under
the Divine influence of Charity and Toleration.

The 20th Degree teaches Veneration for the Deity,
Knowledge of Science and Philosophy, Charity, Honor,
Patriotism, Justice, Truth and Toleration.

The 21st Degree portrays the Crusaders upon their
return from the war in the Holy Land who find their
property appropriated by fraud; its recovery and the
punishment meted out to the plunderers, while the
defenders of the Faith were fighting in Palestine.

The 22nd Degree tells of the work in the cedars of

Lebanon and the preparation of the timbers for the Temple. It exalts the dignity of labor and teaches that rank and nobility go for naught, and that he who toils not with his fellows, shall not eat.

The 23rd and 24th Degrees relate to the ceremonials of the Jewish religion, the building of the Tabernacle and the doctrines and laws given by Moses.

The 25th Degree portrays the sufferings of the Israelites who were bitten by the fiery serpent in the Wilderness and the raising up of the brazen serpent by Moses, that those who looked might live. The profound doctrines of life and death are taught to lead men away from sin and to look for aid to a higher power.

The 26th Degree treats of mercy, charity and kindness.

The 27th Degree relates to the Crusades of Henry VI of Germany which went to the Holy Land in 1191 A.D., and became the Teutonic branch of the Order of the Temple, known as the Knights of St. Mary.

The 28th Degree treats of science and philosophy and inculcates the full exercise of intelligent reason and faith, in reading the book of nature with a well grounded faith in the mercy and wisdom of God.

The 29th Degree portrays the history and valor of the Scottish Branch of Knights Templar. It teaches a lesson of the spirit of humility, patience and selfdenial, with charity and generosity based on truth and honor.

The 30th Degree gives the history of the Order of the Temple with all of its tribulations. Liberty, Equality and Fraternity are its cardinal tenets.

The 31st Degree is the Supreme Court of the Rite. Here are heard the appeals; and trials of all cases above the 30th Degree, are held. Its lesson is the administration of impartial justice and it is the most august tribunal in Freemasonry.

The 32nd Degree gives instruction in the ancient truths and moral philosophy which have come down to us filtered through the Alexandrian school of science and the fundamental principles of the Mosaic and Christian dispensations.

The 33rd Degree is conferred in the Supreme Council of the Rite which is the administrative body of all the Scottish Rite bodies. It prescribes the statutes and rules for the various divisions of the Consistory. It also has a ritual, the fabrication of which is generally credited to Albert Pike, who was Sovereign Grand Commander of the Southern Supreme Council A.A.S.R. for many years.

ABRIDGED MASONIC DICTIONARY

The authorities drawn upon in compiling the following pages were: Encyclopaedia of Freemasonry by Albert G. Mackey, M. D., with Addendum and Pronouncing Dictionary by C. T. McClenachan; Pronouncing Dictionary by T. A. McClure; General History, Cyclopedia and Dictionary of Freemasonry by Robert Macoy; and Biblical Encyclopaedia by John Eadie, D. D., L. L. B.

To each of these authors we submit our thanks for assistance rendered and especially to the publishers of McClure's Pronouncing Dictionary; most convenient for active workers.

In addition to the usual Masonic abbreviations, note the following:

abt.	about	ext.	extending; ed	pl.	plural
anc.	ancient; s	Fr.	French; France	poss.	possibly
b.	born	gen.	generally	prob.	probably
bet.	between	Gr.	Greece; Greek	prop.	properly
bro.	brother	Heb.	Hebrew	prov.	province
Capt.	captivity	H. P.	High Priest	rec.	receive; d
capt.	capture; d	imp.	improper; ly	ref.	reference; red
cent.	century; ies	in.	inch; es	rep.	represents; ed; ing; ative
Ch.	Chapter	inc.	incorrect; ly		
circum.	circumference	incl.	include; ing; ed	run.	running
Co.	Council	L.; LL.	Lodge; es	S.; So.	South; ern
conf.	confounded	Lat.	Latin	Scot.	Scotland
cont.	contraction	lit.	literally	sec.	section
contemp.	contemporary; aneous; ies	m.	miles	sig.; s	signify; ing; ies; icant; ications
		Medit.	Mediterranean		
cor.	corruption; tly	Mid.	Middle	sit.	situated
d.	died	Mt.	Mount; ain	sov.	sovereign; s; ty
des.	descent	mo.	month	subs.	substitute; ed
desc.	descendant; s	Myst.	Mystery; ies	succ.	successor; eeded
dghtr.	daughter	N.	North; ern	sup.	suppose; d; ly
disc.	disciples	opp.	opposite	supt.	superintend; ent
dist.	distinguish; ed	orig.	original; ly	sym.	symbol; ic; ically; izes; ism
E.	East; ern; erly	P.	Pontificate		
Eng.	England; ish	pat.	patron	syn.	synonymous
equiv.	equivalent	philos.	philosophy; er; s; ical	W.	West; ern
est.	establish; ed; ing				

AARON. Bro. of Moses and the 1st Jewish H. P. under the Mosaic dispensation. He is ref. to in the R. A. deg. and is rep. by the presiding officer in the 23d deg. and by the 2d officer in the 24th deg.

AB. Father. Also 11th Heb. month.

A B A D D O N. Destruction; destroyer; place of destruction.

ABBREVIATIONS. The doubling of a letter usually denotes the plural of that word of which the single letter is an abbreviation, as LL. Lodges. To abridge the list these have been omitted as have the titles of the officers of the Grand and Subordinate bodies of Lodge, Chapter, Council, and Commandery and other very familiar abbreviations. (See Three Points.)

A. & A. Ancient and Accepted.

A. & A. S. R. Ancient and Accepted Scottish Rite.

A. C. M. Ancient Craft Mason.

A. D. Anno Domini.

A. Dep. Anno Depositionis.

A. F. M. Ancient Freemason.

A. F. & A. M. Ancient Free and Accepted Mason.

A. H. Anno Hebraico.

A. Inv. Anno Inventionis.

A. L. Anno Lucis.

A. M. Anno Mundi.

A. O. Anno Ordinis.

A. U. T. O. S. A. G. Ad universi terrarum orbis summi Architecti Gloriam.

A. Y. M. Ancient York Mason.

B. B. Burning Bush.

B. D. W. P. H. G. F. Beauty, Divinity, Wisdom, Power, Honor, Glory, Force.

B. L. R. T. Brotherly Love, Relief and Truth.

Br. or Bro. Brother.

C. Chapter; Council.

C. C. Celestial Canopy.

Comp. Companion.

D. Deputy.

D. A. F. Due and Ancient Form.

Deg. Degree or Degrees.

D. M. J. Deus Meumque Jus.

E. Eminent; Excellent; East.

Ec. Eccossais.

E. S. P. T. S. P. L. Ephesus, Smyrna, Pergamos, Thygatira, Sardis, Philadelphia, Laodicea.

E. V. Ere Vulgaire. Vulgar Era.

F. Frere; Brother.

F. A. M. or F. & A. M. Free and Accepted Masons.

F. H. C. Faith, Hope and Charity.

F. M. Free Mason. Old Style.

F. U. R. D. F. P. T. Friendship, Union, Resignation, Discretion, Fidelity, Prudence, Temperance.

G. or Gr. Grand; Guard; Geometry.

G. A. Grand Architect.

G. A. O. T. U. Grand Architect of the Universe.

G. C. H. Grand Chapter of Harodim.

G. E. Grand Encampment; Grand East.

G. O. Grand Orient.

H. A. B. Hiram Abif.

H. E. Holy Empire.

H. J. (Saints John).

H. K. T. Hiram, King of Tyre.

H. R. D. M. or H-R-M. Heredom.

I. H. S. Iesus Hominum Salvator.

Ill. Illustrious.

I. N. R. I. Iesus Nazarenus Rex Iudaeorum.

I. T. N. O. T. G. A. O. T. U. In the name of the Grand Architect of the Universe.

I. V. I. O. L. Inveni Verbum In Ore Leonis.

K. E. P. Knight of the Eagle and Pelican.

K-H. or K. K-D-H. Kadosh, Knight of Kadosh.

K. M. Knight or Knights of Malta.

K. R. C. Knight of the Red Cross, or Rose Croix.

Kt. or Knt. Knight.

K. T. Knight, or Knights Templar.

L. D. P. Lakak Derror Pessah.

L. E. T. Lux e Tenebris.

L. O. P. Liberty of Passage.

M. Mason.

M. C. Master of Ceremonies; Mark of the Craft.

M. C. B. I. See Maccabees.

M. E. Most Excellent; Most Eminent.

M. M. Master Mason.

M. W. Most Worshipful.

N. E. C. North East Corner.

N. J. Northern Jurisdiction.

O. Orient.

O. A. C. Ordo ab Chao.

OB. or O. B. Obligation.

O. C. S. Oriental Chair of Solomon.

P. D. E. P. Pro Deo et Patria.

P. J. Prince of Jerusalem; Provost and Judge.

P. M. Past Master; Perfect Master.

R. A. Royal Arch.

R. A. M. Royal Arch Mason.

R. † or R. C. Rose Croix.

R. E. Right Eminent; Right Excellent.

R. W. Right Worshipful.

S. C. Supreme Council.

S. G. C. Sovereign Gr. Commander.

S. G. I. or S. G. I. G. Sovereign Gr. Inspector General.

S. M. Select Master; Secret Master; Sovereign Master; Speculative Masonry.

S. P. R. S. Sublime Prince of the Royal Secret.

S. S. Sanctum Sanctorum.

S. S. John. Saints John.

S. S. S. Salutem Salutem Salutem, Thrice greeting.

T. G. A. O. T. U. The Grand Architect of the Universe.

U. D. Under Dispensation.

V. or Ven. (Venerable) Worshipful.

V. D. S. A. Veut Dieu Saint Amour.

V. W. Very Worshipful.

ABCHAL. Father of Hiram, the King of Tyre.

ABDA. Father of Adoniram.

ABDAMON. Servant.

ABIF. His Father. Title of honor bestowed upon the chief builder of the Temple.

ABIHAEL. Father of strength.

ABIHU. A son of Aaron.

ABISHUR. See Achisar.

ABRAHAM; ABRAM. Father of elevation; Father of multitude. 10th in des. from Shem. b. at Ur, Chaldea, abt. 2008 A. M. Founder of the Jewish nation.

ACCEPTED. A term orig. syn. with initiated, or received into the society. Now used to dist. a Freemason from an unadmitted operative mason.

ACELDAMA. Field of Blood. A small piece of land for the burial of strangers, just without the walls of Jerusalem, S. of Mt. Zion. Orig. called "potter's field" because it furnished the clay for the potters' ware.

ACHAD. One; or Unity. A Heb. name of God. Adopted as one of the appellations of the Deity.

ACHARON SCHILTON. The new kingdom.

ACHIAS. Cor. of Achijah, the bro. of Jah.

ACHISHAR; ACHIZAR. An officer "over the household" of Solomon. Rep. by one of the officers of a Co. of S. M.

ACMETHA. A Heb. city.

ACRE; ACCHO; ACCA; ACON; or St. Jean d'Acre, called in anc. times Ptolemais, was a seaport on the Bay of Acre, Medit. Sea, "over against" Mt. Carmel, 30 m. S. of Tyre.

ACTUAL PAST MASTER is one who has rec. the deg. of P. M. in a Sym. L. when elected to preside as dist. from a Virtual Past Master or one who has passed through the ceremony in a Ch.

ADAREL. (Adr—Splendor, El— God. Divine Splendor). Angel of fire.

ADMAH. The most E. of the 5 cities of the Vale of Siddim which is now covered by the Dead Sea.

AD MAJORUM DEI GLORIAM. To the greater glory of God.

ADONAI. Pl. of excellence for Adon, the Lord. The Jews, who reverently avoided the pronunciation of the sacred name Jehovah, were accustomed, whenever that name occured in reading, to subs. for it the word Adonai. The Rabbins say "every word indicative of dominion, though singular in meaning, is made pl. in form." It may almost always be considered as allusive to or sym. of the True Word.

ADONIRAM; ADONHIRAM; ADONIRUM; or cor. ADON KHURUM. Chief receiver of taxes and an important officer at the building of the Temple. Although this name has some times been applied to H. A. B., he was prob. the supt. of the workmen in the forests of Lebanon.

AD UNIVERSI TERRARUM ORBIS SUMMI ARCHITECTI GLORIAM. To the Glory of the Grand Architect of the Universe.

AD VITAM. For life.

AENEID. In the 6th book of his immortal Epic, Virgil is sup. to have described the ceremony of initiation into the Anc. Myst.

AERA ARCHITECTONICA. More commonly known as annus lucis—the year of light.

AGAPAE. Love feasts or banquets held during the first 3 cent. in the Christian Church. The ceremonies of the banquet in the R. C. Chapter are arranged with ref. to the anc. agapae.

AGENDA. Order of business. Book of precepts.

AGNUS DEI, Lamb of God, also called Paschal Lamb, is the Jewel of the Generalisimo. It consisted in the 6th cent. of a lamb supporting in his right foot a cross, to which a banneret was attached in the 11th cent.

AHAB. Son and succ. of Omri, King of Israel from 918 to 897 B. C. He married Jezebel, through whose influence the Phoenician worship of Baal was introduced among the Israelites.

AHABATH OLAM. Eternal love. A prayer used by the Jews of the Roman Empire during the time of Christ. Dermott inserted it in his Ahiman Rezon.

AHAD. A name of God.

AHALIAB. See Aholiab.

AHASUERUS. A Persian king. Poss. only a title; or the father of Darius; or Cambyses.

AHAZ. 11th king of Judah. Lived 8th cent. B. C.

AHIAH. He and Elihoreph were the secretaries of Solomon and are rep. by the Wardens in the 7th deg. A. A. S. R.

AHILUD. Father of Josaphat.

AHIMAAZ. Son and succ. of Zadok, the H. P.

AHIMAN REZON. The will of selected brethren. Title of the Book of Constitutions of the "Ancient Masons" compiled by Laurence Dermott, Gr. Sec. in 1756.

AHINADAB. Son of Jetdo.

AHISAMACH. Father of Aholiab.

AHISAR; AHISHAR; AHESHAR. See Achishar.

AHOLIAB. A Heb. weaver who assisted in constructing the tabernacle, the Ark of the Covenant and the tapestries and curtains of the Temple. See Bezaleel.

AICHMALOTARCH. Jewish title of the Prince of the Captivity or rep. of the kings of Israel at Babylon.

AKAR; or ACHAR. (a-kar).

AKIROP. A ruffian.

ALEPPO. A town in N. Syria.

ALEXANDER III., of Macedon, surnamed the Great. b. 356 B. C. d. 323 B. C. Reigned 13 years.

ALEXANDRIA, SCHOOL OF. A school of philos. founded at Alexandria, Egypt, by Alexander the Great, abt. 333 B. C., from which was derived the system of sym. and allegory which lay at the foundation of Masonic philos.

ALFRED the GREAT. b. in Wantage, Berks, 849, the youngest son of Ethelwulf, King of the West Saxons. succ. to the throne on the death of his bro. Ethelred. d. 901.

ALAGABIL. The Builder. The Supreme God. Equiv. to T. G. A. O. T. U.

ALLOCUTION. The address of the presiding officer of a S. C.

ALLOWED. Used in the old manuscript Constitutions for accepted, or approved.

ALL-SOULS' DAY. Nov. 2. A feast day of Ch. of Rose Croix.

ALOHIM. See Elohim.

ALPHA and OMEGA. See Rev. 1, 8; xxi, 6; xxii, 13.

ALS. Powerful. All-powerful God.

AL SHADDAI; AL SHEDI. See Shaddai.

ALYCUBER. Master of the tribe of Menasseh.

AMAL-SAGGHI. Great Labor.

AMARIAH. A H. P. and father of Ahitub.

AMAR-JAH. God spake.

AMBOTH. A sec. of country in Syria.

AMERICAN RITE. According to Mackey, the first 9 deg. conferred in the U. S. by L., Ch. and Co., should be so called, to dist. from the Ancient York Rite and the Modern York Rite.

AMETH. Prop. Emeth.

AMINADAB. A chief in Israel.

AMMONITES. Desc. of the younger son of Lot who dwelt bet. the rivers Jabbok, Jordan and Arnon. The Israelites were accused of seizing part of their territory.

AMRAPHEL. King of Shinar or Babylonia.

ANANIAS. A comp. of Zerubbabel.

ANCIENT CRAFT MASONRY. The first 3 deg. or Ancient York Rite. The deg. of R. A. is not gen. incl. although when considered a complement of the 3d deg. it must, of course, constitute a part.

ANCIENT MASONS. Name assumed by those who in 1738 seceded from the regular Gr. L. of Eng.

ANDERSON, JAMES. Compiler of the Book of Constitutions for the Gr. L. of Eng. 1st published in 1723. b. Aug. 5, 1684, Edinburgh, Scot. d. May 28, 1739.

ANDROGYNOUS DEGREES. Those conferred on both men and women.

ANER. A Heb. chief.

ANGERONA. Roman goddess of silence whose statue has sometimes been used to ornament Masonic edifices.

ANNO DEPOSITIONIS. In the year of the Deposit. Add 1000 to the vulgar era. See Calendar.

ANNO DOMINI. In the Year of our Lord.

ANNO HEBRAICO. In the Heb. Year. Same as Anno Mundi. See Calendar.

ANNO INVENTIONIS. In the Year of the Discovery. Add 530 to the vulgar era. See Calendar.

ANNO LUCIS. In the Year of Light. Add 4000 to the vulgar era. See Calendar.

ANNO MUNDI. In the year of the World. Add 3760 to the vulgar era until Sept., after Sept. add one year more. See Calendar.

ANNO ORDINIS. In the Year of the Order. Subtract 1118 from the vulgar era. See Calendar.

ANTIOCH. Anc. capital of Syria sit. on the Orontes abt. equidistant from Constantinople and Alexandria.

ANTIOCHUS III., the Great, King of Syria. Contemp. with Hannibal, 223 B. C.

ANTIPATER of IDUMEA. Father of Herod the Great. Procurator of all Judea. d. 43 B. C.

ANTIQUITY, LODGE of. The oldest in Eng. and one of the 4 founders of the Gr. L. of Eng. in 1717. Met at the Goose and Gridiron Tavern.

APOCALYPTIC DEGREES. Those founded on the Revelation of St. John or whose sym. and machinery of initiation are derived from that work.

APPLE-TREE TAVERN, where the 4 Lodges of London met in 1717 and organized the Gr. L. of Eng., was sit. in Charles St., Covent Garden.

ARABIA PETRAEA (or Rocky), comprehends what was formerly the land of Midian. Horeb and Sinai were within its bounds.

ARAL; AREL; or ARIEL. Lion of God, meaning Hero.

ARAUNAH. See Ornan.

ARCANA. Secret things.

ARCHELAUS. A Cappadocian, General of Mithridates VI. First cent. B. C.

ARCHETYPE. The thing adopted as a sym. whence the sym. idea is derived, as, the Temple is the archetype of the L.

ARDAREL. See Adarel.

ARELIM. Mighty ones. Pl. of Arel.

ARIOCH. King of Ellaser.

ARK of the COVENANT. See Exod. xxv. 10-23.

ARK. In the ritual of the R. A. deg. three are referred to: 1. The Ark of Safety or of Noah. 2. The Ark of the Covenant or of Moses. 3. The Substitute Ark, or the Ark of Zerubbabel.

ARMY LODGE. See Field Lodge.

AROBA. Pledge; covenant; agreement. (Lat. arrhabo, a token or pledge. Heb. Arubbah, surety; hostage).

ARRAS. A town in N. W. part of Fr. where in 1747, the Pretender est. a Ch. of Rosicrucian Free-masons. See Stuart Masonry and Chapter of Arras.

ARTABAN. A scribe.

ARTAXERXES. In anc. Persic or Zend. sigs. great king.

ARTAXERXES I., LONGI-MANUS. King of Persia. d. 425 B. C.

ARTAXERXES II., Menom. King of Persia. d. 362 B. C.

ARTS, the knowledge of things made known; Parts, the deg. into which Masonry is divided; and Points the rules and usages.

ASAROTA. A variegated pave-ment used in temples and anc. edifices.

ASCALON. A seaport 40 m. W. S. W. of Jerusalem.

ASCENSION DAY or HOLY THURSDAY. 40 days after Easter. A feast day of Ch. of Rose Croix.

ASHER. Happiness. A patriarch. Son of Jacob. His tribe occu-pied the land bet. Phoenicia, Mt. Lebanon and Mt. Carmel.

ASHERALOTH. A sec. of coun-try in Syria.

ASSASSINS or ISHMAELIANS. A secret society of philos. found-ed by Hassan Sabah, abt. 1090, in Persia, who had several amic-able transactions with the Temp-lars and whose government and regulations bore a close resemb-lance to that of the Templars, the Hospitallers and Teutonic Knts.

ASSUR. Anc. name of

ASSYRIA. A powerful empire of Asia, embracing all the coun-tries and nations bet. the Medit. and the Indus River. Ninevah was the capital. See Syria.

ATAH GIBOR LOLAM ADONAI. Thou art strong in the eternal God.

ATHELSTAN, grandson of the great Alfred, b. abt. 895, ascend-ed the throne of Eng. in 925, and d. in 940. Called a pat. of Masonry. See Edwin and York legend.

ATOSSA. Dgtr. of Cyrus, Queen of Cambyses and afterward of Darius Hystaspes, of whom she had Xerxes.

AUDI, VIDE, TACE. Hear, see, and be silent.

AUGUSTUS. Nephew and succ. of Julius Caesar and Emperor of Rome at the time of our Sav-ior's birth.

AURIEL; AURI-AL. See Adarel.

AURIM. See Urim.

AUT VINCERE, AUT MORI. Either to conquer or to die.

AYNON; AGNON; AJUON; and DYON. Prob. meant for H. A. B. in the old manuscript Consti-tutions.

AZARIAH. Captain of Solomon's guards. In some places sig. Helped of God.

BAAL; BEL; or BELUS. Lord, or Master. Chief divinity and rep. the sun among the Phoeni-cians, Canaanites and Babylon-ians. Whenever the Israelites made one of their almost period-ical deflections to idolatry, Baal seems to have been the favorite idol to whose worship they ad-dicted themselves. See 24th deg.

BAANA. One of Soloman's offi-cers.

BABEL. The Noachite Masons date the commencement of their order from the destruction of this tower which occurred abt. 1775 A. M. or 140 years after the deluge.

BABYLON, Gate of Bel; or Sheshach; the seat of universal empire under Nebuchadnezzar, chief of all idolatrous cities and mother of Chaldea, was sit. on the Euphrates, 475 m. nearly due E. from Jerusalem.

BABYLONIA. See Chaldea.

BACULUS. Official staff of the Gr. M. of Templars.

BAFOMET. See Baphomet.

BAGULKAL. Guardian of the sacred ark.

BAHANI. Labor.

BALDWYN II. Succ. of Godfrey of Bouillon as King of Jerusalem. In his reign, 1118, the Order of K. T. was instituted.

BALDWYN ENCAMPMENT. An orig. Encampment of K. T. at Bristol, Eng., said to have been est. from "time immemorial." It became a constituent of the Gr. Conclave of Eng. and Wales in 1860.

BALKIS. Queen of Sheba who is mentioned in connection with the Sign of Admiration in the M. E. M. deg.

BALL. See Stones.

BALTHASAR. See Belshazzar.

BALUSTER. Any official circular or document issuing from a Supreme Council.

BAMEARAH. We have found it.

BANACAS. Captain of the Guard.

BANNOCKBURN, BATTLE of. An Eng. army of 100,000 under Edward II., was defeated (1314) at Bannockburn, by 30,000 Scots under Robert Bruce, King of Scot., which secured independence for Scot. See Bruce.

BAPHOMET. Imaginary idol or sym. which the Templars were accused of employing in their mystic rites.

BARABBAS. A noted Jewish robber and murderer. Matt. xxvii. 16.

BARSABAS. A candidate for the vacancy in the apostleship. Acts. i. 23.

BATH KOL. Daughter Voice. A voice from the Shekinah, in the Holy of Holies which made known the will of God.

BAY-TREE. The laurel. A sym. of the immortal nature of Truth.

BEA MACHEH. To be with God.

BEAUCENIFER. The officer who carried the Beauseant in battle for the anc. Templars.

BEGOAL-KOL. See Bagulkal.

BEL. Cont. of Baal. With Jah and On it rep. the Tetragrammaton.

BELENUS. The god of the sun. Same as Baal.

BELSHAZZAR, last king of Baby-

lon, was the son or grandson of Nebuchadnezzar.

BELUS. Cor. of Baal. A temple of anc. Tyre.

BENAI. See Bonaim.

BENAKAR. A cavern to which the assassins fled for concealment.

BENDEKAR; BENDAKAR; BENDACA; BENGABEE; or BENGABER. An Intendant or Prince of Solomon who owned a quarry once used as a place of refuge by assassins.

BENJAH; BENYAH; BENIAH; or BENAYAH. Son of Jah.

BENJAMIN and JUDAH were the only tribes that returned from the Capt. to rebuild the 2d Temple.

BENKHURIM; BENKHORIM; or BENCHORIM. One that is freeborn.

BERETH; BERITH. Alliance; covenant.

BERTHEMAN; BERTHEMAR. Inspector of the tribe of Asher.

BEZALEEL; Betselal. One of the builders of the tabernacle and the Ark of the Covenant. See Aholiab.

BINAH. The mother of understanding; intelligence.

BIRSHA. King of Gomorrah.

BISHLAM. A Persian officer.

BLUE. Sym. of universal friendship and benevolence. From the color of heaven which embraces the whole globe.

BLUE MASONRY. The first 3 deg.

BLUE MASTER. A Master Mason.

BOAZ (b, in; oaz, strength). A pillar of the porch of the Temple.

BODE, JOHANN JOACHIM CHRISTOPH. One of the most dist. Masons of his time. b. Brunswick. Jan. 30, 1730. d. Weimar, Dec. 13, 1793.

BONAIM. Builders, prob. inferior to the stone-squarers or Giblemites. 1. Kings v. 18.

BONE, cor. pronounced in one syllable, is the Heb. word Boneh, (bonay) builder. Applied to H. A. B.

BOOK of CONSTITUTIONS. That work in which is contained the rules and regulations adopted for the government of the craft.

BOOK OF GOLD. The book in which the transactions, statutes, decrees, balusters, and protocols of the Supreme Council or a Gr. Consistory are contained.

BOOK of the LAW. The Holy Bible to Christians. That sacred book which is believed to contain the revealed will of God. See Scriptures.

BOURBON. A ducal and royal family which ruled France from 1589 to 1793.

BREAD and WINE, Consecrated, the eating and drinking of which is called the "Communion of the Brethren" and is an attestation of sincerity and a covenant of friendship.

BRIGHT MASON. One well acquainted with the ritual, forms of opening and closing and ceremonies of initiation. Does not appear to include the superior knowledge of the history and science of the Institution.

BROACHED THURNEL. A cubical stone with a pyramidal apex. One of the Immovable Jewels in the early part of the 18th cent.

BRUCE, ROBERT, King of Scotland, b. 1274. d. July 9, 1329. Poss. created June 24, 1314, after the battle of Bannockburn, the Order of St. Andrew of the Thistle to which was united the Order of Heredom.

BUH; BUL; Cor. of Bel.

BUNYAN, JOHN. The most celebrated allegorical writer of Eng. Wrote, Solomon's Temple Spiritualized. b. 1628. d. 1688.

BURNS, ROBERT. Scotch poet. b. Jan 25, 1759. d. July 22, 1796. Some portion of his wonderful talent was consecrated to the service of the Craft.

BYBLOS. Anc. name of Gebal.

CABALA. See Kabbala.

CABLE TOW'S LENGTH is 3m. for an E. A. according to the old writers. Now means the scope of a man's reasonable ability.

CABUL. A district containing 20 cities poss. located in the N. W. part of Galilee, adjacent to Tyre, which Solomon gave to Hiram of Tyre for his assistance.

CADUCEUS. The magic wand of Hermes, the guide of souls, entwined by 2 serpents, and surmounted by 2 wings. A sym. of immortality. The rod of the Master of Ceremonies is an analogue.

CAEMENTARIUS. A builder of walls. Has been translated as Freemason.

CAGLIOSTRO, COUNT, or JOSEPH BALSAMO. A Masonic charlatan who flourished in the 18th cent.

CALCOTT, WELLINS. A dist. Masonic writer of the 18th cent.

CALENDAR. The York, American and French Rites use A. L.; the Scotch Rite. A. M. or A. H.; Chapters R. A. M., A. I. or A. Inv.; Councils R. & S. M., A. Dep; Commanderies K. T., A. O.

CALENDAR, Hebrew. See Months.

CALVARY. (Lat. Skull, Heb. Golgotha). A small hill N. of anc. Jerusalem, on the road to Joppa, ½ m. due W. from Mt. Moriah, the site of the Temple.

CAMBYSES, Son of Cyrus, King of Persia, succ. his father in 529 B. C. Conquered Cyprus and Egypt. d. 522 B. C.

CANAAN. Low country. Orig. boundaries were Mt. Lebanon, Arabia, the Jordan, and, at some points, the Medit. At the coming of Christ was divided in 5 prov., Judea, Samaria, Galilee, Perea and Idumea, being 180 m. long, by 75 m. wide.

CAPITULAR DEGREES are those conferred by a Ch. of R. A. M.

CAPTIVITY. The Jews reckoned their national Capts. as 4—

Babylonian, Medean, Grecian and Roman. The 1st, only, is connected with Masonry.

CARAUSIS. A Roman Emperor. A. D. 287. Poss. an encourager of Masonry.

CARMEL, MT. The Garden of God. Highest peak of a ridge rising in the plain of Esdraelon and run. N. W. out into the Medit., S. of Bay of Acre.

CARNAC. An anc. city of Fr.

CARPET. Charts were orig. drawn on the floor with chalk or charcoal and at the close of the L. obliterated. They were subsequently painted on cloth and laid on the floor, hence called carpets.

CASMARAN. The angel of air. Ref. to in 28th deg.

CATECHUMEN. One who had attained the 2d deg. of the Essenian or early Christian Myst. and assumed the name of Constans.

CEPHAS. Stone, or Rock. Gr. Petros; Lat. Petrus. Surname given to Peter.

CHAIN, TRIANGULAR. According to a legend Nebuchadnezzar bound the Jewish capt. with triangular chains as an additional insult, because to them the triangle was the sym. of the Deity.

CHALDEA, capital Babylon, hence called Babylonia, sit. bet. the Tigris and Euphrates rivers, was abt. 400 m. long by 100 m. wide. See Syria.

CHAPTER. In early times Masonic meetings were called, not only Lodges, but Chapters and Congregations.

CHAPTER of ARRAS was created, 1780, in Paris by the Primordial Ch. of Arras and Metropolitan Ch. of Rosicrucian Freemasons. See Arras.

CHARGES OF 1722. Succinct directions for the proper discharge of a Mason's duties which were annexed to Anderson's Book of Constitutions.

CHARLES MARTEL. See Martel.

CHARLES XIII., Ascended the throne of Sweden in 1809. Dist. for his attachment to Freemasonry.

CHART. See Carpet.

CHEDERLAOMER. King of Elam.

CHESED. (gen. cor. into Hesed). Mercy.

CHETH. (Cor. of Gath).

CHIBBELUM. (Cor. of Giblim). A worthy Mason.

CHIEFS OF MASONRY. Formerly, Princes of Jerusalem.

CHOCHMAH. Wisdom.

CICERO. Roman orator and statesman. b. 106, d. 43 B. C.

CITY of the GREAT KING. Jerusalem. Psalm xlviii. 2; Matt. v. 35.

CLANDESTINE. Illegal; not authorized.

CLAY GROUND was sit. abt. 35 m. N. E. from Jerusalem.

CLERMONT, COLLEGE of. A college of Jesuits in Paris, where James II, after his flight from Eng. in 1688, resided until his removal to St. Germain.

CLOUDY. A word sometimes imp. used to report an unfavorable ballot.

COCHLEUS. The form of a screw. The winding staircase which led to the middle chamber.

COCKLE SHELL. See Scallop Shell.

CODRUS. An anc. king of Athens.

COEUR de LEON. Surname of Richard I. of Eng., b. 1157, killed 1199. Leader of the Eng. in the 3d Crusade.

COETUS. An assembly. A word sometimes imp. used for L.

COHEN. A priest.

COLLEGIA ARTIFICUM. Colleges of Artificers. See Roman Colleges.

COLORS, Masonic. Blue, Purple, Red, White, Black, Green, Yellow, Violet.

COMMANDER-IN-CHIEF. Presiding officer in a Consistory of S. P. R. S. His style is Illustrious.

COMMUNICATION. A meeting of a L.

COMO. A city of Lombardy, Italy. Principal seat of the Travelling Freemasons of the Mid. Ages, where they est. a noted school of architecture.

CONCLAVE. An assemblage of Templars.

CONFEDERACIES. The annual meetings of the Masons in the time of Henry VI. of Eng.

CONFERRING DEGREES. Initiation of a candidate into any deg. in due form. See Exemplification.

CONGREGATIONS. The annual meetings of the Craft are so called in the Old Records and Constitutions.

CONSISTORY. A meeting of S. P. R. S.

CONSTANS. To stand firm.

CONSTITUTIONS of 1762. Those drawn up at Bordeaux, Sept. 21, 1762, by 9 commissioners, for the government of the Rite of Perfection.

CONSTITUTIONS of 1786. Regarded as the fundamental law of the A. A. S. R. Poss. est. in 1786 by Frederick II, of Prussia.

CONSUMMATUM EST. It is finished.

CONVOCATION. A meeting of R. A. M.

CORDE GLADIO POTENS. Powerful in heart and with the sword.

CORDON. Fr. name for the Eng. collar.

COWAN. Pretender; intruder; or eavesdropper. Always conveys the idea of contempt.

CRAFT. The whole body of Freemasons wherever dispersed.

CRETE; CANDIA; KIRID; or KRITI. An island of the Medit., S. of Greece, 160 m. by 30 m.

CROSIER. Prelate's official staff.

CROSS, JEREMY L. A teacher of the ritual, b. June 27, 1783,

Haverhill, N. H., d. there in 1861.

CROTONA. A city of Gr. colonists in So. Italy where, in the 6th cent., Pythagoras est. his celebrated school.

CRUSADES. There was, bet. Freemasonry and the Crusades, a much more intimate relation than has gen. been supposed. The communications est. by the Templars with the Saracens led to the acquisition by the former, of many of the dogmas of the secret societies of the E. such as the Essenes, Assassins, and Druses. These were brought to Europe and the influence of the Crusades on the Masons tended materially to assist the restoration of literature and the arts, particularly architecture.

CRUX ANSATA. Cross with a handle. A Tau cross surmounted by an oval. A sym. of life.

CRYPTIC DEGREES. Royal and Select Master.

CUBIT. The Heb. 21 in.; Sacred 36 in.; Profane 18 in.

CULDEES. Primitive Christian priests and their disc. discovered in Britain in the 6th cent. by St. Augustine. Masonic writers have claimed a connection bet. them and the early Masonry of Ireland and Scot.

CURETES. Priests of anc. Crete, whose Myst. bore some resemblance to the Eleusinian rites.

CUSTOS ARCANI. The guardian of the Treasury.

CYRENE. Anc. city in N. Africa, W. of Egypt.

CYRUS the Great. Son of Cambyses and Mandane, dgtr. of Astyages, King of Media, b. 590 B. C. d. 529 B. C. Became founder of the Persian Empire by conquering and uniting Media, Babylonia, Lydia and all Asia Minor. See Temple of Zerubbabel.

DABIR. The Sanctum Sanctorum.

DALCHO, FREDERICK, b. London, 1770, d. Charleston, S. C., Nov. 24, 1836. One of the founders of the S. C. for the So. J.

DAMASCUS, or EL-SCHAMS, capital of anc. Syria, is sit. on the river Baradi 200 m. S. of Antioch, 120 m. N. E. of Jerusalem on the road to Babylon. The resting place of the Jews returning from the Capt.

DANIEL. Heb. prophet, contemp. of Ezekiel abt. 600 B. C. A captive who became Governor of Babylon under Nebuchadnezzar, and 1st ruler of the whole Medo-Persian Empire, inferior only to Darius. Under Cyrus he had been G. M. of the Palace and Interpreter of Visions. Did not return to Judea. Poss. d. in Sushan, Persia, at the age of 90.

DARAQUIEL; DARAKIEL. By the direction of God.

DARIUS I., or Darayavuste, b. 548 B. C., son of Hystaspes, became King of Persia in 521 and d. 485 B. C. Protected the Jews in the rebuilding of the Temple.

DATHAN. See Num. xvi.

DAVID. Father of Solomon and his predecessor on the throne of Israel. Designed the 1st Temple and purchased Mt. Moriah, its site.

DAVID, CITY of. A sec. in the S. part of Jerusalem embracing Mt. Zion.

DEGREE. A step.

DEGREES of CHIVALRY. Those founded on the religious and military orders of knighthood which existed in the Mid. Ages. The Red Cross is not properly such.

DELTA. A triangle. From the 4th Gr. letter. A sym. of God.

DEMIT. Permit to go.

DEO SOLI INVICTO MITHRAE. To Mithras, the only unconquerable god.

DEPHIRAH. Emanation from the Deity.

DEPOSIT of the Substitute Ark is sup. to have taken place in the last year of the building of Solomon's Temple, or 1000 B. C. Hence that date in Cryptic Masonry.

DERMOTT, LAURENCE. G. Sec. afterwards D. G. M. of the "Ancient Masons" and publisher of Ahiman Rezon.

DESAGULIERS, JOHN THEOPHILUS. "Father of Modern Speculative Masonry." b. Mar. 12, 1683, Rochelle, Fr., d. Feb. 29, 1744., Eng.

DETACHED DEGREES. See Side and Honorary Degrees.

DETER. One of Solomon's princes.

DEUS MEUMQUE JUS. God and my right. Lat. translation of Dieu et Mon Droit.

DEUS VULT. God wills it.

DIDYMUS. Another name for the Apostle Thomas.

DIEU ET MON DROIT. God and my right. Motto of Richard Coeur de Leon.

DIEU LE VEUT. God wills it. Battle cry of the Crusaders.

DIMIT. Cor. of Demit.

DIOCLETIAN. A Roman Emperor, b. 245, d. 313 A. D.

DIONYSIAN ARCHITECTS. A fraternity of builders est. in Asia Minor abt. 1000 B. C. by the priests of Bacchus. They are said to have continued their existence to the time of the Crusades, when they passed over to Europe and became merged with the Travelling Freemasons.

DISCIPLINA ARCANI. The Discipline of the Secret.

DISPENSATION. Permission to do that which, without such permission, is forbidden.

DOMINE DEUS MEUS. O Lord! my God.

DOMITIAN. A Roman emperor, b. 51, d. 96 A. D.

DORSON. Inspector of the tribe of Zebulon.

DRUIDS. An anc. Celtic religious sect whose doctrines were the same as those of Pythagoras.

DRUSES. A sect of mystic religionists who inhabit Mts. Lebanon and Anti-Lebanon, in Syria. A theory existed that they were an offshoot from the early Freemasons.

DUE GUARD. (To duly guard). A mode of recognition.

DUNCKERLY, THOS. b. Oct. 23, 1724, London, Eng., d. 1795. Constructed a code of lectures, revised the ritual and collated all the anc. formulas for the Gr. L. of Eng. He reconstructed the R. A. of Dermott, and by his influence the true Word was transferred from the 3d deg. to the R. A. deg.

EBONY BOX. A sym. of the human heart, teaching reserve and taciturnity.

ECBATAM; ECBATANA. Anc. capital of Media (traditionally) founded by Solomon. Darius found there the edict of Cyrus concerning the rebuilding of the Temple at Jerusalem.

ECOSSAIS. Scottish. Scottish Master.

ECOSSISM. Fr. term for the 33 degrees, A. A. S. R.

EDICT OF CYRUS. Issued 536 B. C.

EDOM; or IDUMEA. A Syrian prov. lying S. of the Dead Sea and bordering on Moab.

EDWARD III., the Confessor, King of Eng. Said to have been a pat. of Masonry in 1041.

EDWIN. Son of Edward. Saxon King of Eng. and bro. of Athelstan (895-941). Traditionally the pat. of Masonry in Eng., who called the Congregation at York in 926, which formed the Gr. L. of Eng. See York Legend.

EHEIAH. A Heb. name of God.

EHEYEH ASHER EHEYEH. I am that I am. The name of God in which Moses was instructed at the burning bush.

EL. The Mighty One. One of the names of God and the root of many of the other names of Deity.

ELAH. A valley S. W. of Jerusalem, 3 m. from Bethlehem, on the road to Jaffa.

ELAI BENI ALMANAH. (Ellaibben-ial-mannah).

ELAI BENI EMETH. Sometimes applied to the 26th deg.

ELAM. A city and country E. of Shinar and N. of Persian Gulf. A part of the anc. Persian Empire. Chedorlaomer was one of its earliest kings.

ELCHANAN. God has graciously given. Imp. Elhanan and Elkhannan, Mercy of God. Old rituals, Eleham. Sometimes Eliham, God of the people.

ELEAZAR. Son and succ. of Aaron. H. P. for 20 years.

ELEUSIS. Anc. Gr. village 12 m. N. W. of Athens and now called Lepsina. The home of the Eleusinian Myst.

ELIAH. A Heb. name of God.

ELIAM; ELIGNAM. Father of Bath-sheba, wife of David.

ELIASAPH. A Levite; son of Lael.

ELIHOREPH. One of Solomon's secretaries. See Ahiah.

ELIZABETH. Queen of Eng. b. 1523, d. 1603.

ELIZAPHAN. A Levite; son of Uzziel.

ELLASAR. A city of Chaldea.

ELOHIM. The Creator. The Most Beneficent. The general name of God.

EL SHADDAI. God most mighty. The name by which God was known to the patriarchs before he announced himself to Moses by his tetragrammatonic name of Jehovah.

ELU. Fr. Elected.

EMANUEL. Jesus Christ. Gr. of the Heb. Immanuel, God with us.

EMBASSY of ZERUBBABEL is recorded in the 11th book of the Antiquities of Josephus.

EMESSA. A city of Syria.

EMETH. Integrity; fidelity; firmness. Those devoted to Truth.

EMOUNAH; EMUNAH; AMUNAH. Fidelity; Truth. Fidelity to one's promises.

ENOCH, 7th patriarch, b. 622 A. M., son of Jared and great-grandfather of Noah, is, traditionally, closely connected with the Institution.

ENTERED. Admitted or introduced.

EPHESUS. An anc. city of Asia Minor near the mouth of the Cayster, 30 m. S. of Smyrna. Aijasoluc is near its site.

EPHRAIMITES. Desc. of Ephraim, who inhabited the center of Judea, bet. the Medit. and the Jordan. They were particularly jealous of the tribe of Judah.

EPICTETUS. A Roman Stoic philos. of the 1st cent. b. 60, d. 120 A. D.

EPICURUS. A Gr. philos. b. 340, d. 270 B. C.

EPOPT. Gr. to look into; to behold. One who had passed through the Great Myst.

EQUITAS. Equity.

ESAR HADDON. A king of Assyria.

ESCHOL. A valley in the S. of Judea.

ESDRAS. Ezra.

ESOTERIC. That secret portion which is known only to the initiates as dist. from Exoteric, or monitorial, which is accessible to all.

ESRIM. Twenty.

ESSENES. One of the 3 Jewish sects; the other 2 being the Pharisees and Sadducees. To one of these every Jew was compelled to unite himself. It is sup. that the Savior was an Essene because while repeatedly denouncing the errors of the 2 other sects, he has nowhere uttered a word of censure against the Essenes.

ETERNITAS. Eternity.

ETHIOPIA. A country S. of Egypt and watered by the Upper Nile, including the modern countries of Nubia and Abyssinia.

ETRURIA. An anc. city, also sec. of Italy, now Tuscany and part of Umbria.

EUCLID of ALEXANDRIA. An Egyptian geometrician, b. 328, d. 283 B. C. His name has been always associated with the history of Freemasonry.

EUMOLPUS, King of Eleusis, founded abt. 1374 B. C., the Myst. of Eleusis.

EUREKA. I have found it.

EURESIS. A discovery. That part of the initiation in the Anc. Myst. which rep. the finding of the body.

EXEMPLIFICATION OF THE WORK. When the ceremonies of a deg. are performed by a lecturer or teacher for instruction, by using, gen., a subs. for the candidate. See Conferring.

EXISTENS. Existent.

EXODUS, The, occurred under Meneptah II., abt. 1325 B. C.

EXOTERIC. Public, not Esoteric, or secret.

EZEKIEL, one of the 4 great Heb. prophets, son of Buzi, was carried to Babylon as a capt. 598 B. C.

EZRA; or ESDRAS. One, a famous H. P., the other, a celebrated scribe.

FANATICISM. The Eng. interpretation of the name of the 2d assassin.

FEAST DAYS. St. John the Baptist, June 24; and St. John the Evangelist, Dec. 27.

FESSLER, IGNATZ AURELIUS, a dist. German writer and Masonic reformer, was b. at Czurendorf, Hungary, in 1756. Author of the Rite of Fessler.

FIAT LUX. Let there be light.

FIAT JUSTITIA, RUAT COELUM. Let justice be done though the heavens fall.

FIDES. Faith, or Fidelity. A Roman goddess, "sometimes rep. by 2 right hands joined."

FIELD LODGE, also called Army, Military, or Traveling Lodge. One duly instituted and authorized all powers and privileges during its peripatetic existence.

FIRE-WORSHIP. This was one of the earliest of anc. religions, next to Sabaism, of which it was prob. a development. Everywhere in Scripture fire is a sym. of the holiness of God.

FISH. The letters of the Gr. word for fish form the initials of the five words, Jesus Christ the Son of God, the Savior. Hence its adoption as an early Christian sym. Formerly the G. M. wore a silver fish.

FLAMING SWORD. One whose blade is of a spiral or twisted form. Such was the Tiler's sword until recently, and ref. to that which guarded the entrance to Paradise. Gen. iii. 24.

FLEXIAN or FLORIAN, SQUIN de. The "Judas of the Templars", Prior of Montfaucon, was the 1st accuser of Jacques de Molay.

FORDS of the JORDAN. The "Passage" where the Ephraimites were overwhelmed was prob. due E. from Seikoot and opp. Mizpah.

FOREIGN COUNTRY of a M. M. is (sym.) heaven, the future life, the higher state of existence after death.

FORMULA. A prescribed mode or form, either oral or monitorial of doing or saying anything.

FOUR CROWNED MARTYRS, the Patron Saints of Operative Masonry in early times in Germany and Eng. are said to be 4 "Stone-squarers," who suffered martyrdom for their religion Nov. 8, 287.

FRANCKEN, HENRY A. The 1st propagator of the high deg. in the U. S.

FRATER. Brother. A term borrowed from the monks by the Military Orders of the Mid. Ages.

FREDERICK BARBAROSSA. Frederick I., Emperor of Germany, b. 1123, d. 1190.

FREDERICK the GREAT. Frederick II., King of Prussia, b. Jan. 24, 1712, d. Aug. 17, 1786. Said to have been an active pat. of, and worker in, Freemasonry.

FREE and ACCEPTED. This title was 1st used by Dr. Anderson in the 2d edition of the Book of Constitutions in 1738. See Accepted.

FURLAC. Angel of the earth.

GABAON. A high place. In philos. Masonry the 3d heaven is denominated Mt. Gabaon.

GABOR. Strong.

GABRIEL. Mighty one of God. Chief of the archangels.

GALAAD; GALAHAD. The Keeper of the Seals.

GALILEE. Prov. of anc. Palestine, W. of the Jordan.

GAREB. A Heb. engraver.

GARIMONT. A standard bearer in the 32d deg.

GARINOUS. Cor. of Garimond or Garimund, the Patriarch of Jerusalem (1182), bet. whose hands the Hospitallers took their vows.

GATH. An anc. city in Palestine, 32 m. W. from Jerusalem.

GAUL. Anc. name of Fr.

GEBAL or GIBLOS, now JIBLAH. A city of Phoenicia, on the Medit., under Mt. Lebanon, bet. Tripoli and Berytus. The Byblos of the Gr. where the worship of Adonis was celebrated and whose inhabitants were dist. for the art of stone-carving. See Giblim.

GEBER. One of Solomon's princes.

GEDALIAH, son of Pashur, a prince of Zedekiah's court, persuaded the king to deliver up Jeremiah to death, from which the prophet escaped.

GERSHON. A son of Levi.

GETHSEMANE. Olive garden. Abt. ½ an acre of ground on the W. side of Mt. Olivet, commanding a full view of Jerusalem.

GEVURAH. Valor.

GHEMOUL BINAH THEBOUNAH. Prudence in the midst of vicissitude.

GHIBLIM; GIBALIM; GUIBLIM; Cor. of

GIBLIM. The Giblites, Giblemites, or inhabitants of Gebal. They were the "Master Masons" who put the finishing hand to Solomon's Temple. 1. Kings, v. 18.

GIBOUR. Strength. A name of God.

GILEAD. A part of a mt. ridge, rising 6 m. S. of Jabbok, ext. 5 or 6 m. E. and W. and run. S. from Mt. Lebanon, on the E. of Palestine. The whole country E. of the sea of Galilee is so called.

GOAT, RIDING THE, is an anc. superstititon. The Gr. and Romans portrayed Pan in horns, hoof, and shaggy hide. The early Christians subs. Satan for Pan and in the Mid. Ages the Devil appeared "riding on a goat."

G. O. D. Initials of the 3 Heb. words: Gomer, beauty; Oz, strength; Dabar, wisdom.

GODFREY de ST. ALDEMAR. One of the founders of anc. Knts. Templarism.

GOLDEN FLEECE. This illustrious Order of Knthood was est. in Flanders, in 1429, by the Duke of Burgundy.

GOLGOTHA. A skull. The name given to Calvary by the Jews.

GOMEL. Reward.

GOMORRAH. A city of Palestine destroyed by fire from heaven, 1897 B. C.

GOOSE and GRIDIRON. An alehouse in London, House-Yard, at N. end of St. Paul's. Meeting place in 1717, of L. of Antiquity, and Gr. L. of Eng., June 24, 1717.

GOTHA. (go-tha).

GOTHIC CONSTITUTIONS. See York Constitutions.

GOURGAS, JOHN JAS. JOS., b. in Fr. 1777, d. New York, Feb. 14, 1865. S. G. C. of N. J., 1832-1851.

GRADES. A word sometimes used for deg.

GRAND EAST. The city in which

the governing Masonic body is sit.

GRAND ORIENT. The various Gr. LL. est. by the Lat. races which frequently exercise jurisdiction over the highest deg. from which Eng. and Am. Gr. LL. refrain.

GROUND-FLOOR of the LODGE. Mt. Moriah is so called.

GUIBS; GUIBBS. Name of a ruffian.

GUILD. A fraternity or commonality of men gathered together into one combination, supporting their common charge by mutual contribution. Poss. the Masons arose from the Craft Guilds of Eng. or the Mediaeval Guilds of Europe.

HABAKKUK. A dist. Jewish prophet. Flourished abt. 630 B. C.

HAGGAI. A Jewish prophet, b. in Babylon during the Capt., who came to Jerusalem to aid in the rebuilding. After the suspension of the work he urged the renewal of the undertaking.

HAH. The.

HAHBONEH. The builder.

HAIL or HALE, has 2 very different sigs. Used, 1, as a salutation; 2, to conceal (from the Saxon, hele).

HAM. The youngest son of Noah, whose desc. founded Assyria and Egypt.

HAMATH. A prov. of Syria with a capital of the same name on the Orontes. Orig. the residence of the Canaanites and mentioned as the extreme N. limit of the Holy Land.

HAMELABEL. Affection.

HAPHTZIEL. (half-zi-el) Voluntas Dei.

HARODIM. (Heb. hah, the, or those, and radah, to rule over). Princes in Masonry. A word 1st employed by Anderson in his Book of Constitutions.

HARPOCRATES. Gr. God of silence and secrecy. Usually a nude, bareheaded figure, sitting on a lotus flower with his finger pressed upon his lips.

HAUTES GRADES. Fr. High Degrees.

HAYAH. (hah-yeh).

HEAL. To make valid or legal.

HELENCHAM. (he-len-kam).

HENADAD. Name of a Levite.

HENRY VI., the Cruel, Emperor of Germany, b. 1165, d. 1197. Son of Frederick Barbarossa.

HEREDOM. Holy House, or Temple.

HERIM. Inspector of the tribe of Dan.

HERMES TRISMEGISTUS or THRICE GREAT, was a celebrated Egyptian legislator, priest, and philos. who lived in the reign of Ninus, abt. 2670 A. M. Mentioned as one of the founders of Masonry in all the old manuscript records.

HEROD the GREAT, King of the Jews. b. 60 B. C., d. 2 A. D. Rebuilt the Temple.

HERODEN; HERODIM. Cor. of Heredom.

HESED. A prince of Solomon. See Chesed.

HIEROPHANT or MYSTIGOG. The Chief Priest of the Eleusinian Myst.

HIEROPHYLAX. Guardian of the holy vessels and vestments.

HIGH DEGREES. Orig. meant those above the Master's deg. but in the U. S. gen. applied to those of the Commandery and especially the Consistory.

HIGH TWELVE. The hour of noon or 12 o'clock in the day.

HINNOM. A deep valley S. of Mt. Moriah, known as Gehenna, for which Jehosaphat has been imp. subs.

HIRAM; or HURAM; more correctly KHURAM; or KHURUM. Noble-born.

HIRAM ABBA not HIRAM ABI. Hiram the Master, Father.

HIRAM ABIF. See 1. Kings vii., 13-14. Made Supt. 1012 B. C.

HIRAMITES. Disc. of H. A. B.

HIRAM, KING of TYRE, was the son of Abibal and the contemp. of both David and Solomon. See 2 Sam. v. 11, and 1. Kings v. 8-9.

HOCHMAH. Wisdom.

HO LA TAI. He has suffered, or been wounded.

HOLINESS to the LORD. In Heb. Kodesh Layehovah.

HOLY LODGE. According to the old lectures this was opened in the tabernacle in the wilderness; the Sacred Lodge on Mt. Moriah during the building of the 1st Temple; and the Royal Lodge, among the ruins of the 1st Temple.

HOLY PLACE or sanctuary was sit. bet. the porch and the Holy of Holies of the Temple.

HOLY THURSDAY. See Ascension Day.

HONORARY DEGREES. Those conferred as an honorarium or reward, or as a mark of respect.

HOR, Mt. Sit. on the border of Idumea, abt. ½ way bet. the Dead and Red Seas, where Aaron was buried. A N. E. branch of Mt. Lebanon is also called Mt. Hor. See Seir, Mt.

HOREB. See Sinai.

HUTCHINSON, WILLIAM. b. Eng. 1732, d. April 7, 1814. Noted for his writings on the true philos. of the Institution.

HYKOS or HYKSHOS. An Egyptian dynasty. See Shepherd Kings.

HYSTASPES. The father of Darius.

IAABOROU HAMMAIM. Liberty of passage.

I AM THAT I AM. Heb. Eheyeh Asher Eheyeh (Exod. iii. 14).

I-COLM-KIL. An island S. of the Hebrides. The traditional foundation of the Rite of Heredom.

IDDO. A Heb. captive.

IDUMEA. Edom.

IESUS HOMINUM SALVATOR. Jesus, the Savior of men.

IESUS NAZERENUS REX IUDAEORUM. Jesus of Nazareth, King of the Jews.

ILLITERACY. It is the gen. accepted law that one who cannot write is ineligible for initiation. Hence the written petition.

ILLUMINATI. The enlightened. Often applied in Lat. diplomas as an epithet of Freemasons.

IMMANUEL. God with us. Heb. Immanu, with us, and el, God, Meaning Jesus Christ.

IMPERIUM. Power.

INCOMMUNICABLE. The Tetragrammaton. Not to be attributed except to the True God.

INEFFABLE DEGREES. 4th to 14th inc.

INEFFABLE NAME. The Tetragrammaton or sacred name of God which it is considered unlawful to pronounce.

INFIDELITAS. Infidelity, or unbelief.

INFINITUM. Infinity.

IN HOC SIGNO VINCES. By this sign thou shalt conquer, is a substantial but not a literal translation of the original Gr.

INVENI VERBUM IN ORE LEONIS. In the lion's mouth I found the word.

ISAAC. The free born. Son of Abraham and Sarah. b. 2107 A. M.

ISAIAH. Salvation of Jehovah. A Heb. prophet. Son of Amoz who was the bro. of Amaziah, King of Judah. He lived and prophesied bet. the years 3164 and 3305 A. M.

ISCARIOT, JUDAS. The betrayer of Christ.

ISCHNGI. One of the 5 masters appointed by Solomon after the death of H. A. B. to complete the Temple. (Legendary).

ISH CHOTZEB. Hewers. Phrase employed by Anderson to designate the hewers who with the Giblim and the Bonai constituted the 80,000 F. C. Not to be conf. with the wood cutters on Mt. Lebanon.

ISH SABAL (prop. noche sabal, 1. Kings v. 18). Bearers of burden.

ISH SODI. Man of my choice. A Select Master.

ISPAHAN. A famous city of Persia.

ISSACHER. 5th son of Jacob and Leah. His tribe had a triangular sec. on the Jordan bet. Zebulon and Ephraim.

ITHAMAR. Youngest son of Aaron.

IZABUD. Cor. of Zabud.

IZRACH-JAH (iz-rack-yah).

JAABOROU HAMMAIM. (aquae transibunt) See Iaaborou.

JABULUM; JACHABULUM, Cor. forms of Jubelum.

JACHIN. (Heb. Jah, God, and iachin, will establish). One of the pillars of the porch of the Temple.

JACHINAI. Cor of Shekinah.

JACQUES de MOLAY. See Molay.

JAH. Syn. with Jehovah. Triliteral name of God.

JAHEB. (concedens). A sacred name.

JAI. See Jah.

JAPHETH. Eldest son of Noah. One of the constructors of the ark of safety.

JEBUS. Anc. name of Jerusalem.

JEBUSITES. A warlike race inhabiting the country around Jerusalem which they held until dispossessed by David who made it the capital of Judea.

JEDADIAH. Beloved of God. Solomon's birth name.

JEHOSAPHAT, VALLEY of, lies E. of Jerusalem, bet. Mt. Zion and Mt. of Olives. In reality there was no such valley in anc. Judea. Sym. the place of last judgment. This word played an important part in the old rituals.

JEHOIACHIM, King of Judah, succ. his father Josiah, 609 B. C. d. 598 B. C.

JEHOVAH. The Tetragrammaton, or four-lettered name of God, called also, the Ineffable or Unpronounceable name.

JEKSAN. Son of Abraham and Keturah. (Gen. xxv. 2.) See next heading.

JEKSON. Cor. of Jacquesson, a mongrel compound of Jacques and son, meaning, son of James the Pretender. A sig. relic of the Stuart system. James II. was the son of Henrietta Maria widow of Charles I., and called "the widow's son."

JEO. (yah-oh).

JEPHTHAH. A Judge of Israel and leader of the Gileadites.

JEPHUNNEH. Father of Caleb.

JERICHO, one of the oldest cities in the Holy Land, sit. abt. 20 m. from Jerusalem and 2 from the Jordan, was next in size to Jerusalem.

JEROBOAM. 1st king of the 10 tribes, elected 975 B. C., "the man who made Israel to sin," d. 954 B. C.

JERUSALEM, HEAVENLY. The city of God.

JERUSALEM, NEW. Sym. name of the Christian Church.

JESHUA. See Joshua.

JETDO; or IDDO. Father of Ahinadab and a prophet and annalist of some distinction. See Iddo.

JETHRO. A priest of Midian and father-in-law of Moses.

JEVA; JHAS. Cor. of the name of God.

JOABERT. Chief favorite of Solomon, who incurred the displeasure of Hiram of Tyre.

JOBEL. (jubilans). A name of God.

JOD-HE-VAU-HE. Heb. letters spelling Jehovah.

JOHABEN. Filius Dei.

JOHANNITE MASONRY. That which recognizes the two Sts. John as patrons.

JOKSHAN. Same as Jeksan.

JONES, INIGO. One of the most celebrated of Eng. architects, b. July 15, 1573, London, d. June 21, 1652. An Operative and (prob.) a Speculative Mason.

JOPPA; or JAPHO; now JAFFA. One of the oldest towns of Asia, was the principal port of Judea. Sit. on the Medit. abt. 35 m.

N. W. of Jerusalem bet. Cesarea and Gaza.

JORAM. One of Solomon's 3 architects sent to supt. the cutting and preparing of the timber.

JOSEDEK; or JOZADOK. Father of Joshua.

JOSEPHUS, FLAVIUS. A noted Jewish author who lived in the 1st cent. b. 37 ?, d. 100 ?. Recourse has been had to his Antiquities of the Jews.

JOSHAPHAT. Son of Ahilud. Name of the orator in the 7th deg.

JOSHUA, the H. P. was a lineal desc. from Seraiah and became the associate and colleague of Zerubbabel in rebuilding the Temple. Opposed the interference of the Samaritans.

JOVA; JUA. Cor. of the Tetragrammaton.

JUB. (yub).

JUDAH. The whole of Palestine was sometimes called the land of Judah because that tribe was dist. in obtaining possession of the country. See Benjamin.

JUSTITIA. Justice.

KABBALA; or KABALA. The mystical philos. or theosophy of the Jews. In this sense it is intimately connected with the sym. science of Freemasonry.

KADMIEL. A Levite.

KADOSH. Holy, or consecrated.

KADOSH KADOSHIM. Holy of Holies.

KADOSH L'IHOH; or KADOSH L' YEHOVAH. Holiness to the Lord.

KERIM. One of Solomon's princes.

KHAM. Form of Ham.

KHURUM. Form of Hiram.

KHURUM ABI. Variation of H. A. B.

KILWINNING. The birth-place of Scottish Masonry and where (poss.) the Order of St. Andrew was created. See Bruce.

KISH. Son of Ner, and father of King Saul.

KNIGHTS OF JUSTICE. Anc. technical name of the K. M.

KNIGHTS OF RHODES. One of the titles given to the K. M. on account of their long residence on the island of Rhodes.

KNIGHTS OF ST. JOHN OF JERUSALEM. Orig. title of the K. M.

KNIGHTS OF THE WHITE AND BLACK EAGLE. A title of the 30th deg. The white eagle was the emblem of the E. Empire, and the black of the W.

KODESH KODASHIM. Holy of Holies.

KOHATH. Ancestor of Moses.

KORAH. Son of Izhar, uncle of Moses. Num. xvi. 1.

LABARUM. The monogram of the name of Christ, formed by the first 2 letters of that name in Gr. Sometimes called the Cross of Constantine. It was orig. surrounded by the motto, conquer by this.

LABORARE EST ORARE. To labor is to pray. A saying of the Mediaeval monks.

LADDER. A sym. of progressive advancement from a lower to a higher sphere.

LADDER OF KADOSH consists of the 7 steps; Justice, Equity, Kindliness, Good Faith, Labor, Patience, and Intelligence or Wisdom. Its supports are:— Love of God, and Love of our Neighbor.

LAEL. Father of Eliasaph.

LAKAK DERROR PESSAH. Liberty of passage and thought.

LAMB, PASCHAL, was the lamb offered up by the Jews at the paschal feast. As a Christian sym. called the Agnus Dei, it 1st appeared in Christian art after the 6th cent.

LAMECH. Son of Methuselah and father of Noah.

LANDMARKS. The "unwritten laws of the (Institution) derived from those anc. and universal customs which date at so remote a period that we have no record of their origin." (Mackey.)

LAPICIDA. A stone-cutter. A word sometimes used to denote a Freemason.

LATOMIA. A stone-quarry. A word sometimes inappropriately applied to a L.

LATOMUS, sometimes found as Lathomus and Latonius. Poss. the same as Lapicida.

LAUS DEO. Praise God.

LAWRIE, ALEXANDER. Published in Edinburgh, Scot., in 1804, A History of Freemasonry.

LAZARUS. Brother of Mary and Martha.

LEBANON. A Mt. or rather a range in Syria, ext. from beyond Sidon to Tyre, and forming the N. boundary of Palestine. The Druses still inhabit Mt. Lebanon. (1874).

LEGEND. A narrative, whether true or false, that has been traditionally preserved from the time of its 1st oral communication.

LENITAS. Gentleness.

LEVITES. Desc. of Levi who were employed in the lowest ministerial duties of the Temple.

LIBANUS. (Lat.) Lebanon.

LIBERTAS. Liberty.

LOGOS. The word.

LOW TWELVE. Midnight.

LUN. Cor. of On.

LUSIGNAN, GUY de. King of Jerusalem.

LUX. Light.

LUX EST. There is light.

LUX E TENEBRIS. Light out of darkness.

LUX FIAT ET LUX FIT. Let there be light, and there was light.

MAACHA, King of Cheth, prob. ref. to Maaka, father of Achish, King of Gath. He delivered to Solomon the traitors who had sought refuge in his domain.

MACBENAC; MACHBENAH. (Gaelic.) The blessed son.

MACCABEES. An heroic Jewish family whose name is sup. to be derived from the letters M. C. B. I., being the initials of the sentence, Mi Camocha, Baalim, Iehovah,—Who is like unto thee among the gods, O Jehovah.

MACHOBIM. See Makobim.

MACKEY, ALBERT GALLATIN. "A profound and lucid historian, and writer in all departments of Masonry * * * unequalled by any living writer" (1856). b. Charleston, S. C., Mar. 12, 1807—d. Old Point Comfort, June 20, 1881.

MACZO. Lat. of the Mid. Ages for a mason. Constructor of walls.

MAGI. Men of superior wisdom.

MAGISTER. Master.

MAGNA EST VERITAS ET PRAEVALEBIT. The truth is great, and it will prevail.

MAH. What.

MAHAZ. Bethshemesh. An anc. Syrian town.

MAHER - SHALAL - HASH - BAZ. Name of the son of Isaiah, sig.—Haste to the prey; fall upon the spoil. Sym. of the readiness for action which should dist. a warrior.

MAH-SHIM; MAHUSEN; MAS-SHIN. Standard bearer in the 32nd deg.

MAKADOSH. Sanctuary.

MAKE. "To make Masons" is a very anc. term.

MAKOBIM. Sufferings.

MALACH; MALAK; MALACK. An angel.

MALACHI; or MALACHIAS. The last of the prophets. Lived abt. 400 B. C.

MALAKOTH. The angelic messenger.

MALEK ADHEL SAYFEDDIA. The just king who holds the sword of Faith.

MALEK AFDEL. Excellent king.

MALEK DAHER. Triumphant king.

MALEK MODAFFER, TAKIED-DAN. The victorious king, and devoted to religion.

MALTA. Anc. Melita. A small island (170 sq. m.) in the Medit., S. of Sicily, which was occupied from 1530 to 1798 by the Knts. Hospitallers, then called Knts. of Malta, upon whom it was conferred in the former year by Charles V. They were dispossessed by Bonaparte.

MAMRE. Name of a Syrian plain.

MARTEL, CHARLES, Duke of the Franks. b. 690, d. 741. Governed Fr. 716-741. Defeated the Saracens at Poitiers in 732 for which victory he was called Martel (the Hammer). A pat. of the Op. Masons of the Mid. Ages, according to old records.

MARTYR. A title bestowed by the Templars on their last Gr. M., James de Molay.

MASCAN. Tabernacle.

MASORETIC POINTS. Vowel signs invented for the Heb. alphabet in the 8th and 9th cent. by a school of Rabbins called Masorites.

MASTER AD VITAM. Master for life.

MASTER BUILDER. God.

MASTER OF THE TEMPLE. Orig. the official title of the Gr. M. of Templars. Now the title of the guardian of the Temple Church at London.

MASTER OF THE WORK. Title of the chief builder or architect of a cathedral or other important edifice in the Mid. Ages.

MATHOC. Amiability; sweetness.

MATTANIAH. Former name of Zedekiah.

MATTHIAS. Apostle chosen in place of Judas Iscariot.

MAYAK-AL. Michael.

MECCA. A city in Arabia, 60 m. from the Red Sea and birthplace of Mohammed.

MEDIA. Anc. occupied what is now a part of Persia and was bounded, N. by the Caspian Sea and Armenia, S. by Persia proper, W. by Assyria and E. by Parthia.

MELCHIZEDEK. King of Salem. Gen. xiv. 18.

MELECH, prop. MALACH. A messenger, hence an angel.

MELITA. See Malta.

MEMENTO MORI. Remember death.

MENAHEM. Consoler. One of the kings of Israel. (II Kings. xv. 14.)

MENATZCHIM. Expert Master Masons. 2 Chron. ii. 18.

MERARI. Bitter. Youngest son of Levi.

MERCY-SEAT. The lid or cover of the Ark of the Covenant.

MESOURANEO. (Gr.) Sig. I am in the center of heaven.

MICHA, MACHA, BAALIM, ADO-NAI. See Maccabees.

MICHAEL. Who is like unto God. Chief of the seven archangels.

MIDIAN. Anc. name of Arabia.

MIDDLE AGES. Sup. by the best historians to extend from 400 B. C. to the end of the 15th cent., or abt. 1497.

MILES. Lat. Soldier. Used to designate military knts.

MILITARY LODGE. See Field Lodge.

MILITES CHRISTI. Soldiers of Christ.

MINOS. A mythological king of Crete.

MISCHAN, MISCHAPHERETH, MISCHTAI. Tent of Testimony. Tent of Festival.

MISERERE. Have mercy upon us.

MISERICORDIA. Mercy.

MISERICORS. Merciful.

MITHREDATH. A Persian officer.

MITHRIDATES the GREAT, King of Pontus, b. 135-? B. C., d. 63, A. D.

MIZPEH. A place in the Mts. of Gilead.

MIZRAIM. Improp. Mezraim, Misraim; or Mitzrayim. Anc. Heb. name of Egypt.

MOAB or MOABON. One of the sons of Lot. Gen. xix. 36, 37. Rep. by the J. W. in the 14th deg. as the tried and trusty friend of Hiram.

MODERNS. Title given by the "Ancients" to those Masons who remained faithful in their allegiance to the legal Gr. L. of Eng. at the schism in 1738.

MOLAY, JAMES de. The 22d and last Gr. M. of Templars, b. 1240, Besancon, Burgundy, entered the Order in 1265, and elected G. M. in 1298. After enduring an imprisonment for 5½ years, he was publicly burnt in front of the Cathedral of Notre Dame, Paris, March 11, 1314.

MOLOCH. The chief god of the Phoenicians and a god of the Ammonites. Solomon built a temple to Moloch upon the Mount of Olives.

MONITOR. A manual containing monitorial instruction published for the convenience of LL. The 1st Eng. manual was by Preston, 1772. Other Eng. and Am. authors are Webb, 1797; Dalcho, 1807; Cole, 1817; Hardie, 1818; Cross, 1819; Tannehill, 1824; Parmele, 1825; Chas. W. Moore, 1846; Cornelius Moore, 1846; Dove, 1847; Davis, 1849; Stewart, 1851; Mackey, 1852; Macoy, 1853; Sickles, 1866.

MONITORIAL. Exoteric instruction.

MONTFAUCON, PRIOR OF. One of the 2 false accusers of the Templars. See Flexian and Noffodei.

MONTFERRAT. A country of Italy.

MONTHS, HEBREW. The Judaic year is luni-solar, and commences at 2 different periods. The ecclesiastical, in Nisan, on the new moon following the vernal equinox; the civil, in Tisri, on the new moon after the autumnal equinox, and is the one adopted by Ineffable Masons. The months are:

1. Tisri or Tischri, Sept. and Oct.
2. Khesvan, Marchesvan, or Bul, Oct. and Nov.
3. Kislev or Chisleu, Nov. and Dec.

4. Tebeth or Thebet, Dec. and Jan.
5. Schebet or Sebat, Jan. and Feb.
6. Adar, Feb. and Mar. (Ve-adar).
7. Nisan or Abib, Mar. and Apr.
8. Ijar, Jyar or Zius, Apr. and May.
9. Sivan, May and June.
10. Tamuz or Thammuz, June and July.
11. Ab, July and Aug.
12. Elul, Aug. and Sept.

Since the lunar year is less. than the solar year by abt. 11 days, the Jews intercalated a month after their 12th mo., Adar, whenever the 15th day of the following mo., Abib, fell before the vernal equinox. This mo. was called Ve-adar, or the 2d Adar, and was inserted every 2d or 3d year as required.

MORIAH, Mt. The name of the site of anc. Jerusalem, but later applied only to an eminence in the S. E. part of the city whereon Abraham was directed to offer up his son, Jehovah appeared to David who purchased the site for an altar, and Solomon built the Temple.

MORPHEY. Inspector of the tribe of Ephraim.

MOSES. (Heb. drawn out; Egyptian, saved from the waters). The lawgiver of the Jews., b. 1574 B. C.

MOSAIC SYMBOLISM. Craft Masonry finds its sym. teachings almost exclusively in the symbolism instituted in the wilderness by Moses, who gave "a holy use to the sym. whose meaning he had learned in his ecclesiastical education on the banks of the Nile."

MOURNING, PERIOD of. 40 days by the A. A. S. R.; that period being a bond by which the whole world, ancient and modern, Pagan, Jewish, and Christian, is united in religious sympathy.

MYSTAGOGUE or HIEROPHANT. The one who presided at the Anc. Myst.

MYSTES. One who had been initiated into the Lesser Myst. of Paganism. See Epopt.

NAAMAH. The dgtr. of Lamech and inventor of the art of weaving, according to the legend of the Craft.

NADAB. One of the sons of Aaron.

NAPHTALI. As the territory of this tribe adjoined Phoenicia, there must have been frequent and easy communication bet. the Phoenicians and Naphthalites, resulting sometimes in intermarriage. This will explain the fact that Hiram was the son of a widow of Naphtali and a man of Tyre.

NAZARENE. An inhabitant of

NAZARETH. A town in Galilee from 50 to 70 m. N. of Jerusalem now called Nasera and sit. abt. midway bet. Mt. Tabor and Cana.

NEBUCHADNEZZAR, King of the Chaldeans, a nomadic tribe orig. from the Caucasian Mts., took Babylon abt. 630 and Jerusalem in 606 B. C. He afterward conquered Tyre and Egypt. d. 562 B. C.

NEBUZARADAN. A captain or general of Nebuchadnezzar who commanded the Chaldean army at the siege of Jerusalem.

NECUM. See Nekam.

NEC PRODITUR, NEC PRODITUR, INNOCENS FERAT. Not the traitor, not the traitor, let the innocent bear it.

NEDER. Promise.

NEHEMIAH. A Heb. prophet who commenced his career as a reformer abt. 444 B. C.

NEKA. Strike.

NEKAM, prop. NAKAM. Vengeance, or vengeance is taken.

NEKAMAH. Vengeance.

NEMBROTH. A cor. of Nimrod.

NEOPLATONISM. A philos. school founded at Alexandria, Egypt, among whose disc. were Philo, Judaeus, and Jamblichus. Much of the sym. teaching of the higher deg. has been taken from this school and these disc.

NE PLUS ULTRA. Nothing more beyond.

NE VARIETUR. Lest it should be changed.

NIL NISI CLAVIS. Nothing but the key is wanting.

NIMROD. In the Old Constitutions ref. to as one of the founders of Masonry, and in the Scriptures as the architect of many cities. He was the grandson of Ham, and is sup. to have been the founder of Babylon, the 1st king and the 1st conqueror.

NINEVAH. The capital of anc. Assyria, was sup. founded by Nimrod, in the 15th cent. B. C.

NOACHITES or NOACHIDAE. Disc. of Noah who subs. Noah for Solomon, and Peleg, chief builder of the Tower of Babel, for H. A. B.

NOFFODEI; NOFFO DEI; or NOSSO de FLORENTIN; and Squin de Flexian were the 2 first to make false accusations against the K. T., which led to the downfall of the Order.

NONIS. (no-niss) Poss. the initials of several words.

NON NOBIS, DOMINE! NON NOBIS, SED NOMINI TUO DA GLORIAM. Not unto us, O Lord! not unto us, but unto Thy name give Glory. Commencement of Psalm 115 and the anc. Templars' shout of victory.

NOTUMA. Anagram of Aumont, who is said to have been the 1st G. M. of Templars in Scot. and restorer of the Order after the death of De Molay.

OATH, TILER'S. That taken by an unknown visitor to assist in gaining admission into a L.

OBED. One of the 9 favored officials selected after the death of H. A. B.

OBLONG SQUARE. A parallelogram whose angles are equal, but 2 of whose sides are longer than the others.

OHEB ELOAH. Love of God.

OHEB KAROBO. Love of Neighbor.

OLIVER, GEORGE, D. D. "Father of Anglo-Saxon Masonic Literature," was b. in Pepplewick, Nov. 5, 1782, and d. in Eastgate, Lincoln, Mar. 3, 1867.

OMNIA TEMPUS ALIT. Time heals everything.

OMNIFIC WORD. The Tetragrammaton.

ON. City of the Sun. A city in Lower Egypt bet. the Nile and the Red Sea, called also Bethshemesh and Heliopolis, and being the prime seat of the Anc. Myst. it was naturally sup. that On was the Egyptian name for Jehovah.

ORDO AB CHAO. Order out of Chaos.

ORIENT. The East.

ORIGIN OF FREEMASONRY. Among other sources the following 12 have been held by Masonic writers at different times: 1, the Patriarchial religion; 2, Ancient Pagan Mysteries; 3, Temple of King Solomon; 4, Crusaders; 5, Knights Templar; 6, Roman Colleges of Artificers; 7, Operative Masons of Middle Ages; 8, Rosicrucians of 16th cent.; 9, Oliver Cromwell; 10, Pretender (for the restoration of the House of Stuart); 11, Sir Christopher Wren; 12, Dr. Desaguliers and his associates, in the year 1717.

ORNAN the Jebusite, an inhabitant of Jerusalem (Jebus), was the owner of the threshing-floor on Mt. Moriah which David bought for the purpose of erecting an altar. The Temple was built on the same spot.

ORPHEUS. A Thracian who introduced the sacred rites of initiation and mystical doctrines into Gr. and from whom the Orphic Myst. derived their name. Pythagoras promulgated the doctrines "enigmatically and through images."

OZI. Mightiness. Anc. name of God.

PALESTINE, called THE HOLY LAND. (For 1st Masonic period see Ancient Israel). In 7th cent. fell into power of the Mohammedans and afterward the Turks. Became a Christian kingdom in 1099 when Godfrey de Bouillon took Jerusalem, and so continued for over 80 years. In 1187, reconquered by Saladin and in 1291, the Crusaders were finally expelled.

PALMER. A pilgrim from the holy war in time of the Crusades and known by a palm branch bound round his staff. See Pilgrims.

PALMYRA, SYRIA, anc. Tadmor, pos. founded by Solomon, was sit. 120 m. N. E. of Damascus, 20 m. W. of the Euphrates, and 120 from Aleppo. Although one of the finest and most magnificent cities of the world it lay on a kind of island, separated from the habitable earth by an ocean of barren sands.

PARROT MASON. One who commits to memory the questions and answers of the catechetical lectures, and the formulas of the ritual, but pays no attention to the history and philos. of the Institution. See Bright Mason.

PARSEES. Desc. of the orig. fire-worshippers of Persia, or the disc. of Zoroaster, who emigrated to India abt. the end of the 8th cent.

PARTHIANS. Inhabitants of Persia.

PARTS. See Arts.

PASCHAL FEAST. When celebrated by the Christians is in commemoration of the resurrection of our Lord.

PASSWORD AND WORD. The former is for recognition only; the latter is given for instruc-

tion as it always contains a sym. meaning.

PAST. Applied to one who has held an office for the period for which he was elected.

PAST MASTER. An honorary deg. conferred on the Master of a L. at his installation into office. See Actual Past Master.

PATMOS. An island of the Egean Sea, W. of Asia Minor, 20 to 25 m. in circum. to which John the Evangelist was banished by Domitian, A. D. 94.

PATRIARCH. Father of a race or clan. In the early history of the Jews, the ancestor or father of a family retained authority over his children and his children's children so long as he lived, whatever new connections they might form.

PAX VOBISCUM. Peace be with you.

PAYENS, HUGH de. The founder and the 1st Gr. M. of the Order of Knts. Templar; was born at Troyes, Naples; elected G. M. in 1118, and d. in 1129.

PELEG or PHALEG. Son of Heber. Rep. as the architect of the Tower of Babel.

PENNY. The coin given in payment for the laborers daily wage had a value of about 12 or 14 cents, U. S. currency. Is now simply the sym. of the reward of faithful labor.

PENTALPHA. The triple triangle or pentalpha of Pythagoras forms the outlines of the 5 pointed star. This should not be conf. with the Seal of Solomon or Shield of David, whose outlines form a star of 6 points. A talisman of health.

PERNETTY, ANTOINE JOSEPH, poss. author of Knight of the Sun, was b. 1716, Roanne, Fr., d. 1800, Valence, Dauphiny.

PHAAL CHOL. Separated; driven apart.

PHALEG. See Peleg.

PHARAOH. Title of the sov. of anc. Egypt.

PHARAOH HOPHRA. For 25 years a sov. of Egypt contemp. with Zedekiah, King of Judah, with whom he formed an alliance against Nebuchadnezzar.

PHARAOH NECHO. Succ. to the sov. of Egypt 617 B. C. Contemp. with Josiah, King of Judah, whom he defeated.

PHARASH-CHOL; PHARASH-KOL; PHARAS-KOL; PHARAXAL. Division and subsequent reunion.

PHENICIA. "the birthplace of commerce", was a Syrian prov. 80 m. long by 12 broad, N. of Palestine. on the W. declivity of Lebanon, bordering upon the Medit. and of which Tyre and Sidon were the principal cities. It has been asserted that the language spoken by the Jews and the Phenicians was almost identical.

PHILIP II., or PHILIP AUGUSTUS, King of Fr., b. 1165, d. 1223.

PHILIP IV., le Bel or the Fair, ascended the throne of Fr. in 1285, and d. in 1314, execrated by his subjects for his cruelty, avarice and despotism. The persecutor of the Templars.

PHILISTIA or "the land of the Philistines," was sit. on the Medit. bet. Joppa and the border of Egypt. Its inhabitants were prob. of Egyptian origin.

PHILO JUDAEUS. A Jewish philos. of the school of Alexandria, b. abt. 30 B. C. Frequent use of his esoteric philos. was made by the early inventors of the high deg. in constructing their systems.

PHINEAS. Son of Eleazar and grandson of Aaron. H. P. for 20 years.

PHOENICIA. See Phenicia.

PIKE, ALBERT, poet and most dist. Masonic author and historian, was b. at Boston, Mass. Dec. 29, 1809, and d. in 1891.

PILGRIMS made the journey to any shrine but once, while Palmers were in the habit of passing from shrine to shrine living on charity. Pilgrimage being frequently an act of penance, the person performing it was called a "Pilgrim Penitent." When the Turks seized Syria it was necessary for the pilgrim to fight his way and he became a "Pilgrim Warrior." He frequently ended his warlike pilgrimage by assuming the vows of a Knt. Templar.

PILGRIM'S SHELL. See Scallop Shell.

PLATO. A Gr. philos., b. in Athens or Aegina, 428 B. C., was a disc. of Socrates and became an eminent teacher. d. 347 B. C.

POINTS. See Arts.

POLKAL. Altogether separated.

POOR FELLOW-SOLDIERS OF JESUS CHRIST. Title first assumed by the K. T.

POPES OF ROME. Pontificate.
Honorius II. 1124-1130
Eugenius III. 1145-1153
Celestine III. 1191-1198
Innocent III. 1198-1216
Boniface VIII. 1294-1303
Clement V. 1305-1314

POSTULANT. (Lat. postulans, asking for). Candidate's title in the 30th deg.

PRECEPTORY. The house or residence of the K. T.

PRECEPTOR. The Superior of such residence and officer over its jurisdiction.

PRESTON, WILLIAM. b. Aug. 7, 1742, Edinburgh; d. April 1, 1818, London. Author of a course of lectures on the first 3 deg. for the Craft of Eng. Used by the Gr. L. of Eng. as the authoritative system from abt. 1772 to 1813.

PRETENDER. James Stuart, (b. 1688, d. 1765), the son of James II., who abdicated the throne of Great Britain, and Charles Edward (b. 1720, d. 1788), his son, are known in history as the Old and the Young Pretender.

PRICE, HENRY, b. abt. 1697, Eng., d. 1780 Mass. Founder of Masonry in New England by organizing a Provincial Gr. L. July 30, 1733.

PRINCE OF CAPTIVITY. Rightful heir to the throne of Israel during the Babylonish Capt. At the time of the restoration, Zerubbabel was the lineal desc. of Solomon.

PRINCEPS. Chief.

PROBATION. The interval bet. the reception of one deg. and the succeeding one.

PRO DEO ET PATRIA. For God and my country.

PROFANE. (Lat. pro and fanum. Outside of the temple). Uninitiated.

PRO TEMPORE. For the time being.

PROTOTYPE. Same as Archetype.

PTOLEMAIS. Anc. name of Acre.

PULSANTI OPERIETUR. To him who knocks it shall be opened.

PYTHAGORAS. One of the most celebrated of the Gr. philos. and the founder of what has been called the Italic school, was b. at Samos abt. 586 (?) B. C. He is said to have submitted to the initiations in Egypt, Chaldea, and Asia Minor, and on his return to Europe est. his celebrated school at Crotona in S. Italy. Tradition says he d. (506 (?) B. C.) of starvation in Metapontum, whither he had fled after the lawless destruction of his school.

QUADRIVIUM AND TRIVIUM. The 7 liberal arts and sciences. The 1st, arithmetic, geometry, music and astronomy; the 2d, grammar, rhetoric and logic.

QUOD NON VETAT LEX, HOC VETAT FIERI PUDOR. What the law does not forbid doing, shame forbids.

RABBANAIM. The chief of the architects.

RABBATH, chief city of the Ammonites, was sit. in the mts. of Gilead. Its modern name is Amman, and lies abt. 20 m. S. E. of Szalt. Also called Rabba.

RABBINISM. The system of philos. taught by the Jewish Rabbis subsequent to the dispersion.

RABBONI. Lit. My Master. Translated, a most excellent Master. Used by the Jews in anc. times to designate their learned men. See John xx. 16.

RAGON. J. M. One of the most dist. Masonic writers of Fr. His contemp. called him "the most learned Mason of the 19th cent." b. Bruges, Belgium, in the last ¼ of the 18th cent.; d. Paris, abt. 1866.

RAHAB. A name of Egypt.

RAMOTH GILEAD. A famous city in the mts. of Gilead, within the territory of Gad, abt. 15 m. from Rabbah.

RAMSAY, ANDREW MICHAEL, called the Chevalier Ramsay, was b. at Ayr, Scot., June 9, 1668. d. May 6th, 1743, at St. Germain de Laye. The founder of a Masonic Rite and the inventor of deg., especially a system known as the Royal Arch, which is entirely different from that practised in Great Britain and the U. S.

RAPHAEL, A messenger. Title of an officer in a Rose Croix Ch.

RAPHODOM. (raff-oh-dom).

RAZAH-BELSIJAH. (rah-za-bel-sy-ya).

RE and THMEI. Light and Truth.

RECUSANT. In Masonic law, sometimes used to designate a L. or a Mason that refuses to obey an edict of the Gr. L. Insubordinate.

RED CROSS KNIGHT. When in the 10th cent. Pope Urban II., won by the enthusiasm of Peter the Hermit, said: "His cross is the sym. of your salvation; wear it, a red, a bloody cross, as an external ·mark on your breasts or shoulders, as a pledge of your sacred irrevocable engagement", the red cross on the breast immediately became the sign of him who was engaged in the Holy Wars, and Crusader and Red Cross Knt. became convertible terms.

RED LETTERS. The A. A. S. R. edicts, summonses or other documents, written or printed in red letters, are sup. to be of more binding obligation, and to require more implicit obedience, than any others.

REFRESHMENT, CALLING to. Now means cessation from labor.

REHOBOAM. Son and succ. of Solomon, ascended the throne of Judah at the age of 41, and reigned 17 years.

REHUM. Called by Ezra, the chancellor. Prob. Lt. Gov. of Judea, who wrote to Artaxerxes to stop the building of the 2d Temple.

RESPLENDENS. Resplendent.

RESTORAVIT PACEM PATRI. Meaning, He restored peace to his country.

REUBEN. The eldest son of Jacob, whose tribe lay E. of the Jordan.

REVIVAL OF MASONRY. The occurrences which took place in London, 1717, when that important body, since known as the Gr. Lodge of Eng., was organized.

REX REGUM DOMINUS DOMINORUM. King of Kings, Lord of Lords.

RHODES. An island (40 m. x 15 m.) in the Medit., off S. W. coast of Anatolia. Was in possession of Saracen pirates in 1308, when they were expelled by the Knts. Hospitallers, who made it the seat of the Order, which it continued to be until 1522. In that year it was retaken by the Saracens and the knts. removed to Malta, but their residence at Rhodes, for over 200 years, caused them, at times, to be called the Knts. of Rhodes.

RIBLAH. A town on the N. border of Palestine, 30 m. S. of Hamath.

RITE, MASONIC. The method and order observed in the government of a system. There were 38 more or less important rites built upon the 3 sym. deg.

RITUAL. The mode of opening and closing; of conferring the deg.; of installation and other duties, constitute a system of ceremonies which is called the Ritual.

ROMAN COLLEGES OF ARTIFICERS. Guilds or corporations of artisans organized by Numa, the 2d king of Rome abt. 700 B. C. Poss. the cradle of the modern Masonic L., but only as to the outward form and mode of working.

ROSE CROIX. Rose Cross.

ROSE on the CROSS, sig. Christ crucified.

ROYAL LODGE. See Holy Lodge.

RULE of the TEMPLARS. The code of regulations for the government of the anc. K. T. was drawn up by St. Bernard and by him submitted to Pope Honorius II., and the Council of Troyes, by both of whom it was approved.

SABAISM. Worship of the sun, moon and stars.

SABAOTH. (Hosts). Jehovah Tsabaoth, Jehovah of Hosts. Indicates power and majesty.

SABBAL. The Burthen.

SABIANISM. See Sabaism.

SACRED LAW. The 1st Tables of Stone, or Commandments delivered to Moses on Mt. Sinai.

SACRED LODGE. See Holy Lodge.

SACRED NAME. The Heb. noted the attributes of the Deity under different names, thus; his divine essence, Jehovah; his omnipotence, El, Elah or Eloah; his excellency, Elion; and his mercy, Elchannan.

SADOC. See Zadok.

SADONIAS. (sa-do-ne-as).

ST. ALBAN or ALBANUS, the protomartyr of Eng. was b. in the 3d cent. at Verulam, now St. Albans, in Hertfordshire, Eng. Freemasons have claimed him as being intimately connected with the early hist. of the Craft in that island.

ST. ANDREW. Bro. of St. Peter and one of the 12 apostles. Tradition says he was crucified on a cross shaped thus, X.

ST. ANDREW'S DAY. Nov. 30.

ST. BERNARD of CLAIRVAULX. b. in Fr. 1091. d. 1153. Pat. and protector of the K. T. in the Mid. Ages.

ST. GEORGE'S DAY. April 23.

ST. GERMAIN. A town abt. 10 m. from Paris, where James II., est. his court after his expulsion and where he d., 1701.

ST. JEAN d'Acre. See Acre.

ST. JOHN the ALMONER. Son of the King of Cyprus. b. in Cyprus in 6th cent. Pat. of the Masonic Order of the Templars.

ST. JOHN the BAPTIST. The only pat. saint of Freemasonry prior to the 16th cent. His festival occurs June 24.

ST. JOHN the EVANGELIST. One of the pat. saints of Freemasonry subsequent to the 16th cent. His festival occurs Dec. 27.

SAINTS JOHN. St. John the Baptist, and St. John the Evangelist.

ST. PAUL'S CATHEDRAL, London, was rebuilt (1675-1710) by Sir Christopher Wren, which fact has induced some writers to advance the theory that Freemasonry took its origin at that reconstruction.

SAKINAT. The Divine Presence. The Shekinah.

SALADIN or SALAH-EDDIN. Sultan of Egypt and Syria. Opposer of the Crusaders. b. 1137, d. 1194 (?). "Salah-ed-din, King of Kings; Salah-eddin, Victor of Victories; Salah-eddin, must die." A motto in 29th deg.

SALEM. Poss. Jerusalem, although the place of which Melchizedek was king might have been Shalem of Gen. xxxiii. 18.

SALIX. Initials forming part of a sentence.

SALSETTE. An island in the Bay of Bombay celebrated for its stupendous artificial caverns used in the Anc. Myst.

SALUTEM. Health.

SAMARIA, the metropolis of the kingdom of Israel or of the 10 tribes, sit. near the center of Palestine abt. 40 m. N. of Jerusalem, was built by Omri, King of Israel, abt. 925 B. C.

SAMARITANS were orig. the desc. of the 10 revolted tribes living in Samaria, but after they had been carried into capt. by the Assyrian, Shalmaneser, their place was filled by idolatrous foreign colonies who assumed the name. Hence their assistance in rebuilding the Temple was refused.

SAMOTHRACE or SAMOTHRACIA. An island in the Egean Sea, 17 m. in circum., lying off Romania and not far from Thrace. Modern Samandraki.

SANCTUM REGNUM. Holy Kingdom.

SANCTUM SANCTORUM. Holy of Holies.

SANCTUS. Holy; consecrated.

SANHEDRIM. The highest judicial tribunal among the Jews and consisted of 72 persons beside the high priest. Sup. orig. with Moses on the occasion of a rebellion in the wilderness.

SARACENS. Orig. only an Arab tribe; later applied to all Arabs who embraced Mohammedanism.

SCALLOP SHELL. The recognized badge of a pilgrim in the Mid. Ages.

SCHISMATIC. Any body of Masons separating from the legal obedience and est. a new one not authorized by the laws of Masonry is properly schismatic.

SCHORLABAN. White Ox, or morally, Innocence.

SCRIBE or SOFER, in the earlier Scriptures was a kind of military secretary; but in the latter he was a learned man, and doctor of the laws, who expounded them to the people.

SCRIPTURES. Formerly it was not the custom to open the Book of the Law at random although the use of a particular passage was not always constant or universal, as: 1st deg., Psalm cxxxiii; Gen. xxii; 2nd deg., Amos vii. 7, 8; Gen. xxviii; 1 Kings vi. 8; 2 Chron. iii. 17; 3rd deg. Ecc. xii. 1-7; Amos v. 25, 26; 2 Chron. vi.; In Eng. 1st, Ruth iv. 7; 2nd, Judges xii. 6; 3rd, 1 Kings 13, 14.

SEAL of SOLOMON, or SHIELD of DAVID, consisting of two interlaced triangles forming the outlines of a 6 pointed star was the great Oriental talisman. It was adopted by the Christians as rep. the 2 natures of our Lord—his divine and his human.

SEIR, Mt. A desolate chain stretching from the S. shore of the Dead Sea to the E. gulf of the Red Sea. Mt. Hor was one of its summits.

SELEC. A Giblemite.

SENNACHERIB. (705-681 B. C.) Son and succ. of Sargon as king of Assyria when Hezekiah reigned in Judah.

SERAIAH. A prince of Judah and the H. P. when the Temple was destroyed by the Chaldeans.

SHADDAI. All-powerful; Omnipotent. The name by which God (Exod. vi. 3) was known to the Israelites before he communicated to Moses the Tetragrammaton.

SHALAL SHALOM ABI, meaning, He restored peace to his father.

SHALASH ESRIM. Twenty-three. Ref. to a day in the month Adar.

SHALMANESER, King of Assyria, 727-722 B. C.

SHAVEH. A valley in Palestine.

SHEALTIEL. Father of Zerubabel.

SHEKINAH. A visible manifestation (as by a beam of light or a cloud) of the divine presence. See Bath-Kol.

SHELOMOTH. Peacefulness.

SHEM. The Name. The Jews in their sacred rites often designated God by the word Name, as, Shemchah Kadosh, Thy name is holy; Shem hamjukad, the appropriated name; Shem haggadol, the great name; Shem hakkadosh, the holy name; and Shem hamphorash, the separated name or the Tetragrammaton,

SHEM, HAM, JAPHETH. The 3 sons of Noah, who assisted him in constructing the ark of safety.

SHEPHERD KINGS; or HYKOS. Name given to the kings of Egypt of a foreign race, whose rule (abt. 2000 B. C.) lasted for 511 years.

SHESHBAZZAR or Sesh-Bazzar. Poss. another name for Zerubbabel.

SHETHARBOZNAI. See Tatnai.

SHIBBOLETH has 2 meanings, 1, an ear of corn; 2, a stream of water.

SHIELD OF DAVID. See Seal of Solomon.

SHIMSHAI. A Persian officer.

SHINAR. Anc. Chaldea.

SHITTIM, pl. of Shittah of the Scriptures, is the Acacia, a sacred wood among the Heb.

SHOULKAIN. Stolkin.

SHUSHAN, anc. and magnificent city, sit. on the river Ulai (now Kerrah) in the prov. of Elam, Persia, was the capital and residence of the kings.

SIC TRANSIT GLORIA MUNDI. meaning, Thus passes away earthly glory.

SIDE DEGREES are those not placed in the regular routine of the acknowledged deg., and are not recognized as a part of anc. Masonry. They constitute no part of the regular ritual and are not under the control of any legal, administrative body of the Institution.

SIDDIM, a valley of Palestine now covered by the Dead Sea, is sup. to have been the site of Sodom and Gomorrah.

SIDON. A city of Phoenicia, sit. at N. W. angle of Canaan, abt. 20 or 30 m. from Tyre. (Modern, Saide.)

SIGNET of TRUTH. Zerubbabel's signet. (Haggai II., 23). Zerubbabel was the sym. of the searcher after truth.

SIMEON. One of the tribes of Israel. Occupied 19 cities within the bounds of Judah, principally S. of Dan, on the coast. In Hezekiah's time they possessed parts of Mt. Seir.

SINAI. A mt. of Arabia Petraea bet. the horns of the Red Sea. One of a group called Horeb or the Sinaitic range. Where Moses received the Law from Jehovah, and was directed to construct the tabernacle.

SION, Mt. See Zion.

SIROC. A shoe latchet, meaning, nothing even of the slightest value.

SIT LUX et LUX FUIT. See Lux Fiat.

SKULL. Among the articles of accusation sent by the Pope to the bishops and papal commissaries upon which to examine the K. T., those from the 42d to 57th refer to the human skull, "cranium humanum", which the Templars were accused of using in their reception, and worshipping as an idol.

SOCRATES. An anc. Athenian philos. b. abt. 469 B. C., d. 399.

SOLDIERS of CHRIST, Milites Christi, is the title by which St. Bernard addressed the K. T.

SOLI SANCTISSIMO SACRUM. Sacred to the most holy sun.

SOLOMON, King of Israel, son of David and Bathsheba, ascended the throne 3989 A. M. or 1015 B. C., at the age of 20, and reigned

40 years, having abandoned the path of truth after the building of the Temple.

SOLSTICES. June 21 and Dec. 22.

SOLUS. Alone.

SPES MEA IN DEO EST. My hope is in God.

SQUIN de FLEXIAN. See Flexian.

STARE SUPER VIAS ANTIQUAS. To stand on the old paths.

STAUROS. A cross.

STELLATO SEDET SOLO. He sits on his starry throne.

STIRLING. A city in Scot. The seat of the Stirling Anc. L., which conferred the R. A.; Red Cross: K. M.; and K. T. until abt. the beginning of the 18th cent.

STOLKIN. Inspector over the tribe of Benjamin and a "searcher out" of criminals.

STONES, BLACK AND WHITE, were used by anc. Gr. and Romans to give sentence in the courts. White for acquittal. Black for condemnation.

STONE-SQUARERS. See Giblim.

STUART MASONRY. This title is given by Masonic historians to that system which is sup. to have been invented by the adherents of the exiled house of Stuart for the purpose of being used as a political means of restoring, 1st, James II., and afterward his son and grandson, James and Charles Edward, respectively, known in history as the Chevalier St. George and the Young Pretender.

SUBLIME DEGREES. The 11 of the A. A. S. R. from 4 to 14 inc. are sometimes so called. (Now called Ineffable).

SUBLIME GRAND LODGE. A title formerly given in the A. A. S. R. to what is now simply called a Lodge of Perfection.

SUCCOTH. An anc. city of Palestine abt. 45 m. N. E. of Jerusalem. (Now, Seikoot).

SUPREME COUNCIL. Title of the Supreme authority of the A. A. S. R.

SWORD, TILER'S. See Flaming Sword.

SYMBOLIC DEGREES. The first 3.

SYMBOLISM, THE SCIENCE of. That which is engaged in the investigation of the meaning of symbols, and the application of their interpretation to moral, religious and philos. instruction.

SYRIA. Once the words Babylonia and Chaldea were equiv. to Assyria. Later the region E. of the Euphrates was known as Assyria, while the W. portion was called Syria and extended from the Euphrates to the Medit. bet. Mt. Taurus and Arabia and Egypt. This was divided into Syria, Palestina, (incl. Canaan and Phoenicia), Coele-Syria (bet. 2 ridges of Mt. Lebanon), and Upper Syria.

TAANACH MEGIDDO. Prob. the names of 2 anc. Syrian cities.

TABAOR; TOFFET; EDOM. 3 obsolete names.

TABEEL. A Persian officer.

TABERNACLE. Tent. The 3 mentioned in Scripture history are: 1, The Anti-Sinaitic, perhaps used from the begin. of the exodus; 2, The Sinaitic, constructed by Aholiab and Bezaleel under the direction of Moses, and accompanied the Israelites in all their wanderings; and 3, The Davidic, erected by David in Jerusalem, to which the holy furniture was removed from the Sinaitic. This was superseded by the Temple. Masonic tradition enumerates another. 4, That erected by Zerubbabel on his arrival at Jerusalem with his countrymen, prior to rebuilding the Temple.

TABLE LODGE. Frequently, in early days, the banquet, (which now follows the work), was served during the session or on a special occasion, under the most rigid Masonic rules and regulations and was called a Table Lodge.

TABOR. Inspector over the tribe of Gad.

TADMOR. See Palmyra.

TALJAHAD; TALLIUD. The Angel of water.

TAPIS. Name given in Germany to the carpet, which see.

TARSEL. Old form of Tessel.

TARSHATHA. See Tirshatha.

TATNAI and SHETHAR-BOZNAI. The former was a Persian satrap of the prov. W. of the Euphrates in the time of Darius and Zerubbabel, the latter, an officer under his command. The 2 united with the Apharsachites in trying to obstruct the building of the 2d Temple.

TAU. The last Heb. letter and in the anc. alphabet was a figure like X or —|—, and later, T. This tau, tau cross, or tau mark, was an almost universal sym. among the anc. and to the Heb. a sign of salvation.

TAU, TRIPLE. A figure formed by 3 of these crosses meeting in a point, resembling a letter T, resting on the transverse bar of an H.

TEMPLARIUS. Lat. title of a K. T. Constantly used in the Mid. Ages.

TEMPLAR ORIGIN OF MASONRY. The theory that Masonry orig. in the Holy Land during the Crusades, and was instituted by the K. T. was 1st advanced by the Chevalier Ramsay.

TEMPLE DEDICATIONS. Jewish history records 5. 1, Solomonic, B. C. 1004; 2, In time of Hezekiah, B. C. 726; 3, Zerubbabel's, B. C. 513; 4, After Judas Maccabaeus had driven out the Syrians, B. C., 164; Herod's, B. C. 22.

TEMPLE, DESTRUCTION of the. That of Solomon stood 416 years, although plundered by Shishak, King of Egypt, 30 yrs. after its completion. It was frequently profaned and pillaged, and finally totally destroyed by the King of Babylon, 588 B. C. 73 years later, or B. C. 515, a new edifice was completed by Zerubbabel and Joshua, the H. P. This stood nearly 500 years and being much decayed, Herod the Great restored and enlarged it, being 46 yrs. in entirely completing the building. This was razed by the Romans A. D. 70, and the site is now occupied by the Mosque of Omar.

TEMPLE, FIRST.   Solomon's.

TEMPLE of EZEKIEL.   An ideal seen by the prophet in the 25th year of the Capt., while residing in Babylon.

TEMPLE OF HEROD. From this one the K. T. derived their name. See Temple Dedications; also Destruction of.

TEMPLE of ZERUBBABEL.   In 3466 A. M. and 536 B. C. Cyrus gave permission to the Jews to return to Jerusalem, and one year later, Joshua, the H. P., Zerubbabel, the Prince or Governor, and Haggai, the Scribe, laid the foundations of the 2d Temple which was not completed for 20 years or until 515 B. C. This is called, by way of distinction, the Temple of Zerubbabel.

TEMPLE, SECOND.   Zerubbabel's.

TEMPLUM HIEROSOLYMAE. Lat for the Temple of Jerusalem.

TENGU. (ten-gew).   Initials of a sentence.

TERCY.   One of the 9 Elus.

TESSERA HOSPITALIS. The token of the guest, or the hospitable die, was an alliance of friendship bet. 2 persons formed by dividing an article into 2 parts and exchanging the pieces after inscribing their names thereon, and was a perpetual covenant.

TETRAGRAMMATON. Sig. A name of 4 letters. Jehovah in Heb. consists of 4 letters, hence called the Tetragrammaton or four-lettered name. Also the Ineffable or Unpronounceable name.

THAMMUZ or TAMMUZ. A deity worshipped by the apostate Jews in the time of Ezekiel. Sup. identical with Adonis.

THEBES, or LUXOR, in Egypt; flourished 1600-1800 B. C.; capt. by Persians 525 B. C.; destroyed 86 B. C.

THEBOUNAH. (the-boo-na).

THERAPEUTAE. A Jewish sect, near Alexandria, Egypt, in 1st cent. A. D., whose doctrines bore a striking resemblance to those of the Essenians.

THOKAH.   Strength.

THORY, CLAUDE ANTOINE. A Masonic historian, b. Paris, May 26, 1759; d. Oct., 1827.

THREE POINTS, or DOTS, in triangular form, placed after letters indicate that such are the initials of a title or technical word in Masonry and are simply a mark of abbreviation.

THRESHING-FLOOR. A spot of hard ground used for threshing corn. David paid 600 shekels of gold for the one on Mt. Moriah. See Ornan.

THUMMIM.   Truth.   See Urim.

THURIBLE. A metallic censer for burning incense. Used in the philos. deg.

THURIFER. The bearer of the thurible.

TIBERIAS. An anc. city in lower Galilee. on the W. shore of Sea of Galilee.

TIGRIS. A river of Syria, 1150 m. long, flowing into the Euphrates.

TIRSHATHA. Title of the Persian governors of Judea. It was borne by Zerubbabel and Nehemiah.

TITLES. The Knight devotes his hand, his heart, his brain to the service of Masonry, and professes himself the sworn soldier of truth; the Prince aims to be chief, first, leader among his equals, in virtue and good deeds;

the Sovereign, one of an (Institution) whose members are all sovereigns, is supreme only because the law and Constitutions are so which he administers, and by which he, like every other bro., is governed. The titles Puissant, Potent, Wise, and Venerable indicate that power of virtue, intelligence and wisdom which those ought to strive to attain, who are placed in high offices by the suffrages of their brethren.

TITO. Prince of Harodim, is rep. as having been a favorite of Solomon, who appointed him the 1st Provost and Judge.

TOUB. Light.

TRAMPING MASONS. Those using their privileges for interested purposes and travelling from city to city.

TRANSMISSION, CHARTER of. A doubtful deed said to have been granted by James de Molay, just before his death, to Mark Larmenius, by which he transmitted to him and to his succ. the office of G. M. of Templars. It is preserved in Paris.

TRAVELLING FREEMASONS. There is no portion of the history of the Craft so interesting to a Masonic scholar as that which is embraced by the Mid. Ages of Christendom, beginning with abt. the 10th cent., when the whole of civilized Europe was perambulated by those associations of workmen who passed from country to country and city to city, under the name of Travelling Freemasons, for the purpose of erecting religious edifices. See Roman Colleges; Como; Guild.

TRAVELLING WARRANTS. Those granted to Military LL.

TRIAD. In the anc. mythologies this consisted of a union of 3 deities—a creator, a preserver, and a destroyer.

TRIBES of ISRAEL. All 12 were engaged in the construction of the 1st Temple, but before its destruction 10 revolted and formed the nation of Israel. Those of Judah and Benjamin retained possession of the Temple and Jerusalem under the name of the kingdom of Judah.

TRIFELS. A ruined castle, 4 m. from Madenburg, Austria, where Richard I. was a prisoner for more than a year.

TRUTH. A knowledge of God.

TSADOC. See Zadoc.

TSEDAKAH. Justice.

TSIDONI. A Seeker or Inquirer.

TSIDUN. See Sidon.

TSUR. A city of Palestine.

TUBAL CAIN. See Gen. iv. 22.

TUB BAANI AMAL ABAL. It is just to reward labor.

TURCOPOLIER. The 3d dignity in the Order of Knts. Hospit. of St. John or K. M.

TYRE. An anc. city of Phoenicia, founded 1300 B. C. abt. 90 m. N. W. of Jerusalem and 20 or 30 S. W. of Sidon.

UNHELE. To uncover or reveal.

UNIVERSI TERRARUM ORBIS ARCHITECTONIS PER GLORIAM INGENTIS. By the Glory of the Grand Architect of the Universe.

UNUTTERABLE NAME. The Tetragrammaton or Divine Name. More commonly, the Ineffable Name.

URI. Father of Bezaleel.

URIEL. Fire of God. An archangel.

URIM and THUMMIM. Light and Truth. Sacred lots to be worn concealed in or behind the breastplate which revealed the will of God.

VASHTI. Queen of Persia and wife of Ahasuerus.

VEUT DIEU SAINT AMOUR. 4 words sup. to be repeated by the Fraters of the Temple.

VEADAR. See Months, Heb.

VERITAS. Truth.

VESPASIAN, TITUS FLAVIUS SABINUS. Emperor of Rome 70-90 A. D.

VEXILLUM BELLI. A war-flag.

VINCERE AUT MORI. To conquer or to die.

VIRTUAL PAST MASTER. See Actual Past Master.

VIRTUS JUNXIT, MORE NON SEPARABIT, meaning, Whom virtue unites, death cannot separate.

VIVAT. Lit. May he live.

WASHINGTON, GEORGE. Init. Nov. 4, 1752, Passed, Mar. 3, 1753, and Raised, Aug. 4, 1753, in the L. of Fredericksburg, Va.

WEBB, THOMAS SMITH, the "ablest ritualist of his day" and the inventor and founder of the system known as the Am. Rite, was b. in Boston, Mass., Oct. 13, 1771, and d. July 6th, 1819.

WILLIAM I., the Conqueror, King of Eng., b. 1027, in Normandy; crowned Dec. 25, 1066 in London, and d. 1087 at Nantes.

WORD. If the Word is a sym. of Divine Truth; if the search for the Word is a sym. of the search for that Truth; if the Lost Word sym. the idea that Divine Truth has not been found, then the Substitute Word is a sym. of the unsuccessful search after Divine Truth and the attainment in this life of what is only an approximation to it.

WORD, THE TRUE, is the sym. of life eternal as the Lost Word is the sym. of death.

WREN, SIR CHRISTOPHER, one of the most dist. architects of Eng. (b. Oct. 20, 1632, d. Feb. 25, 1723), was a Speculative as well as an Operative Mason. His crowning work is St. Paul's Cathedral; which see.

XERXES, King of Persia, (486-465 B. C.) was the son of Darius I.

XINXE, meaning, the seat of the soul.

YAH; YEVA; YOD; Cor. names of Deity.

YAPHETH. See Japhet.

YAVERON HAMMAIM, meaning, the passage of the river.

YOD. A Heb. letter which in a triangle constitutes the symbol of Deity.

YORK CONSTITUTIONS. Those purported to have been adopted at York, 926. Also called Gothic Constitutions on account of the style of architecture introduced into Eng. by the Craft.

YORK LEGEND. The theory that abt. 926 an assembly of Masons was held at York (in the N. of Eng.) when a code of laws was adopted which became the basis of all subsequent Constitutions. See Edwin.

YORK RITE, the oldest of all, organized in 1717 and used for 50 yrs. by the Gr. L. of Eng., consisted of the first 3 deg. only. The last contained the True Word. (See Dunckerly). After the addition of the R. A., Mackey calls it the Modern York Rite, while that of the U. S., where 6 had been added to the 3, the American Rite.

YZEBRATH. Lord of Hosts.

ZABUD. Son of Nathan the prophet, the friend of the king. Friend and counselor of Solomon. 1. Kings iv. 5.

ZACCHAI. The Deity.

ZADOK or TSADOC. Chief priest, who anointed Solomon to be king. President of the Sanhedrim, lived abt. 260 B. C.

ZAPHNATH - PAANEAH. Savior of the world. Egyptian title of Joseph.

ZARTHAN. See Zeredatha.

ZEBEDEE. Father of the apostles James and John.

ZEBULON. 6th son of Jacob.

ZECHARIAH. The son of Iddo. Priest and prophet (b. in Babylonia) who joined Zerubbabel on his return to Palestine.

ZEDEKIAH. 20th and last king of Judah. 2 Kings xxiv. 17, to xxv. 11.

ZEHOLIM. A Heb. city.

ZEMZEM. The holy well in Mecca.

ZENDAVESTA, the bible of the anc. Persians and of modern Parsees, is ascribed to Zoroaster.

ZERAIAS. One of Solomon's 3 supt's in the forests of Lebanon.

ZERBAL. Sup. name of Solomon's Captain of the Guard.

ZEREDATHA. A town on W. bank of the Jordan near Bethlehem and opp. Succoth.

ZERUBBABEL, Born in Babylon; or Sheshbazzar, the prince of Judah; was the grandson of Jehoiachin or Jeconiah, deposed King of Judah. The "Prince of the Captivity" led 42,360 of his Jewish subjects back to Jerusalem where they arrived, after a march of 4 mos., June 22, 535, B. C. See Temple of Zerubbabel.

ZION, Mt. (or Sion) was the S. W. of the 3 hills on which Jerusalem was built. Often called the "City of David" and sometimes used as syn. with Jerusalem.

ZIZA. (zee-zah).

ZIZON. Balustrade.

ZOAN. (Gr. Tanis). Egyptian city on the Nile, founded 3700 B. C. Residence of the Pharaohs.

ZOROASTER or ZARATHUSTRA. Legislator and prophet of the anc. Bactrians out of whose doctrines the modern Parsee religion developed. He lived in Bactria, an anc. country of Asia, bet. the Oxus river and the Caucasian Mts. The greatest discrepancies exist as to the age in which he flourished, being from 6350 B. C. down to 550 B. C.

ZURTHOST. Modern Parsee name of Zoroaster whom they call their prophet.

The following books are recommended for those desiring further Masonic light as being authentic and conservative:

Encyclopaedia of Freemasonry.................................Mackey
Masonic Jurisprudence ....Mackey
Masonic Parliamentary Law..................................Mackey
Poetry of Freemasonry.......................................Morris
History of Freemasonry......................................Hughan
Concise History of Freemasonry..............................Gould
History of the Knights Templar.............................Addison
Morals and Dogma..Pike
Book of the A. A. S. R................................McClenachan

"Adieu! a heart-warm, fond adieu!
Dear brothers of the mystic tie!"